DATE DUE

NOV 0 3 2003	
JUL 0 8 2006	

Learning, Creating, and Using Knowledge:

Concept Maps™ as Facilitative Tools in Schools and Corporations

by

Joseph D. Novak
Cornell University

LEA **LAWRENCE ERLBAUM ASSOCIATES, PUBLISHERS**
1998   Mahwah, New Jersey   London

Lawrence Erlbaum Associates, Inc., Publishers
10 Industrial Avenue
Mahwah, New Jersey 07430

Cover Design by Kathryn Houghtaling Lacey

Library of Congress Cataloging-in-Publication-Data

Novak, Joseph Donald
Learning, creating, and using knowledge : concept maps as facilitative tools in schools and corporations / Joseph D. Novak
    p. cm.
Includes bibliographical references and index.
    ISBN 0-8058-2625-4 (cloth : alk. paper). — ISBN 0-8058-2626-2 (pbk : alk. paper)
    1. Learning, Psychology of. 2. Cognitive maps (psychology) 3. Instructional systems—Design. 4. Constructivism (Education)
    I. Title
    LB1060.N677 1998
    370.15'23—DC21   98–22965
                                                  CIP

Books published by Lawrence Erlbaum Associates are printed on acid-free paper, and their bindings are chosen for strength and durability.

Printed in the United States of America
10 9 8 7 6 5

For Joan

Contents

List of Figures

List of Tables

Preface

For more than the past 40 years, I have enjoyed working in the fields of biology and education with over 350 graduate students and visiting professors and numerous colleagues at several universities. The past 3 decades as Professor at Cornell University and now Professor Emeritus have been especially rewarding. More recently, I have been working with corporations to apply ideas and tools my colleagues and I have developed in the field of education to improve knowledge creation and utilization in corporations. This book represents a synthesis of much that I have learned with a focus on what I believe to be a universal problem facing society; namely, how can we more effectively help people learn, create, and utilize knowledge?

In some ways, the work we have done in the field of education has been successful, and many of the ideas and tools we developed are being applied in both school and university education in countries all over the world. In other ways, my work in education has been a constant frustration because there remains a huge discrepancy between what I believe we know that can improve education, and the quantity and quality of applications of this knowledge in school and university settings. I believe there have been enormous advances in the past 3 decades in our understanding of how people learn and in our understanding of the nature of knowledge and the process of new knowledge creation. Little of this knowledge is currently being utilized either in academic or in corporate settings. It is my hope that this book shall make some contribution both to the understanding of this new knowledge and to its utilization.

The ideas and tools presented in the book are equally applicable to governmental and nongovernmental organizations other than schools, and also to religious organizations. However, my work with these groups has been limited, and it would be too overwhelming to include examples and illustrations from these institutions as well. We are currently launching a major project in religious education and this work may be the subject of a future book.

Given the enormous pressures that are being brought to bear on businesses and societies through the rapidly accelerating globalization of business, I expect the adoption and development of ideas tools presented will have more rapid acceptance and application in the business world than has been true for the academic world. Recent work with one of the Dow Jones 30 companies where these ideas and tools are beginning to be applied widely suggests the enormous potential that exists in utilization for the enhancement of corporate effectiveness. My hope is that in the long term there will be new partnerships between business and education, and indeed the boundaries between these groups may fade to the benefit of both schooling and business.

Every current, major societal problem is rooted in educational failure. It is my hope that this book will contribute in a fundamental way to the improvement of education in every context—and eventually to amelioration of at least some of the social problems and suffering that exists in the world.

ACKNOWLEDGMENTS

For the past four decades, I have been blessed with many excellent graduate students, including the team that helped to develop the concept mapping tool in the early 1970s. I have also enjoyed stimulation, support, and insights from many visiting professors from all parts of the world. These people have been my mentors and we have learned together. The College of Agriculture and Life Sciences at Cornell University has been a hospitable home for my work for the last 30 years. Professor Alan McAdams of the Johnson Graduate School of Management has been especially helpful in assisting me in understanding business issues and problems. My colleagues at Procter and Gamble have also been excellent mentors. My three children, two grandchildren, and my wife Joan have also been a source of energy, ideas, and inspiration. Much of the credit for the ideas in this book belongs to my mentors, but the shortcomings are my own. I extend my warm and grateful thanks to all of these good folks.

—*Joseph D. Novak*

1

An Overview of the Book

INTRODUCTION

This book is for anyone who cares deeply about education. It is for anyone who believes education can be significantly improved and who is frustrated with the parade of educational innovations of the past half century that seem to have accomplished so little. During the 1970s, standardized test scores were steadily declining while school budgets were increasing. From 1955 to 1985, per-pupil expenditures rose 300% after adjustment for inflation, and the growth in school budgets continues. For 3 decades, Americans have pumped money into schooling. In 1984, Goodlad wrote in his report on American schools,

> There is even a growing mood that some schools are now beginning to improve rather than continuing to get worse. . . . The change in mood may stem from little more than the belief that conditions in our schools have bottomed out. The only way to go now is up. (p. xv)

But the evidence now is that little progress has been made in school improvement. Almost daily we read in our papers reports on new studies that indicate American children lag behind those in most industrialized nations. Our national illiteracy rate and school dropouts rates are also among the highest for all developed nations. Why? Why has progress been so slow even, in the exceptional schools?

Have you wondered why so many people you encounter seem unable to think out the simplest of problems? Indeed, have you wondered why you may have failed to see the solution to a problem that, retrospectively, appeared so simple? Contrast this with observations we all have made where very young children have seen solutions before we have. Why is it that finding and executing solutions to common problems appears to be so uncommon? In short, why do people have so much difficulty in organizing, using, and creating knowledge? This is a question for which

1

I propose answers. It is a difficult question, and the answers I give are not always simple. And to understand the solutions I propose will require learning more about the nature of learning and the nature of knowledge and knowledge creation than you may want to know at this point in your life. But, stay with the book; in the end, I believe you will say, as so many have over past decades, "This makes sense. Why aren't we doing more of the things proposed?" My hope is that after you study this book, you will help to change the way we educate, use, and create knowledge.

It is a cliché to say that we are today in a crisis. There have been so many crises in the past and yet somehow the world goes on. But great empires have fallen; the cultural and economic power of the Orient gave way to the dominance of the West; and maybe we shall see history repeat itself. As Prestowitz (1988) argued, the United States is trading places with Japan. In a decade, the United States moved from the largest creditor nation in the world to the largest debtor nation—and the debt increases continue! The economic consequences of stupidity are enormously negative. Perhaps more than any time in the history of capitalism, the well-being of U.S. citizens, and all who depend on us, is at stake. We need to learn how to educate ourselves better, both as individuals and as organizations. American companies need to become "knowledge-creating" companies, as Nonaka and Takeuchi (1995) advised.

In his book, *Post Capitalist Society,* one of America's economic gurus, Peter Drucker (1993), advised that we need radically different schools from those we see today. These schools must have the following specifications:

- The school we need has to provide universal literacy of a high order—well beyond what *literacy* means today.
- It has to imbue students on all levels and of all ages with motivation to learn and with the discipline of continuing learning.
- It has to be an open system, accessible both to highly educated people—to people who for whatever reason did not gain access to advanced education in their early years.
- It has to impart knowledge both as substance and as process—what the Germans differentiate as *Wissen* and *Können.*
- Finally, schooling can no longer be a monopoly of the schools. Education in the post-capitalist society has to permeate the entire society. Employing organizations of all kinds—businesses, government agencies, nonprofits—must become institutions of learning and teaching as well. Schools, increasingly, must work in partnership with employers and employing organizations. (p. 198)

You may want to amend or add to Drucker's specifications, but it is difficult to deny the value of any of those listed. How can society move to achieve these revolutionary schools? There are no easy answers. A basic assumption of this book is that we must look to new partnerships and exchanges of ideas between schools and business, and we must build educational change into both on the basis of a comprehensive theory of education. This book attempts to provide such a theory and framework.

There is today unprecedented movement toward globalization of the world's economies. This process accelerated rapidly in the 1990s and is likely to continue to increase as new technologies continue to facilitate global communications and global commerce. Although I see little evidence that schools, especially universities, are leaping to address the new educational challenges, it is likely that corporate America, and corporations throughout the world, will rush to employ the most powerful ideas and tools available to enhance their effectiveness. Continued globalization of the economy will require this—the alternative being increased corporate bankruptcy. The next decade should be an exciting time for everyone, especially for educators who seek to grasp the challenges we face. It is my hope this book will contribute to better education of all the peoples of the world.

SYNOPSIS OF THE BOOK

A graphic summary of the book is presented in Fig. 1.1. This is an example of a concept map, many of which will be shown in the following chapters. Concept maps are a knowledge representation tool, and this map represents a general overview of this book. Concept maps should be read from the top to the bottom, proceeding from the higher order—more general—concepts at the top to the lower order—more specific—concepts at the bottom. Concepts maps also have crosslinks that show relationships between ideas in different segments of the map. Figure 1.1 shows that three key concepts or ideas will be presented in this book: (1) the nature of knowledge, its capture, creation and use; (2) the nature of human learning; and (3) a theory of education that will tie together aspects of the latter two ideas and explain how these interrelate. Review the map before you proceed in reading the synopsis of the book.

Chapter 2 discusses the need for a Theory of Education to help us deal with the many questions, issues, and problems faced in educating people, educating them in a manner that will empower them to become powerful, confident, and committed knowledge creators and knowledge users. There are five *elements* in my theory of education, each of which interacts with all the others, and all must be considered simultaneously to create a powerful educational event. The five elements presented are: (1) learner; (2) teacher; (3) knowledge; (4) context; and (5) evaluation. Each of these and their interactions are discussed in chapter 2.

This chapter also stresses the crucial role that *meaningful* learning, as distinct from rote learning, plays in successful education. In fact, the idea of meaningful learning is the very foundation for the theory of education presented. Although the

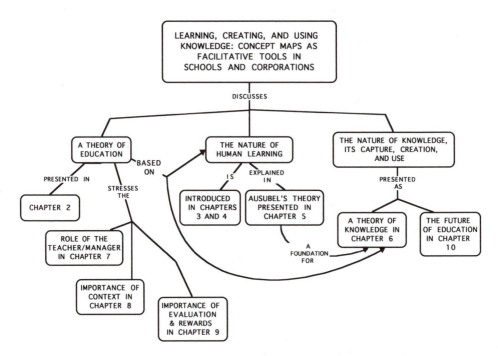

FIG. 1.1. A concept map showing a graphical representation of the content of this book. Concept maps should be read from top down. Arrowheads may be omitted except on horizontal or upward linkages.

learner must choose to learn meaningfully, the teacher (live or vicarious) can do much to encourage and facilitate meaningful learning.

Theory can improve practice directly by providing an explanatory framework to guide practice, and indirectly, by helping to improve research in education. If we are going to make the quantum leap forward in education necessitated by evolving social and business demands, educational research must be dramatically improved.

Chapter 3 defines meaningful learning and the fundamental elements that knowledge is made from—facts, concepts, propositions, and principles. The nature of human memory and the role of the three memory systems are discussed. Our early work in the development of the concept map tool to represent knowledge and applications in school and corporate settings are described briefly. Finally, the role of meaningful learning for the empowerment of individuals and organizations is sketched out.

Chapter 4 develops further how humans construct new meanings and the role that concepts and propositions play in the process. Humans construct, over time, complex concept and propositional frameworks as they develop, idiosyncratically, their knowledge structures, or as psychologists refer to them, their cognitive structures.

The monumental works of Jean Piaget and his ideas on cognitive development are presented briefly, along with a brief discussion of emerging newer ideas.

Chapter 5 presents, in detail, David Ausubel's assimilation theory of meaningful learning, along with numerous examples and some modifications that derive from our studies. Ausubel (1962, 1963) was one of the pioneers who helped to move psychology away from behavioral models of learning based largely on animal studies in the 1930s through the 1960s, to cognitive models that focus on how humans construct new meanings and use knowledge in creative problem solving. The nature of creativity and intelligence as seen through assimilation theory is discussed. For readers new to the field of learning psychology, this chapter may prove to be a challenge. However, to acquire a deep understanding of how humans create and use knowledge, careful study of chapter 5 can prove rewarding. In spite of many newer theories advanced to explain human learning, I still see Ausubel's theory, perhaps with minor modifications and additions, as the most comprehensive and most powerful.

Understanding meaningful learning is the foundation needed to understand the nature of knowledge and knowledge creation. Chapter 6 presents a theory of knowledge that builds on the theory of learning presented in chapter 5. The Vee heuristic is presented as a tool to help illustrate the structure of knowledge and the 12 elements involved in knowledge creation. Each of the 12 elements are defined and examples are given to show how the Vee can be used to represent the knowledge-creation process, or the structure of knowledge in any specific domain of knowledge.

Different forms of knowledge, such as tacit contrasted with explicit knowledge, are discussed. Methods for capturing tacit knowledge are presented, and various approaches for capturing and using knowledge are discussed. Both academic and business examples are used to illustrate the principles and methods involved. Special attention is given to capturing and using knowledge from consumers. A fundamental principle of meaningful learning is that new learning must build on specific relevant knowledge the learner already has. Thus, understanding what knowledge individuals possess, be they school learners or consumers, is crucial to moving them to new levels of understanding and competence.

Chapter 7 focuses on the third element involved in educating and empowering people—the teacher. I take the position that management, if it is to be effective, is essentially teaching. Therefore, the issues and ideas discussed apply equally to teaching and management. For example, I believe both require emotional sensitivity, commitment, honesty, and caring. Of course, there are teachers and managers who have been judged successful who do not evidence consistently these characteristics. There are always exceptions when we are dealing with the complex feelings, thoughts, and actions of people. This chapter seeks to put forward ideas that evidence suggests will be most effective most of the time with most people. The ideas presented are consistent with and build on the theory of learning and theory of knowledge presented in earlier chapters.

All educative events take place in some space, time, social, and cultural milieu. Chapter 8 deals with issues related to the context for effective teaching or management. Once again, emphasis on the emotional experience is stressed. The effective teacher or manager can do much to help develop a context that will maximize the effectiveness of the learner or employee. Gender, race, and other social and cultural factors may present a challenge to the teacher or manager, but conscious, deliberate efforts to ameliorate deleterious influences can pay off in developing more effective learners and employees. Moreover, there are costs associated with ignoring or dealing ineffectively with contextual issues influencing learning and performance. In the school setting, these include high drop-out rates, failure to learn, and ego destruction that can lead to individual disempowerment and a lifetime of failure. The societal costs for this are enormous. In business or government, failure to develop strong positive environments for workers reduces productivity, leads to high turnover rates that are costly, and fails to capture and utilize optimally the energy, talents, and creativity of workers. Furthermore, practices that discriminate on the basis of gender or race are illegal in the United States and other countries, and recently very large corporations have paid very large penalties for such discrimination. In worst cases, corporations go bankrupt, and governmental institutions fail at a high cost to everyone affected.

Chapter 9 deals with the last, and in some ways most crucial, element involved in educating or managing. The methods we use to evaluate and reward learning and performance can enhance or undermine all of our best efforts in dealing with the other four elements of educating. In school settings, the widespread use of multiple-choice type tests, most of which have limited validity at best, tends to encourage rote learning and learning patterns that can stifle rather than enhance creativity. In business settings, similar problems can occur in selection or promotion of workers. Ineffective assessment of consumer knowledge, interests, and desires can lead to failures in developing the kind of products or services that go beyond consumer demands and lead to corporate growth and greater societal contributions. Alternative forms of evaluations are discussed and their merits presented.

The last chapter of the book looks to the future. What are the chances for enhanced educating and managing? Given my thesis that significant advances in education are unlikely unless teacher education and school practices are guided by a comprehensive theory of education, and given the snail's pace at which this is occurring, it is difficult to be optimistic about substantive improvements in schools in the near term. There are other factors that are operating now that could alter the normally slow advances in school educational practices. Globalization of the economy is placing an accelerating demand on businesses to be more creative to remain competitive. Enhancing the creativity of our work force can best be accomplished by education that confers a capacity for and commitment to high levels of meaningful learning for everyone. This must include minority groups, who are rapidly becoming majority groups in large cities, and these groups too often receive the most boring, rote-learning-dominated programs.

Other factors operating that could influence the rate of change is privatization of public schools. However, the evidence to date is that for-profit corporations do no better than the public schools in effecting student achievement, even when assessed by relatively simplistic evaluation measures. Increasing use of technology, in combination with privatization, also has had limited success at best. So where is the new innovation to come from that can and must lead to the very substantive improvements that are needed in schools? My prediction is that competitive pressures in business will, in the next decade or so, drive businesses to adopt radically new ways and new ideas for creating, sharing, and using knowledge. I believe we shall also see adoption of the kind of theory and methods discussed in this book in education and management in corporations. Subsequently, either by example or a new genre of privatization, or both, education in schools and tertiary institutions will be driven toward truly significant advances.

If schooling as we know it now ranks a 2 or 3 on a scale of 10, where 10 represents the best we can do by applying fully the ideas and tools we have now, I predict we shall see improvements to a level of 7 or 8 in 20 years. Considering that almost no progress has been made in the past 40 years, I recognize how optimistic my prediction is. My hope is that this book will make some small contribution to achieving this goal.

2

The Need for a
Theory of Education

My thesis in this book is the same as it was in my earlier book, *A Theory of Education* (Novak, 1977a): Education, in any setting, is an enormously complex human endeavor; there are more ways to make changes that will be harmful or of little value than ways to make constructive improvements in education. A comprehensive theory of education is needed to give vision and guidance for new practices and research leading to steady improvement of education. The ideas in this book should apply to all educational settings, including schools, universities, corporations, technology-mediated education, and nonformal education, such as museums or hobbies.

Theories are ideas that explain why some set of phenomena in the universe behaves as it does. The sciences have been enormously successful in devising theories, and although even the best theories evolve and change over time, these still make possible a steady advance in knowledge about how the natural world works and in prediction and control over an ever-widening range of events or phenomena. The theory of education presented in this book explains why educational experiences we judge as effective are effective, and why those experiences we judge as ineffective are ineffective. For example, the theory of learning I present explains why learning by rote is ineffective for long-term retention and application of knowledge and why meaningful learning is effective and necessary for creative thinking. As with all theories, there are no simple, direct answers (consider, for example, the theory of evolution), and yet I hope to explain, on a theoretical basis, what is in the ballpark of being better and what appears to be outside of this ballpark. The theory of education presented will be a composite of a theory of learning, a theory of knowledge, and a theory of teaching and management, each of which complements and supports the others.

Educating is more than science; it is also an art. It requires personal judgments, feelings, and values. Increasingly, of course, we are coming to recognize that the latter are also involved in science. Keller (1983) chose to title her biography of Nobel Laureate biologist Barbara McClintock *A Feeling for the Organism,* expressing not only the careful research done by her, but also her commitment and sensitivity to understanding plants. Issues of sensitivities and values are becoming increasingly important in the sciences also, especially with the growing application of scientific ideas and tools for manipulating plant and animal (including human) genes. Throughout this book I make reference to issues that concern both the science of educating and the art of educating.

I will claim that *the central purpose of education is to empower learners to take charge of their own meaning making.* Meaning making involves thinking, feeling, and acting, and all three of these aspects must be integrated for significant new learning, and especially in new knowledge creation. In some ways, this is not a new idea. In the monograph published by the Educational Policies Commission (EPC) in 1961, this statement was made:

> The purpose which runs through and strengthens all other educational purposes—the common thread of education—is the development of the ability to think. This is the central purpose to which the schools must be oriented. . . . the development of every student's rational powers must be recognized as centrally important. (p. xiv)

One of the difficulties with the EPC report is that it failed to recognize the central role that meaningful learning and acquisition of powerful conceptual frameworks in basic disciplines play in the ability to engage in rational thought. It also failed to recognize that students need explicit guidance in learning about learning and in the use of tools and strategies to facilitate meaningful learning. This guidance in learning and the use of tools to facilitate learning and understanding is becoming especially important in the corporate world. Learning and integrating new knowledge in collaborative settings is especially important in the highly competitive global markets in which corporations are operating. These are some of the issues focused on in this book.

Successful education must focus on more than the learner's thinking. Feelings and actions are also important. We must deal with all three forms of learning. These are acquisition of knowledge (cognitive learning), change in emotions or feelings (affective learning), and gain in physical or motor actions or performance (psychomotor learning) that enhance a person's capacity to make sense out of their experiences. A positive educational experience will enhance a person's capacity for thinking, feeling, and/or acting in subsequent experiences. A maleducative or miseducative experience will diminish this capacity. Humans engage in thinking, feeling, and acting, and these combine to form the meaning of experience (Fig. 2.1). This book focuses on how to enhance the meaning of experience for any person.

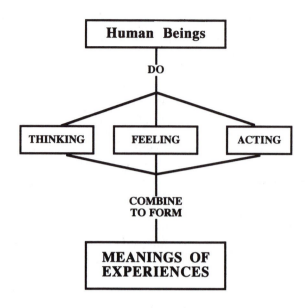

FIG. 2.1. Our meanings for experiences are a composite of our thinking, feeling, and acting.

THE FIVE ELEMENTS OF EDUCATION

In 1973, Joseph Schwab proposed that education involved what he called "four *commonplaces*" (p. 502–503). His commonplaces were learner, teachers, subject matter, and milieus. Each commonplace was necessary to consider and could not be reduced into one of the others (analogous to finding the lowest common denominator in fractions). Schwab's commonplaces, and many of his other ideas, have proven to be of value to educators. They provide a kind of checklist to assure that we are covering all the key checkpoints necessary to understand or to design an effective educational intervention.

Our studies in schools and other settings, notably corporate settings, however, have shown that much of what happens in teaching and/or learning depends on the forms of appraisal used. Therefore, I wish to propose evaluation as a fifth element in education. I prefer the term *elements* to commonplaces because it connotes the idea that each is a building block for myriads of combinations that form educational events, much as the 100 or so elements of chemistry form an infinite variety of molecules.

My five elements are: (a) learner, (b) teacher, (c) knowledge, (d) context, and (e) evaluation. I add the last element because so much of what happens to people in life is based on evaluation. For better or worse, the evaluations we are subjected to determine whether or not we can drive an automobile, graduate with honors or enter a university or graduate program or succeed in a corporate or other work setting. Unfortunately, so much of the testing that is done is really poor at evaluating human competencies, and I deal with this issue throughout the book. Nevertheless, I see evaluation as an additional key element in education. Figure 2.2 shows a concept map with these elements. Concept maps, a knowledge representation tool that was developed in 1972 in our research program (Novak & Musonda, 1991) are used extensively in this book. Strategies for developing and using concept maps have been described in numerous publications and in *Learning How To Learn* (Novak & Gowin, 1984). As we shall see, concept maps and Vee diagrams can also be powerful tools to aid learning as well as tools for evaluation.

Two additional factors operate in education: money and time. These are factors that influence any human enterprise and are not uniquely relevant to education. In general, we can improve any endeavor if we have more money and/or more time to pursue that endeavor. Moreover, the past few decades have illustrated that simply spending more money on education may not lead to significant improvement in

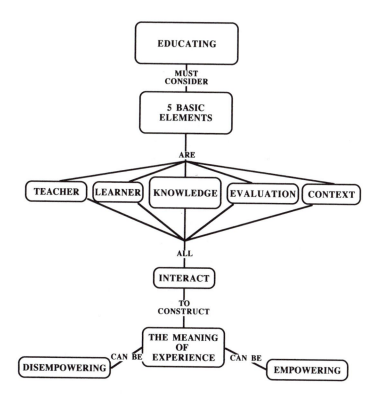

FIG. 2.2. The Five Elements that comprise an educational event: learner, teacher, knowledge, evaluation, and context. All elements are present in an educative event and combine to construct or reconstruct the meaning of experience.

student achievement (Hanushek, 1981, 1989). Lengthening the school day and/or the school year might lead to improvement in achievement; while I favor a 12-month school calendar, evidence for this is equivocal. It would certainly increase the cost of education. My thesis is that more money and time are not the primary needs for improvement of education. The debate on whether expenditures are related to student achievement is one that has gone on and will continue (cf. Hanushek, 1981, 1989; Hedges, Laine, & Greenwald, 1994; Wainer, 1993). What is needed are promising new ideas and determination to apply these ideas and to set standards. A viable theory of education can help to generate and identify promising ideas and strategies to improve education in any setting. It can also help to set and reach functional high standards. Whatever money or time resources are made available can then be used much more efficiently. Resnick and Nolan (1995) observed that, "Countries known for their outstanding students have several practices in common; clear, consistent demanding standards head the list" (p. 6). However, as Howe (1995) pointed out, setting academic standards without dealing with poverty and limited resources in poor districts will not solve our educational problems. But money alone is not the solution. Wainer (1993) cited data from the National Heritage Foundation that show the 10 states with the highest per-pupil expenditure rank 31st to 49th in rank on SAT scores, whereas the 10 states with lowest per-pupil expenditure rank 2nd to 22nd in SAT rank.

I am not alone in recognizing the need for theory. Brown (1994), in her presidential address to the American Educational Research association, pointed out that the advances in learning theory of the past century are not being applied in schools, a position with which I agree. Shuell (1993) called for an integrated theory of teaching and learning to improve education, but I contend this is not enough. We need a theory that integrates all five elements of the educative process leading to honest, authentic, and productive achievement, and this is the goal of this book.

In the corporate world, similar problems prevail. Although corporations recognize that continued change in the ways in which manufacturing and marketing are done to meet the competition require continued education of employees, they tend to look for short-term solutions that train employees in new methods or techniques. What they seldom do is educate employees to understand the ideas that underlie the new methods or techniques. This training usually takes the form of memorizing new rules, procedures, or rationales, without the requisite conceptual understanding necessary for employees to take command of their work—and to contribute their own creative ideas. The result in a rapidly changing market environment can at times be ineffective at best and disastrous in worst cases.

THEORY OF EDUCATION FOR HUMAN BEINGS

Human beings do three things: they think, feel, and act. A theory of education for human beings must consider each of these and help to explain how to improve the ways in which humans think, feel, and act. Throughout this book, I consider each of these forms of human experience and how they relate to education.

In schooling, work, or any educational setting where we have a teacher, even if it is a textbook or a computer program serving as a proxy for a teacher, we must recognize that the learner's world and the teacher's world are never the same. Thus, we must recognize that the interplay between learner and teacher involves two different sets of interacting elements. Figure 2.3 shows this relationship. One emerging potential of technology-mediated education is that faulty ideas or biases that may be introduced by the teacher might be reduced. In earlier work using audio tape as an instructional vehicle, we found that carefully designed lessons could be highly effective without teacher intervention (Novak, 1972; Novak & Musonda, 1991). One disadvantage of technologically mediated instruction is that machines do not express emotions, the caring, warmth, and excitement that an effective human teacher can share. We must recognize that teaching and learning are interactive events and involve the thoughts, feelings, and actions of both teacher and learner. This is illustrated in Fig. 2.3.

Also shown in Fig. 2.3 is a fundamental idea in my theory of education. Any educational event is a shared action to seek to exchange meanings and feelings between the learner and the teacher. This exchange or negotiation will be emotionally positive and intellectually constructive when learners gain in their understandings of a segment of knowledge or experience; conversely, it will be negative or destructive when understanding is obfuscated or feelings of inadequacy emerge. And because learner and mentor share thoughts, feelings, and actions, the teacher will also experience positive feelings and a sense of power over knowledge when the educative event is successful. When learner and teacher are successful in negotiating and sharing the meaning on a unit of knowledge, meaningful learning occurs. In its simplest form, my theory of education states: Meaningful learning underlies the constructive integration of thinking, feeling, and acting leading to human empowerment for commitment and responsibility. I show this in Fig. 2.4 to give emphasis to this idea. This book sets forth the key concepts, principles, and philosophy underlying this theory. It is a book for learners, for teachers, and for managers. When education is most effective, managers become teachers, teachers are also learners, and learners are also teachers. This can be especially true where learners are engaged in cooperative learning activities, and I discuss this idea again in later sections. Fundamental to constructive interaction between teachers and learners is authenticity and honesty because this is fundamental to building the trust needed for both teacher and learner to share meanings and develop new more powerful meanings.

Meaningful learning is a key concept in my theory of education, a concept that is both simple and universally known, but also extraordinarily complex and never

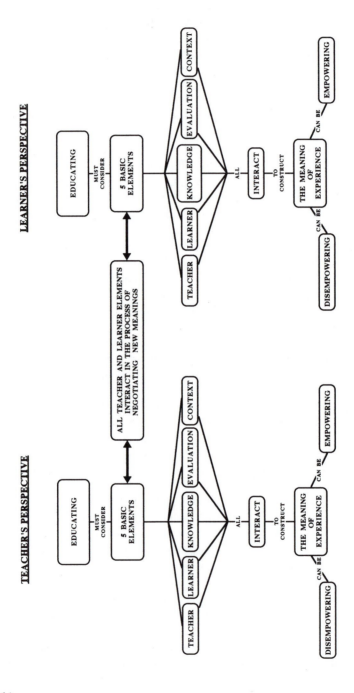

FIG. 2.3. Teacher and each learner has his or her own perspectives on the five elements operating in an educative event. The challenge is to reach a shared perspective on each element.

fully understood (as for example, the concepts of energy or evolution in the sciences). Throughout this book I try to add clarity to the idea of meaningful learning, and also distinguish this from memorization or rote learning, so prevalent in much of schooling. So many of the games people play in school or work settings are inherently fraudulent and do not lead to enhancement of learner or teacher. In addition, I seek to show how meaningful learning contrasts with rote learning in terms of the neurobiology of brain functioning, albeit the latter remains a domain of considerable speculation today (see Gazzaniga, 1989, 1995). Rote learning may be useful on occasions, such as when we memorize a poem, the score for a piece of music, or multiplication tables. But the real value of rote learning comes when we also move to understand the meaning of what we have memorized, and it is meaning that confers power to our learning. The person who simply plays the notes he or she has memorized is, at best, a technician, whereas the artist understands and interprets the meaning of the music intended by the composer. The good teacher helps to move the learner beyond rote learning by negotiating meanings with the learner.

For almost a century, most of the scientific research on learning was done with animals in laboratory settings. The idea was that as basic knowledge about learning processes were elucidated through studies with animals, this knowledge could later be applied to improving the education of human beings (Skinner, 1938, 1987). One of the prominent psychologists who had his early training in this scientific behavioral psychology later observed:

> What was important was the promissory note that, once we understood simple conditioning [in animals], we would understand complex behavior [of humans]. The promissory note turned out to be a rubber check. At least, by 1966, nobody has been able to cash it in. (Mandler, 1967, p. 6)

Nevertheless, the dogmas generated by behavioral psychologists remain very much in vogue and continue to guide practice in schools and corporations. For

A THEORY OF
EDUCATION

MEANINGFUL LEARNING UNDERLIES
THE CONSTRUCTIVE INTEGRATION OF
THINKING, FEELING, AND ACTING
LEADING TO EMPOWERMENT FOR
COMMITMENT AND RESPONSIBILITY

J.NOVAK

FIG. 2.4. Briefly stated, this is my theory of education.

example, Glasser (1994) observed this problem in corporations:

> To review briefly, boss-managers, like almost all human beings, believe in and manage according to the traditional theory of human behavior; stimulus-response (S–R) psychology. They follow it mostly because it supports their common-sense belief that people can be made, through reward or punishment, to do what the manager wants them to do whether they like it or not. And, to some extent, they follow it because no one has ever offered them another theory. They have nothing to turn to if they suspect, as I am sure many do, that what they believe may be wrong. Therefore, it is not that they believe in S–R theory so absolutely that they cannot change. It is more that, for almost all people, stimulus-response theory is all there is. (p. 48)

Glasser suggested a new kind of control theory that is predicated on the need to help people construct new meanings and see value in a new idea, thing, or procedure. He asserted, *"You cannot make anyone do what he or she does not want to do. You can only teach him a better way and encourage him to try it. If it works, there is a good chance he will continue"* (p. 50, italics in original).

One reason I prefer the word *act* to *behave* is that it implies a conscious, deliberate, and emotion-laden event, not the kind of passive event we associate with a trained rat or bird. Very little human activity is behavior in the animal sense. Most of it is deliberate action, and at least in the mind of the actor, the action makes sense.

IMPROVING EDUCATIONAL RESEARCH
AND EVALUATION

Agriculture and medicine are two areas in which we have seen dramatic advances in the last few decades. We spend far more on research in these fields than on research in education, and much of what has been spent on educational research has yielded little of value. Most research in education is method driven rather than theory driven. That is, researchers have often compared two or more methods of instruction, usually with little or no theoretical justification for the design of the instruction, or they have used a variety of tests or scales as methods for assessing achievement, often with little or no theory behind the choice of these instruments. Most of this research has led to the conclusion that no significant differences were found between methods or groups, or conflicting results are reported comparing one study to another. Many of the tests used produce not facts, but poor artifacts about human performance.[1] The net result has been that teachers and the public are skeptical at best regarding educational research findings and most of the research that has been done has had little or no lasting effect on the improvement of education.

A major limitation of educational research has been the weak or inappropriate evaluation tools employed. Almost all educational research utilizes some form of questionnaire or multiple-choice or true-false test for evaluation of attitudes,

---

[1]For dozens of examples of this kind of research, see Gage, 1963.

knowledge, or aptitude. And yet we know that most of the test results have near zero correlation with real-life performance and at best they measure only about 10% of the range of human abilities.[2] Unfortunately, many people's lives and futures are determined by this kind of evaluation, not only in the United States but even more so in developing countries. Sternberg (1996a), a distinguished professor of psychology at Yale Universtity observed:

> As an elementary school student, I failed miserably on the IQ tests I had to take. I was incredibly test anxious. Just the sight of the school psychologist coming into the classroom to give a group IQ test sent me into a wild panic attack. (p. 17)

With strong parental support and a wise fourth-grade teacher, Sternberg did go on to succeed in schools and later achieved wide recognition for his outstanding work.

As an alternative to typical testing, concept mapping is proving to be a powerful tool for evaluation, and this, together with other new evaluation methods that are beginning to emerge, show promise both for educational research and practice. It is impossible to improve practice based on research when the evaluation tools used in the research have limited validity at best, and in some cases are negatively correlated with valuable human performance such as creativity.

Education is an enormously complex set of events. Comparing my research experiences in botany as a graduate student with my experience over the past 4 decades as a researcher in education, I would say educational research is an order of magnitude more complex and difficult than most research done in botany. Moreover, botany and other sciences have relatively well-defined theoretical foundations, and also well-defined theory-based methodologies for gathering data, to say nothing about comparatively sophisticated instrumentation. In spite of the morass that educational research has represented (see, for example, Kaestle, 1993), I now feel highly optimistic about future improvement in educational research and subsequent improvement in educational practice. My optimism is based in part on an increasingly powerful theoretical foundation for education and a slow but steady movement toward its application, driven by new global economic pressures.

There is a great need for strengthening the linkages between researchers and practitioners. We already know much that could be extremely useful for the improvement of teaching and learning. There are many skilled and creative teachers in schools, universities, and corporations. Slowly but surely, managers in private and public organizations are learning to be teachers of the kind I seek to encourage with this book. An important challenge is to find better ways to increase the flow of information between researchers and practitioners, and the flow must be in both directions. Federal, state, and local budgeting to encourage this exchange and broaden the context of educational research are needed. New initiatives along the lines of the highly successful Federal Hatch Act (passed in 1865) and the Extension system that has been so successful for our advances in agriculture could yield

---

[2]For a critique of typical educational testing, see Hoffman (1962), Keddie (1973), and Gould (1981).

enormous advances in education. What has been needed is a vision or, more specifically, a comprehensive theory of education to guide the changes needed. The foundations for theory/research-based improvement of education are being laid. We need to seek better institutional structures needed to advance and build on these foundations. There are no easy solutions to the political problems that will need to be solved to effect this advance. With the growing importance of education in every phase of our lives, including our economic well-being,[3] I am confident that solutions will be found.

With the accelerating globalization of business and the growing importance of creating and using knowledge to remain competitive, we shall see in the next decade exponential growth in corporate interest in educating—that is educating that empowers people to be more creative as well as more content. I see a future where new partnerships will be formed between businesses and educational institutions, where a new kind of sharing and seeking solutions will take place. The first decade of the 21st century is likely to be revolutionary in many respects, and most importantly in how we learn better to educate people for whatever the needs may be.

---

[3]See, for example, Marshall & Tucker (1992), Sengé (1990), Drucker (1993), and Nonaka & Takeuchi (1995).

3

Meaningful Learning
for Empowerment

Meaningful learning results when the learner chooses to relate new information to ideas the learner already knows. Its quality is also dependent upon the conceptual richness of the new material to be learned. *Rote* learning occurs when the learner memorizes new information without relating it to prior knowledge, or when learning material that has no relationship to prior knowledge. There is a continuum in learning from pure rote to highly meaningful, and Fig. 3.1 represents this continuum.

Meaningful learning has three requirements:

1. Relevant prior knowledge: That is, the learner must know some information that relates to the new information to be learned in some nontrivial way.
2. Meaningful material: That is, the knowledge to be learned must be relevant to other knowledge and must contain significant concepts and propositions.
3. The learner must choose to learn meaningfully. That is, the learner must consciously and deliberately choose to relate new knowledge to knowledge the learner already knows in some nontrivial way.

This raises the question: What are nontrivial relationships? For example, if a learner knows that Ohio, California, and New York are states, it is comparatively trivial to learn that Michigan is also a state, unless one goes further and recognizes that states are relatively large geographic units and there are only 50 in the United States, including Alaska and Hawaii. The learner needs to seek to build an organized knowledge structure that moves toward recognition of the differences between towns, cities, states, and countries.

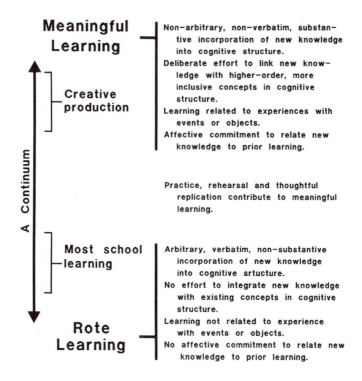

FIG. 3.1. Characteristics of human learning showing variation on a continuum from very rote to highly meaningful. Only high levels of meaningful learning lead to creative production.

When knowledge structures are well-organized, higher order concepts that are more inclusive and more general subsume lower order concepts that are more specific and less general. Figure 3.2 illustrates these relationships for the study of history, where the superordinate concept is HISTORY, and two levels of subordinate concepts are shown. The hierarchical organization is, of course, dependent on the context we are dealing with, and a remarkable characteristic of our minds is that we may use the same concepts in many different contexts and many different hierarchies. For example, for the study of geography, the concept *European* might hold a more subordinate position on a concept map dealing with geography of the world, and it would also have a somewhat different meaning in this context.

FACTS, CONCEPTS, PROPOSITIONS, AND PRINCIPLES: COMPONENTS OF KNOWLEDGE

The universe consists of objects and events. Objects are composed of atoms and molecules whereas events involve objects and exchanges of energy. For example, this page and the words on it are objects composed of carbon, cellulose, and other substances. Energy was required to produce this page.

Your reading of this page is an event that requires mental activity, and this requires energy in the form of biochemical changes in your brain cells. Human beings are unique from all other animals in their ability to perceive regularities in objects and events and to code these regularities with labels. These labels for regularities in events or objects are usually words (some 460,000 in the English language), but may also be signs such as +, -, Σ, Δ, and so forth. The labels represent *concepts,* which I define as perceived regularities in events or objects, or records of events or objects, designated by a label (Fig. 3.3). For example, there are various shapes and kinds of things we call a chair, but once a child acquires the concept *chair,* that child will label correctly almost anything with a seat, back, and legs as a chair (see Macnamara, 1982).

No one has ever seen an atom disintegrating, but we can observe regularities in records of events (such as counts of a geiger counter) that we interpret to mean atomic decay or disintegration. Similarly, no one has ever seen a dinosaur, but we have bones, footprints, and other records whose regularities allow us to construct the concept of a dinosaur. Much of what humans know is constructed from records of events or objects rather than direct observations. We use the term *fact* to indicate a valid record. It is a fact that water boils at 212° Fahrenheit, but if our thermometer reads only 200°F in boiling water, we may be some thousands of feet above sea level, or we may have a faulty thermometer. In the sciences, and especially in the social sciences, it is not always easy to see regularities in events or objects because often, our records are faulty. Facts are not always easily distinguished from artifacts. The pottery fragments studied by anthropologists are human constructions (not naturally occurring objects) and these records of human activity are artifacts. Their meanings must be interpreted, and interpretations may vary widely.

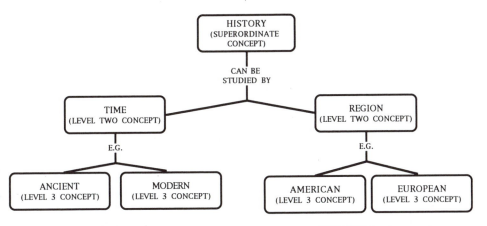

FIG. 3.2. A concept map dealing with the superordinate concept HISTORY showing second- and third-level subordinate concepts.

CONCEPT

A PERCEIVED REGULARITY IN
EVENTS OR OBJECTS, OR
RECORDS OF EVENTS OR OBJECTS,
DESIGNATED BY A LABEL

J. Novak

FIG. 3.3. My definition for Concept.

Principles are relationships between concepts. Principles tell us how events or objects work or how they are structured. In physics, for example, we have the principle: force equals mass times acceleration (F = ma). This principle involves the concepts force, mass, and acceleration. In education, we know that learning is in part a function of study time, but the relationship is complex and we cannot write a mathematical formula to express this principle.

HUMAN MEMORY SYSTEMS

The human brain is a complex organ. It contains at least 300 trillion cells, and each of the cells that functions in storage of information has some thousands of axons and dendrites that permit these cells to store and pass along information. Part of the brain, the lower or limbic region, records information about our feelings, positive or negative. Brain cells are also connected to the skin, heart, lungs, and other organs of our body, as well as to the many muscles of our body that produce our movements or actions. In some wonderful way, the brain serves to integrate our thinking, feeling, and acting. The challenge of education is to help us most constructively to achieve this integration in a wide variety of contexts.

Our knowledge storage system consists of at least three parts: (a) sensory or perceptual (PM) memory; (b) short-term or working memory (STM); and (c) long-term or permanent memory (LTM). Each of these memory systems depends on the others, and what is stored in LTM strongly influences what will be perceived, how it will be processed in STM, and finally how it will be stored in LTM. Study Fig. 3.4 and notice that the arrows show interaction between all of our memory systems.

Many of our human limitations derive from our perceptual limitations. Most of us cannot hear sounds below 80 hertz or above 20,000 hertz, nor can we see light in the ultraviolet or infrared range. No amount of learning can overcome these inherited biological limits on our sensory organs. Nevertheless, there remains an enormous range of events we can respond to within our limitations, and instruments we have developed permit us to extend greatly the sights, sounds, and feelings we can record and respond to. Whereas it is true that instruments yet to be developed may give us wonderful new powers to observe regularities in as-yet-unobserved events or objects, there is perhaps even greater promise in learning how to use the information we now can gather by learning to improve our use of our working memory and the quality of the organization of knowledge stored in our long-term memory.

In 1956, Miller published an article entitled, "The magical number seven, plus or minus two." In this article, Miller presented data to show that our short-term or working memory system can only operate on about seven chunks of information at a time. In a later article, Simon (1974) asked, "How big is a chunk?" Simon's answer was basically that the size of a chunk depends on the knowledge you have in long-term memory. This has been confirmed by numerous studies including my own work. For example, people who recognize numbers as symbols can remember

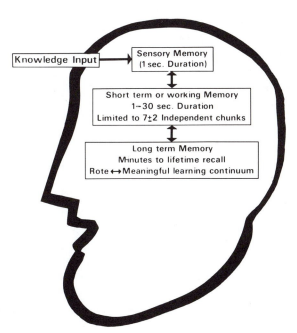

FIG. 3.4. A representation of the three memory systems involved in learning. Note that each system interacts with the other, both limiting and facilitating the acquisition of information. From Novak, 1980. Copyright © 1980 by the National Association of Biology Teachers.

six to eight numbers after a short (5 to 10 second) exposure to a list. The learning time must be long enough to perceive the material through sensory memory, but not long enough to rehearse or repeat the information, until it is set into long-term memory. The same is true for letters, but often letters can be chunked as words or word-like units, and hence 9 or 10 letters might be recalled after a short exposure. In my work, I find that the letters Q C V M E P Y T O are often chunked by people as Q, C, V, Me, Pyto, and all 10 letters can be recalled. Familiar words may contain several letters but each word is a psychological chunk, and five to nine words may be recalled after a short exposure. Very familiar strings of words can also be processed as single chunks. For example each of the following statements could be a chunk: Jack and Jill went up the hill; to be or not to be, that is the question; pi is equal to the circumference divided by the diameter; profit is equal to the price minus the costs. If all of these statements are already well-known by you, you could easily recall all four after a quick reading because they would represent only four chunks in your short-term or working memory. Most people would not have stored in their long-term memory easily recallable meanings for all of these statements, and hence most would have difficulty recalling all four statements after a single quick reading. Certainly every reader has had the experience of listening to a lecture where all of the words used by the speaker were familiar, but when presented rapidly, especially when long sentences are used, the meanings of the sentences cannot be processed in STM and the lecture is incomprehensible.

To return to the idea that meaningful learning requires relevant prior knowledge, we can see that for any learner, the quantity and quality of the relevant knowledge he or she has will vary from topic to topic. Therefore, even with intense willingness to learn meaningfully, any learner has limitations on the degree of meaningfulness that can occur in a given learning task. Refer again to Fig. 3.1. Highly meaningful learning that includes novel problem solving and creativity is only possible in domains of knowledge where the learner has considerable, well-organized prior knowledge. Thoughtful practice or rehearsal also contribute. The dependence of meaningful learning on the adequacy of our prior relevant knowledge is both a blessing and a curse. The more we learn and organize knowledge in a given domain, the easier it is to acquire and use new knowledge in that domain. The curse is that when we try to learn new knowledge in a domain where we know little, and/or what we know is poorly organized, meaningful learning is difficult, usually time consuming, and tiring. Too often, we may escape the challenge by resorting to rote learning, even though we know that what we learn will soon be forgotten and it will not be of value in future learning. Such fraudulent learning may allow us to pass school exams, but contribute little or nothing to future learning or acting.

Human beings are not only remarkable in their acquisition, storage, and use of knowledge; they also manifest complex patterns of feelings or emotions. Feelings, or what psychologists call *affect*, are always a concomitant of any learning experience and can enhance or impair learning. We know relatively little about the memory systems humans have for feelings, although we do know that the amygdala region of the brain is heavily involved, as are also the endocrine or hormone systems of the body. The involuntary or autonomic nervous system is also involved in some complex, but not well understood manner. There is a complex interplay between our knowledge or thinking systems of the brain and those systems involved with emotion or feelings. Much remains to be learned about those systems of our body that produce and store emotional experiences.

Human beings act. They consciously and deliberately move. I prefer the term *act* to *behave,* because the latter is so commonly used to describe animal movements, many of which are controlled genetically or by the environment, and not consciously by a thinking brain. Except for the patellar or knee-jerk reflex and a few other movements, most human movement is under control of our minds. Herrigel (1973) spoke well of this control in his book, *Zen in the Art of Archery.* We know that the lower brain regions and the spinal cord are involved in learning and storing information that controls our muscles, but as with feelings, our knowledge of the nature of this memory system is poor. Nevertheless, the complex interaction that takes place between stored information about knowledge, feelings, and actions is very important in education. This interaction needs to be considered. Figure 3.5 illustrates these interacting systems. Recall also that learning is one element in education that interacts with the other four elements: teacher, knowledge, context, and evaluation (See Fig. 2.2).

An example of a learner seeking to integrate a new experience occurred when my granddaughter bought a new lock for her school locker. My 6-year-old grandson also wanted one of these combination locks. We tried to suggest an easy-to-use keyed lock instead, but he insisted on getting one like his sister's. These locks have a combination such as: right 10, left 36, right 22. Joseph began trying to open his lock and continued try after try. Then he asked me to try, and I opened it quickly. Knowing that it was possible to open the lock, Joseph proceeded to try and try again. I noticed that he was not always getting the number exactly on the mark before turning to the next number and pointed out this requirement for successful action (i.e., opening the lock). He persisted to try and try again, but still his lock would not open, and he came back to me for help. I asked him to show me and explain what he was doing, and I noticed he was not turning the lock one full rotation before turning to the second number. This was a key piece of knowledge that was missing from the lock code attached to the lock, but one I recalled from previous experience with this type of lock. Once he got this information—wow! The lock opened on the next try. Joseph was so excited, he kept on closing and opening the lock, showing his sister, parents, and grandmother how easily he could open the lock. In short, he had achieved successful integration (with a bit of help from his mentor—me) of thinking, feeling, and acting—and the result for Joseph was euphoria!

Any human experience that results in strongly negative feelings can contribute to a breakdown of the normal interplay between how we think, feel, and act. If such

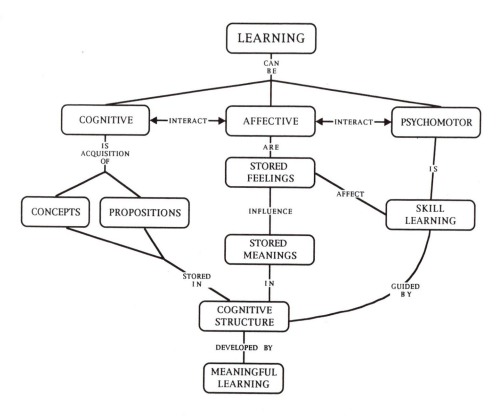

FIG. 3.5. Humans have three distinct but interacting systems for learning, each of which has its own forms of information storage. Meaningful learning underlies development of cognitive structure, which strongly influences our affective and psychomotor learning.

experience is repeated over and over, or is extraordinarily emotionally intense, we may observe actions that signal deviation from acceptable norms or in extreme cases, psychotic actions and what we label as mental illness. Most mental illness is notoriously difficult to cure, partly because so little is known about the ways in which our thinking, feeling, and acting systems store information and influence one another. The best cure is prevention, and an important source of illness is maledu-cation. For example, in one of our studies, we found that every bulimic or anorexic subject we interviewed used primarily rote-mode learning strategies and had a sense of disempowerment over their learning (Hangen, 1989). One of my objectives in building a theory of education is to help to improve education not only to empower humans, but also hopefully to reduce maladaptive practices and in the extreme, psychotic actions.

CONCEPT MAPS AND KNOWLEDGE ORGANIZATION

During the early 1970s, my research program struggled with the problem of making records of what children know about a domain of knowledge before and after instruction. I tried every conceivable form of paper and pencil test and found that these poorly represented the children's knowledge. Interviewing children on how or why they selected their answers showed that many chose the right answer for the wrong reasons and most knew either more or less about the subject than the test question answers indicated. We moved to the use almost exclusively of interviews patterned after the work of Jean Piaget (Pines, Novak, Posner, & Vankirk, 1978), but then we were faced with numerous audio tapes or typed transcripts of these tapes. It was exceedingly difficult to analyze these records and find patterns or regularities that could help us understand how and why children were learning or failing to learn the new subject matter. Working from Ausubel's (1963, 1968) theory of meaningful learning, we decided to examine interview transcripts for concept words and propositions given by the students, for these would indicate prior knowledge and postinstruction knowledge. After trying several ways to organize the concept words and propositions, my research group came up with the idea of *concept mapping*. Figures 3.6 and 3.7 show examples of an early concept map we constructed and a more recent map constructed by a sixth grade student in a remedial program. From 1972 onward, concept maps have played an increasingly important role in our research and instructional programs. They are used extensively in this book to show key ideas and relationships between ideas. I return to a discussion of the study of children's concept development in chapters 4 and 5.

We found that concept maps were a good way to help a teacher organize knowledge for instruction, and a good way for students to find the key concepts and principles in lectures, readings, or other instructional material (cf. Novak, 1991; Robertson, 1989; Wandersee, 1994; Jonassen, Beissner, & Yacci, 1993). Moreover, as students gained skill and experience in constructing concept maps, they began to report that they were learning how to learn. They were becoming better at meaningful learning and found they could reduce or eliminate the need for rote learning. Concept maps were helping to empower them as learners. They also help to empower the teacher, for they are useful as a tool for teachers to negotiate meanings about knowledge with students, and also to design better instruction.

More recently, we have begun to use concept maps in a variety of corporate settings. For example, Fig. 3.8 shows a concept map of the structure of a New York company illustrating internal communication problems. In essentially every company we have worked with, we find the same problems prevail as described by Crosby (1992): Management of organizations don't understand their organizations (pp. 5–6). Every organization I have worked with has found profit in trying to develop a concept map of the organization that is structured to show what the organization is all about. How can one engage in creative management when he or

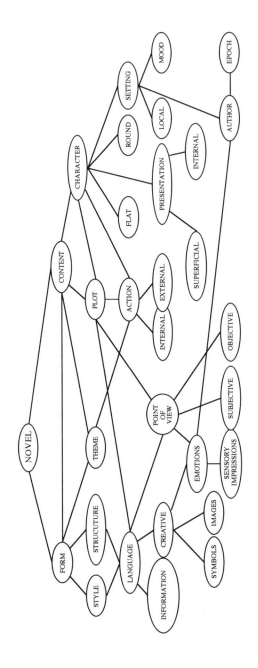

FIG. 3.6. An early concept map constructed to show the structure of a novel. Novels can be compared and critiqued using such a conceptual framework. In later maps, lines linking concepts are always labeled to show specific relationships between concepts; that is, to form propositional statement Reproduced with permission from Moreira, 1977.

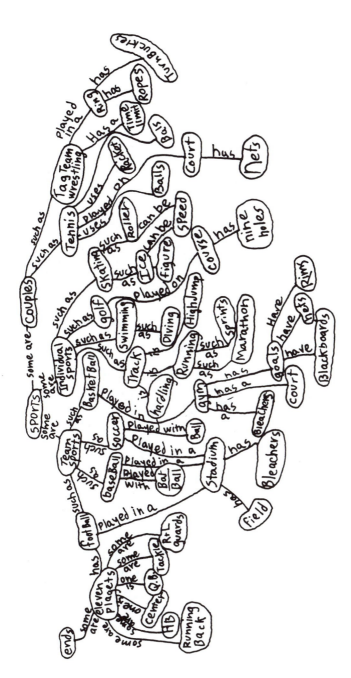

FIG. 3.7. A concept map constructed by a sixth-grade boy in a remedial reading program. Note that most lines are labeled and that concepts plus labels form propositions or statements of principles this boy believes. We see this as a representation of the quantity and quality of knowledge this boy has regarding sports. After experience constructing and sharing concept maps with his class, this boy's performance surged ahead. From Novak and Gowin, 1984. Reprinted with the permission of Cambridge University Press.

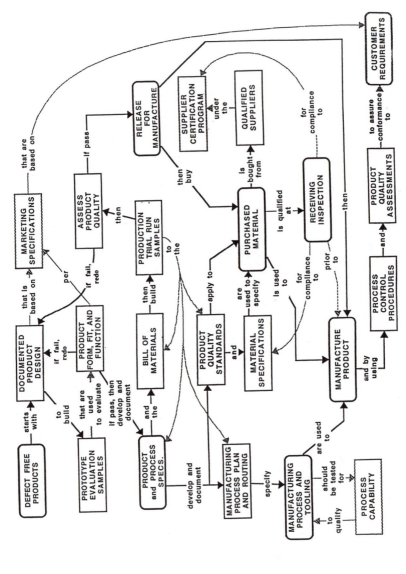

FIG. 3.8. A concept map of the structure of a New York company illustrating internal communication problems. Dotted lines indicate weak or missing communications between sectors of the company, or sectors that need strengthening.

she does not comprehend the nature and purpose of the organization? I shall return to this issue in later chapters.

Our research, and more recent studies by many others in countries all over the world, has shown that young children learn quickly how to make good concept maps, whereas secondary school or university students often have difficulty, partly as a result of years of habit with rote learning (Novak & Wandersee, 1990). We have also found that to benefit from concept maps presented in text or lectures, learners needed to construct their own maps and learn this method of organizing their own knowledge. Our work and other studies led to the publication of *Learning How to Learn* (Novak & Gowin, 1984), now translated into Spanish, Italian, Chinese, Thai, Japanese, Portuguese, Arabic, and Finnish, with a French translations in progress. Concept maps will play a key role as a tool to represent knowledge held by a learner, and also the structure of knowledge in any subject matter domain. Begin to build your skill by starting now to make your own concept maps for this book or for other subjects you are learning. Appendix I provides suggestions on how to make good concept maps. A variety of computer software is now available to assist in construction of concept maps. Figure 3.9 shows a concept map for key ideas about concept maps. For more information on how to construct good concept maps, see *Learning How to Learn* (Novak & Gowin, 1984).

MEANINGFUL LEARNING IS EMPOWERING

Knowledge that we have learned meaningfully, that we have constructed from a union of our actions, feelings, and conscious thought, is knowledge we control. Think of any domain of knowledge where you can relate what you know to how that knowledge operates to make sense out of experience in that domain, and you have an example of knowledge you have learned meaningfully. This is knowledge you control and with which you feel a sense of ownership and power. Then think of a domain of knowledge that you learned mostly by rote. By contrast, this will be knowledge that you have largely forgotten, or for which you see little relationship to experience and over which you feel little sense of power or control. Unfortunately, so much of school learning for most people has been essentially by rote, and this disempowerment has made most of us fearful of learning in one or more fields like science, history, mathematics, music, or athletics. The goal of this book is to provide a theory that can guide us to develop educational experiences that are meaningful, that facilitate meaningful learning, and that reduce the need for rote learning. Education should lead to a constructive change in a person's ability to cope with experience; this is the objective this book addresses.

Paulo Freire (1985), in his work with illiterate adult peasants in Latin countries, developed a pedagogical strategy beginning instruction in language with a few words that had important meaning in the day-to-day lives of the people. These *generative* words, as he called them, could then be used as language building blocks

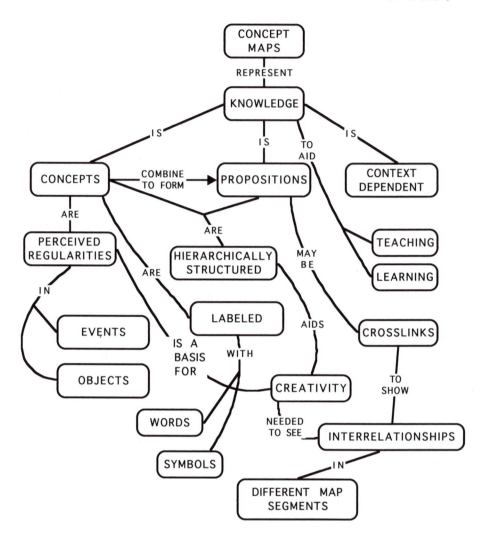

FIG. 3.9. A concept map showing key ideas and principles exhibited in a good concept map.

and gradually the people gained control over reading and writing their own language. The acquisition of literacy led to both increased self-confidence and increased political power. Freire's work to empower the peasants led to his imprisonment in Brazil, and later exile. Freire's teachings and writings (see, e.g., *The Politics of Education,* 1985) have gained worldwide recognition not only for their power in helping adults acquire literacy, but for their general value for empowerment of people.

Most education, Freire asserted (1970), assumes the person is an empty vessel to be filled with information (Fig. 3.10). This banking concept of education proceeds by rote memorization of material that has little or no relevance nor meaning for the learner. It leads to domestication (Freire's term), which makes the learner always dependent on the master for new learning or decision making. By contrast, working with generative words that have significance and meaning in the life of the learner leads to the learner's control over the acquisition and use of new knowledge. This empowers the learner to become autonomous and in charge of his or her destiny. Needless to say, education for empowerment is often a risky business. It also tends to threaten the status quo. Too often in schools and other organizations, people and/or ideas that are innovative are threatening, resulting in a coalescence of forces to quiet or remove the threat.

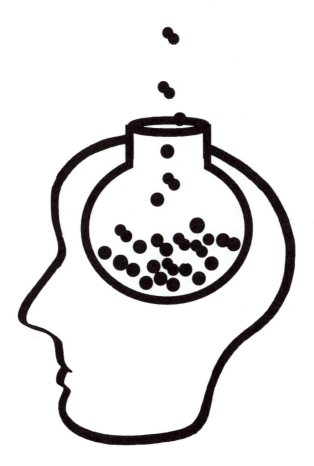

FIG. 3.10. Much of teaching proceeds as if our minds were an empty vessel that needs to be filled with information.

ORGANIZATIONAL LEARNING

At the present time, most education takes place in some organizational setting. In schools, churches, corporations, and other groups, many of the constraints on effective learning are imposed by the structure and functioning of the organization. Organizations are an important aspect of the context of education, as well as exerting influence on what is learned, how it is learned, and how it is evaluated. Sengé (1990), focusing on business organizations, observed that organizations do not know how to learn, and others have shown similar limitations in organizational learning that, in turn, constrain the learning of individuals operating in these organizations. The theory, ideas, and tools put forward in this book address applications to organizations as well as to individuals.

A major problem faced by organizations is how to deal with information, especially information acquired by staff in the course of their years of experience in the organization. Although this is a problem in school settings, it is especially critical in corporate settings where knowledge has become more important than the traditional resources of land, labor, and capital. As Nonaka and Takeuchi (1995) observed:

> Knowledge is created only by individuals. An organization cannot create knowledge on its own without individuals. It is, therefore, very important for the organization to support and stimulate the knowledge-creating activities of individuals or to provide the appropriate contexts for them. Organizational knowledge creation should be understood as a process that "organizationally" amplifies the knowledge created by individuals and crystallizes it at the group level through dialogue, discussion, experience sharing, or observation. (p. 239)

In recent years, I have put a good deal of my time into working with corporations to help them become more effective at capturing, storing, sharing, and creating new knowledge. This work is discussed throughout the book, showing how the ideas that empower learners are also the ideas that are needed to empower organizations.

4

The Construction of
New Meanings

THE MEANING OF MEANING

From infancy onward, healthy human experience is a constant search for meaning. The 1- or 2-year-old child begins to recognize that older people use sounds to represent things or events, and soon the powerful hereditary potential begins to be expressed as mama, dada, doggie, and so on. Human beings have the innate capacity to do something no other animal species is capable of doing, albeit there is some debate on this. They can recognize and use language labels (or sign language) to represent regularities in events or objects. It is this incredible ability that distinguishes *Homo sapiens* from all other species of animals. The marvels of change in living things over the eons of time have somehow led to an animal species that has this unique language capability. *Humanness* implies this capacity, and it also implies a capacity to discern these regularities with feelings. Humans think, feel, and act. Every experience they have involves thinking, feeling, and acting. This is as self-evident as the sun rising in the East and setting in the West. What is not obvious is why and how humans construct their meanings for events or objects.

The meaning of an event or object depends on what we already know about that kind of event or object. School, work, joy, and fear are labels for regularities in experience, but their meanings may be radically different depending on a person's experience. Meaning, to a person, is always a function of how he or she has experienced the combination of thinking, feeling, and acting throughout life experiences. How humans choose to act depends on how they think and feel about an object or event to which they relate. School, work, joy, and fear involve experiences that can lead to radically different meanings to children growing up in radically different environments. It is evident that the context of experience has an important

35

impact on the meaning of an experience. Here we see the important interaction of the learner and the context of the learning.

From birth onward, each human being creates his or her own meanings. Each of us has had a unique sequence of experiences, hence each of us has constructed our own idiosyncratic meanings. However, there is sufficient commonality in our meanings that we can use common language labels to share, compare, and modify meanings. Of course, the more disparate the sequences of experiences of individuals, the more difficulty they experience in sharing meanings. This is the root source of racial, ethnic, cultural, religious, geographic, and other barriers we experience in societies. This will be discussed further in chapter 8.

Some of the key concepts associated with the acquisition of meanings will be presented, and I shall move to discussion of Ausubel's (1962, 1963, 1968) theory of meaningful learning. A few of the key concepts in his theory are shown in Fig. 4.1.

ELEMENTS OF MEANINGFUL LEARNING

Concept Learning and Representational Learning

We have defined concept as a perceived regularity in events or objects, or records of events or objects, designated by a label. One of the issues in the psychology of

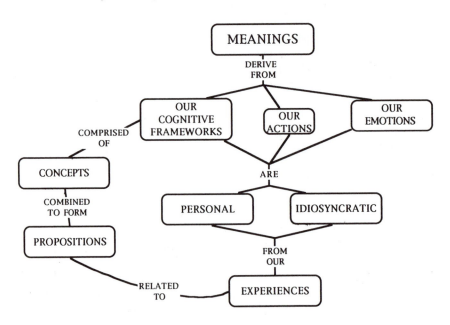

FIG. 4.1. The meanings we hold are a product of our idiosyncratic sequence of experiences and hence vary, at least to some degree, between all people.

concept learning has been which comes first, the perception of the regularity or the acquisition of the label? Piaget in his numerous writings argued that the perception of the regularity must come first, and this was dependent on the cognitive developmental stage of the learner (Wallace, 1976). Vygotsky (1962), on the other hand, held that the availability of a label for a concept can be helpful in acquisition of the concept. For example, if we suggest to a child that dogs, cats, and lions are all carnivores, the child may inquire further as to what other animals are or are not carnivores, thus accelerating acquisition of the concept. Some persons will never acquire a word to represent this concept.

Macnamara (1982) saw in his studies of how children acquire names for things that either the perception of a regularity or the name (word) for a regularity may come first, but facility in proper use of the word requires that both the word label and its associated meaning be integrated. Because meaning is always context-dependent, the meanings of a concept label will always have some idiosyncratic elements, for no two people experience an identical sequence of events (contexts) in which a given concept label is applied. Whorf (1956) was one of the first and most prominent researchers to recognize that the cultural context in which a person lives shapes the meaning of that person's concepts.

Representational learning is a form of meaningful learning where the learner recognizes a word, sign, or symbol as a label for a specific object or event or category of events or objects. Proper nouns are learned through representational learning (e.g., Fido is our dog). Representational learning may preceed concept learning, where a label is learned before the generic attributes or regularities in events or objects are recognized (Ausubel, 1968). Once a child learns that all dogs have certain common characteristics, he or she has acquired the concept *dog.* Similarly, children may recognize similarities between dogs, cats, lions, and tigers long before they learn the word *carnivore* to label or represent this group of flesh-eating animals. Thus concept learning may occur before representational learning.

In learning foreign languages, we may learn synonyms for English words through representational learning, but the subtle connotative meanings for the foreign language words may be acquired much later. Learning the vocabulary used in a new field of study frequently involves much representational learning, but the full conceptual meaning of technical vocabulary may take years, and for some students little more than representational meaning may be achieved. When definitions for vocabulary words are learned by rote, representational learning does not automatically advance to conceptual learning. However, representational learning may provide language labels that may serve to facilitate concept learning (Vygotsky, 1962).

Unfortunately, much school learning that should be concept learning is little more than representational learning for many students. They learn definitions for concepts, but they do not acquire the meanings for the concepts. For example, many biology students learn that a cell is the basic unit of structure of living things, but they really cannot explain what that definition means in ways that make sense to them. They have not acquired the concept *cell.* All of us have done this at times, and often tests do not require us to have more than definitions for labels for concepts, and not the meaning of the concepts per se. We look further at this issue in chapter 9.

Young children are very competent at learning new concepts. I recall when two of my children were under 3, they both referred to a thing adults call umbrellas as *underbrellas.* I'm not sure if it was because it was easier for them to pronounce this word that they chose to use it or if it was because the word made sense as a concept label. After all, people do walk and stand under umbrellas!

It is important for teachers and administrators to remember that they live in a culture in some ways significantly different from their students or subordinates. Therefore, the same word can have significantly different meanings for each person. This is why we emphasize the constant need to negotiate meanings between teacher and learner (refer to Fig. 2.3). The problem is confounded further in that almost every word in the English language (or any language) serves as a label for two or more concepts. For example, we may use the word *red* to refer to a color, high temperature (as in red hot), a political position, and numerous other regularities in events or objects. Many times a student will fail to understand a teacher because the teacher is using one or more words that are being identified by a student as labels for concepts other than those the teacher intends to convey. Technical vocabulary frequently contains many words that are applied to common concepts, sometimes totally unrelated to the technical concept meanings.

One reason we are enthusiastic about concept mapping as an instructional and evaluation tool is that concept maps can be enormously useful to teachers, administrators, and learners to move toward sharing the same concept meanings for the words or symbols presented. They can also be helpful to move the learner from mere representational meaning to richer conceptual meaning. Even with relatively sophisticated learners, concept maps can help to share meanings of concepts and to facilitate creation of new knowledge. We found this to be the case with a research group studying plant root growth at Cornell University. Figure 4.2 shows an example of a global map created by the group to facilitate their discussions and research. Even with highly educated specialists in a knowledge domain, it is common for individuals to find it difficult to share meanings about concepts used in that domain. Concept maps are proving helpful in research settings both for academic and corporate groups.

Propositional Learning

Propositions are two or more words combined to form a statement about an event, object, or idea. Propositions can be valid (e.g., the sky appears blue), invalid (e.g., Paris is the capital of England) or nonsensical (e.g., the door looked). Propositions

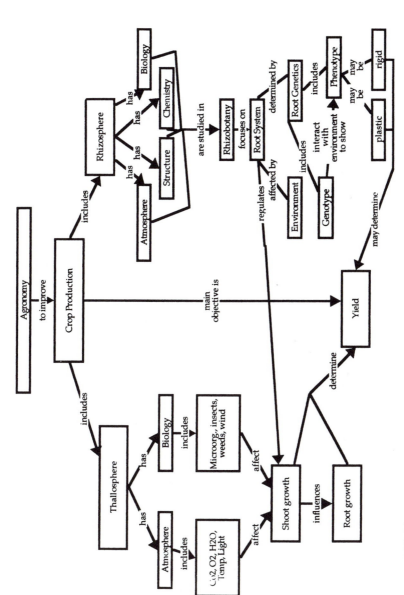

FIG. 4.2. A concept map prepared by the Rhizobotany research group at Cornell University showing key concepts and principles of agronomy and the relationship of the Rhizobotany program to the field of agronomy.

are the principal units that make up meaning. We can liken a concept to an atom and a proposition to a molecule. There are only 100 or so elements in the universe, but there are an infinite variety of molecules that make up an infinite variety of substances. In an analogous way, there are only 460,000 words in the English language, but they can be combined to form an infinite variety of propositions. Poets, novelists, and other writers will never exhaust the possibilities for creating new works.

The meaning we acquire for a given concept is formed from the composite of propositions we know that contain that concept. The richness of meaning we have for a concept increases exponentially with the number of valid propositions we learn that relate that concept to other concepts. This is one reason why we represent learning on a continuum (see Fig. 3.1), where rote learning may be no more than verbatim memorization of a concept definition, whereas meaningful learning can involve relating new concepts through valid propositions for a person's lifetime. Refer to Fig. 4.2 and consider how the propositions shown here may enrich your meaning for the concept *root*. Concept maps are a tool for representing some of the concept-propositional or meaning frameworks a person has for a given concept or set of concepts. If a person could draw all possible concept maps in which a given concept is related to other concepts, for all possible contexts, we would have a good representation of the meaning the concept has for that person. This is obviously impossible. As a matter of fact, none of us know the full potential meaning for concepts we have because a new context or a new, related proposition could yield meanings we had never thought about before. Virtually everyone who prepares a concept map for some domain of knowledge they possess discovers that they knew propositions they had never thought about before, and also that some of their concepts have much more ambiguous meanings than they recognized before. For both teachers and learners, the construction of concept maps can be very revealing of knowledge frameworks they possess. Figure 4.3 shows a concept map presenting some of the ideas just discussed.

Concept learning occurs in two ways, concept formation and concept assimilation. By age 30 months, most children have recognized and accurately learned to label some 200 to 300 regularities with word labels. (See Macnamara, 1982.) In the young child, this recognition of regularities and use of language labels to designate these regularities is a kind of learning Ausubel (1968) called concept formation. The child is discovering through trial and error the language labels older persons use to label the regularities the child recognizes in the surroundings. This is an incredible learning feat that only humans can perform, and all nonbrain damaged children do it successfully by age 3! The child is constructing meanings for words, but simultaneously constructing concepts. There is, in my view, no difference in the process the child uses to learn names for things or events than that which adults use to construct new concepts. Both are fundamentally meaningful learning processes. It is part of the genetic capacity of every normal human being to construct

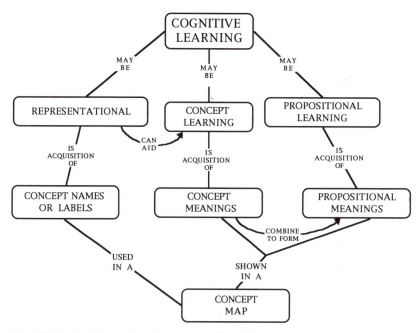

FIG. 4.3. The three forms of cognitive learning, all of which interact.

their own idiosyncratic concept meanings from regularities observed in events or objects. Older learners and more sophisticated learners (such as researchers) also construct concepts from records of events or objects. And concept meanings grow as concept labels are linked to one another to form propositions or statements about events and/or objects. These ideas are shown in Fig. 4.4.

Ausubel (1968) distinguished between primary concepts and secondary concepts. Primary concepts are formed by young children by directly observing objects or events and recognizing regularity in these in the hypothesis testing phase of concept formation and subsequent incorporation of concepts into cognitive structure. Dog, mom, growing, and eating are examples of primary concepts formed by young children. As the child builds cognitive structure, he or she can acquire secondary concepts by the process of concept assimilation. Here concepts and propositions in the child's cognitive structure function to acquire new concept meanings including concepts that have no visible exemplars such as molecule, love, and history. By school age, almost all concept learning is concept assimilation.

Concept meanings grow as concept labels are linked to one another to form propositions. New concepts can be acquired by concept formation or by concept assimilation, where the meanings for new concept labels are acquired when these labels are associated into propositions containing already known concepts. When we use a dictionary to acquire the meaning of an unfamiliar concept label (word), we are engaged in at least the first stage of concept assimilation. Unfortunately, sometimes the synonyms or definition given are not familiar and we cannot begin to grasp the meaning of the new concept (word). Even if the synonyms or definitions are familiar, however, we have only the first beginning of developing a full, functional meaning for the concept. Some concepts, such as evolution, bureaucracy, or capitalism, may undergo growth and changes in meaning over our lifetime. Concept assimilation for most significant concepts is a process of meaning building that is never finished. After age 3, however, it is the process by which most new concept learning occurs (see Fig. 4.5). Schooling, when it is effective, can markedly accelerate concept assimilation.

When my grandson was 5 years old, he asked me at lunchtime one day, "Grandpa, what's annoy?" Joseph has a sister who is 6 years older, so you can easily imagine a context where he heard the word *annoy*. Trying to use concepts and propositions I thought might have meaning for Joseph, I explained that something that bothers you or something unpleasant being done to you is annoying, along with several other examples. Before I finished, it seemed evident that Joseph was no longer paying attention to me, and I thought my attempt to help him assimilate the meaning of *annoy* probably failed. The next day we were boating, and Joseph fell asleep with his life jacket on. When we got to the shore, I laid him down on a hammock to let him continue sleeping. After 15 minutes or so, he got up and walked over to me, tugging on the life jacket and said, "Grandpa, take this thing off. It's

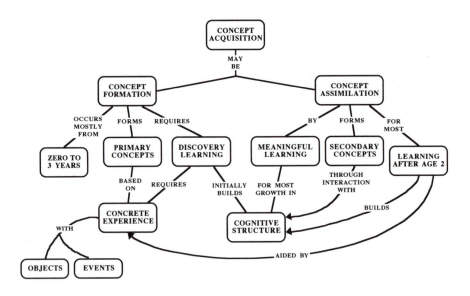

FIG. 4.4. The two forms of concept acquisition and their relationship to experience and cognitive structure.

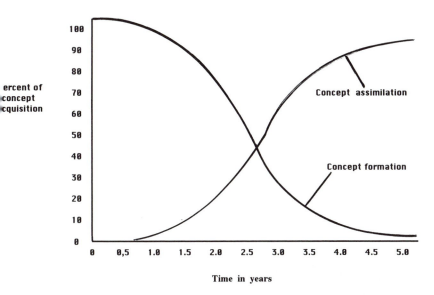

FIG. 4.5. Early concept learning is totally by the process of concept formation, where the child builds through discovery primary concepts that permit later learning by concept assimilation. By school age, almost all concept learning is by concept assimilation.

annoying me." Not only had he assimilated the meaning of *annoy,* he even got the verb tense correct! And from that day on, Joseph evidenced that the meaning for this concept was a thoroughly functional part of his cognitive structure.

More recently, Brown and others recognized the constraints that the context of learning places on concept development, describing what they call situated cognition (Brown, Collins, & Duguid, 1989). They argued that "knowledge is situated, being in part a product of activity, context, and culture in which it is developed and used" (p. 32). My children's development of the concept of *underbrella* was a clear case of situated cognition. The word made sense in terms of the context in which they used it. In widely differing cultures or contexts, the same word may have substantially different meanings or connotations, sometimes leading to embarrassment of either speaker or listener. Using English synonyms for foreign words (or vice versa) can be equally embarrassing at times. Even within English-speaking cultures, the same words may have different meanings. I recall my first experience in an Australian shop when the clerk asked, "Are you right?" She was not inquiring about my health. She meant what American clerks mean when they say, "May I help you?"

Young children can be enormously persistent in pursuing meanings for concepts and propositions. My wife, Joan, recalls an experience with our granddaughter, Rachel, when she was 2½ years old. Joan said, "We are going to the grocery store to get some groceries." Rachel asked, "Why?" Joan replied, "Because we need to get some more food to eat." And Rachel asked, "Why?" Joan replied, " We need to eat to stay healthy and to grow." Rachel asked, "Can't we grow without eating?" Joan replied, "No, we need food to grow." Rachel asked, "If we keep eating, will we keep growing?" Joan replied, "To some extent." Rachel asked, "Why?"

And so the conversation continued on and on, until Joan became exhausted and refused to answer more "why?" questions. Now to some extent, asking "Why?" is a great way for a child to get an adult's attention, and this, too, is significant motivation. Any reader who has been around 2- or 3-year-olds recently probably has had similar experience. But asking "Why?" is also a great way for a child to acquire meanings for new concepts and propositions. So most parents and grand-parents have a pretty high level of tolerance for the persistent "Why?" questions of their young children.

Development of Cognitive Frameworks

At the time of birth, the billions of neurons of the human brain have already been formed. Growth of associated glial cells and formation of myelin around neurons will result in continuing growth in brain size and weight, with most growth occurring between birth and age 2, and almost no brain growth occurring after age 7. Learning and associated cognitive development begins at birth and continues until senescence or death. There have been speculations on the influence of listening to classical music or other environmental influences on a child's cognitive development prior to birth, but no valid evidence exists to support such speculations. Soon after birth, however, cognitive development begins, and by age 15 months most children begin to use language to express their ideas. Again, I refer to Macnamara (1982), who provided a careful description of research on language acquisition.

Piaget's Developmental Theory

The best known studies on cognitive development are those done by the Swiss scientist, Jean Piaget. Piaget's PhD degree dealt with the phylogeny of mollusks (snail and clam types), but after working with Binet on developing intelligence tests, Piaget turned most of his energy to the study of cognitive development in children. Piaget's theory deals with the development of cognitive operational capacities, which are generic in character and are presumed to apply in a wide variety of instances. Piaget (1926) proposed that children undergo four major developmental stages. The first he called the sensory-motor stage (ages 0 to 2 years), during which time most of the child's development is primarily physical. During the sensory-motor stage, according to Piaget, the child comes to recognize, among other things, that objects do not disappear when they are moved out of sight. This cognitive capacity to recognize the permanence of objects is a key charac-teristic of the end of this Piagetian stage.

During the age period 2 to 7, children move through what Piaget called the preoperational stage. This stage is characterized by the child's egocentric view of objects and events in the world and their inability to *decenter*, that is to see an object or an event from a perspective other than their own. For example, when a liquid is poured from a short, wide container into a tall, narrow container, the child will frequently say that the tall container contains more liquid. The child fails to decenter from the height dimension and thus erroneously concludes that the tall container holds more liquid.

Piaget's third developmental stage occurs between the ages of 7 to 11. In this concrete operations stage, the child can decenter and recognize, for example, that the taller vessel is also narrower and that no liquid was lost in the transfer from the short, wide container. However, these cognitive operations require concrete, visible props and the child cannot reason hypothetically to recognize that any form of a container will not alter the amount of substance when it is transferred from one container to another.

The final cognitive developmental stage Piaget described is the formal operational stage, roughly from age 11 or 12 onward. In this stage, the child (or adult) can make inferences or predictions in hypothetical cases as well as for concrete events or objects observed. For example, a child could predict that a given amount of liquid or sand poured into cylinders of varying diameters will be higher or lower in a ratio inversely proportional to the diameter of the cylinder. Formal operational subjects can control variables and predict that a pendulum bob on a long string will move back and forth more slowly than a bob on a short string and that the weight of the bob makes no difference.

Piaget's developmental theory has had enormous popularity in educational circles, especially after the early 1960s when his work was rediscovered (Ripple & Rockcastle, 1964). Hundreds of researchers came forth with studies that showed, in general, that older subjects were more successful at various tasks than younger subjects. Explicit curricular recommendations were made suggesting inclusion or exclusion of specific instructional events based on the cognitive operational capacity presumably required for understanding the events. (See, e.g., Shayer & Adey, 1981.)

My own studies, and my interpretation of other studies, led to a lack of enthusiasm for Piaget's developmental stage theory at best. For example, consider the data shown in Fig. 4.6. This figure makes it very difficult to argue that cognitive development as indicated by Piagetian tasks follows the scheme proposed by Piaget. If most 12 year olds (7th grade) are in the concrete operational stage and most 17-year-olds (12th grade) should be formal operational, why do we get the results shown in Fig. 4.6? It has appeared to me much more valid and more parsimonious[1] to interpret these kinds of data through Ausubel's (1968) assimilation theory of learning and development (Novak, 1977b). Considering cognitive development more broadly, my view is that Vygotsky's (1962, 1986) ideas are much

---

[1]For a discussion of parsimony, see page 96.

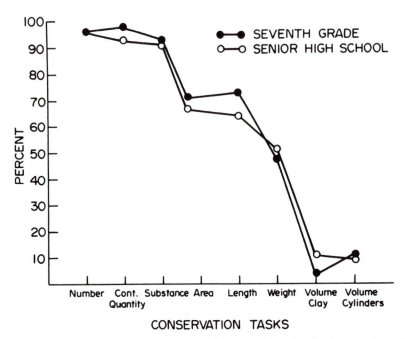

CONSERVATION TASKS

FIG. 4.6. Percent of seventh-grade students and twelfth-grade students performing correctly on eight different Piagetian conservation tasks. Notice that there is essentially no difference in performance between seventh grade and senior high school students on the various Piagetian conservation tasks. From "A study of levels of concrete and formal reasoning in disadvantaged junior and senior high school students," by F. H. Norland, A.G. Lawson, & J. B. Kahle, *Science Education*. Copyright © 1974 by John Wiley & Sons. Reprinted with permission.

more powerful for educators than those of Piaget. Although Piaget and Vygotsky were born in the same year (1896), Vygotsky died in 1934 and Piaget continued to be active in research and writing until his death in 1980. Many of Vygotsky's writings were available only in Russian and inaccessible to most scholars in the west. Recently, new applications of his work have appeared (Moll, 1990). His emphasis on the special contribution that school learning can play, in contrast to Piaget, was evidenced in our own studies.

> Our hypothesis is the notion that although learning is directly related to the course of child development, the two are never accomplished in equal measure or in parallel. Development in children never follows school learning the way a shadow follows the objects that cast it. In actuality there are highly complex dynamic relations between developmental learning and processes that cannot be encompassed by an unchanging hypothetical formulation. (Vygotsky, translated by Kozulin, 1990, p. 91)

It is this complex interplay between developing cognitive structure and school learning that has been the focus of our research programs for the past 4 decades.

Since the publication of Ausubel's (1963) *The Psychology of Meaningful Verbal Learning,* which placed emphasis on the role of concept and propositional learning in schools, we have found more power and parsimony in his ideas than in those of Piaget and his followers. Although other learning theorists, such as Anderson (1983, 1990) and Sternberg (1986) may currently be more popular, I still find greater power and relevance in Ausubel's (1963, 1968) ideas for understanding educational issues and applications. Wittrock (1974), a former student of Ausubel's, has put forth a *generative theory* of learning, but this builds heavily on Ausubel's ideas, with some changes in terminology. Arguments for the relevance and power of Ausubelian ideas are developed throughout this book.

Many teachers and other school people leaped to embrace Piagetian developmental stages as a way to explain why so many students fail to learn and retain usable ideas taught in school. The inadequacy of the student's developmental readiness, both in individual cases and in groups, has been a convenient scapegoat for what in many cases could be better explained as inadequate prior preparation or inappropriate instruction. Numerous researchers are now showing the power of children's thinking in language development (Macnamara, 1982), philosophy (Matthews, 1980, 1984), science (Chi, 1983) and many other areas (Carey, 1985; Donaldson, 1978; Novak & Musonda, 1991). Based on the collective body of evidence, it seems reasonable to conclude that by age 3, all normal children can think hypothetically and deductively ("formal operationally," in Piaget's [1976, p. 24] terms) in domains where they have acquired adequate conceptual/propositional frameworks. Obviously, older children and adults in general possess much richer and more varied knowledge structures than most young children, so there are cognitive developmental differences between young children and older children or adults. Nevertheless, the educative potential of even young children is probably enormously greater than we observe under current educational practices. Bloom (1968, 1976, 1981) has been a strong proponent of the idea that students of all ages can learn much more than traditional school practices achieve. His efforts to help students learn for mastery of subject matter at any grade level place central importance on instructional strategies to improve school learning. I return to issues of instructional design in later chapters.

Flavell (1985), who has done much to help bring clarity and understanding of Piaget's monumental work to English readers, provided a cogent statement on the status of Piaget's work:

It can be argued, with Piaget, that the cognitive systems of infants are indeed fundamentally and qualitatively different from those of older humans. Although Piaget also believed that the cognitive systems of early-childhood, middle-childhood, and adolescent-adult thinkers are likewise qualitatively different from one another, there is growing doubt in the field that these differences, too, are not that radical and stage-like. Older minds may appear to be more qualitatively different from younger ones than they really are. One reason for this is that older minds have accumulated much more organized knowledge, or expertise, in many more knowledge domains than younger ones have, and we now know a number of specific ways that the possession of expertise in a domain [of knowledge] can dramatically improve the quality of one's cognitive functioning within that domain. We would hesitate to say that older minds truly are qualitatively different from younger ones—constitute distinct and different cognitive systems—if disparities in domain-specific expertise were largely responsible for the appearance of qualitative difference. For one thing, the older mind might look almost as immature as the younger one when operating in domains in which it, too, is an utter novice. More generally, both child and adult minds can vary considerably over domains and occasions in the quality of their cognitive performance. At present, therefore, it is difficult to identify really clear-cut, stage-like "cognitive metamorphoses" during the childhood and adolescent years. It is far easier, instead, to defend and document the existence of very important and substantial "developmental trends" during these years. (p. 114)

It should be recognized that although Piaget may have been on the wrong track with his idea of cognitive developmental stages, his monumental studies over 70 years have done much to advance our understanding of how children's minds develop and the necessity for each child to construct her or his own conceptual meanings from experience. We owe much to Piaget for his continuing research efforts to understand how students construct meanings at a time when such research was shunned or ridiculed in much of North America. Partly for this reason, his work was too long ignored in North America. Application of Piaget's ideas to education laid some of the groundwork for what became in the 1970s a revolutionary change in the study of education.

Throughout this book, I deal with some of the cognitive developmental principles and trends and show how they relate to education and to knowledge creation. Human development involves physical, emotional, and cognitive changes, and these in turn are influenced importantly by how we construct new meanings. Therefore, I move next to an extensive discussion of Ausubel's (1968) learning theory, for I believe this remains the most powerful, most comprehensive theory available to understand better ways for educating.

5

Ausubel's* Assimilation Learning Theory

When Ausubel's work came to my attention in the early 1960s, the emphasis on the role of concepts in meaningful learning appealed to me; but it took more than 3 years and six seminars in which Ausubel's work was emphasized before I began to feel comfortable interpreting his theory to others. His work began to make real sense after a 5-day conference[1] on concept learning in 1965 at which I had extensive opportunity to talk privately with him. A sabbatical leave during 1965 and 1966 at Harvard University offered opportunities to study and analyze the work of Jerome Bruner and others. These experiences, and particularly the new interpretations that my students and I were seeing in our research data, led to a growing conviction that Ausubel's learning theory, especially as presented in his 1968 book, was a powerful model of learning to guide education.

David Ausubel first introduced his theory of Meaningful Learning in 1962 under the title, "A Subsumption Theory of Meaningful Learning and Retention." In 1963, he published *The Psychology of Meaningful Verbal Learning*, elaborating on the ideas presented earlier. Finally in 1968, a more comprehensive view of his ideas was published in *Educational Psychology: A Cognitive View* (Ausubel, 1968).

It should be remembered that the late 1930s to the early 1960s when Ausubel was formulating his ideas was also the heyday of behavioral psychology. Not only in the field of psychology in general, but also in educational psychology, behaviorism was the overwhelmingly dominant paradigm, and, along with it, positivistic

---

*Some of the ideas expressed in this chapter represent my views on Ausubel's theory. The description in this and subsequent chapters more closely follows that in a description of assimilation theory of cognitive learning to be found in the second edition of his *Educational Psychology: A Cognitive View* (Ausubel, Novak, & Hanesian, 1978). See also Novak (1994).

[1]A report of this conference was published in Klausmeier and Harris (1966), *Analysis of Concept Learning*.

epistemology was also strongly in control. Positivism and other epistemologies dealing with the nature of knowledge and the nature of knowledge creation are discussed at length in chapter 6. The key idea in positivistic views is that there is one true answer to questions, and these answers will be self-evident if we simply observe and record events carefully. Current ideas see that the nature of questions we ask, the kinds of records we make, and especially the ways we interpret these records are dependent on a whole set of contextual and conceptual factors. The views that Ausubel put forward in the early 1960s were strongly in discord with the prevailing behaviorist ideas and Ausubel experienced considerable difficulty in finding publication outlets in respectable journals of psychology or educational psychology. Recall also that Kuhn's book, *The Structure of Scientific Revolutions,* was published in 1962, and the movement toward newer epistemologies was only in its infancy at the time Ausubel's work emerged.

The prevailing behaviorist dominance not only created a hostile climate for many of Ausubel ideas, but also helped to prevent wide acceptance of Piagetian ideas, which had been put forth since the 1920s in Geneva, Switzerland. In fact, it could be said that Piaget was not discovered in this country until the mid-1960s (Ripple & Rockcastle, 1964).

Not surprisingly, Ausubel's ideas on learning made slow progress in the 1960s, even though there was a relatively immediate recognition of the importance of his work in some circles and the beginning of a substantial worldwide acceptance of his ideas outside of North America. Remember also behavioral psychology did not succeed in dominating the thinking in most European and Asian countries.

Our research group first became familiar with Ausubel's (1963) work in 1964 when we began careful study of his *Psychology of Meaningful Verbal Learning.* The theory put forward in this work explained many of the difficulties we found in interpreting data we were gathering on student problem solving. Working initially with an information processing model of learning (Novak, 1958), we assumed that problem solving was a function of two independent traits, knowledge stored in the mind, and information processing capability. What we found suggested in Ausubel's theory was that these two processes are confounded in the process of new learning, where integration of new and old knowledge is a function of both the quantity and the quality of cognitive structure organization. This interpretation closely followed the pattern of our research results. Further elaboration of this movement away from information processing models and toward Ausubel's assimilation theory has been presented elsewhere (Novak 1977a).

After moving in 1967 from Purdue University to Cornell University, our research group there proceeded not only in the study of problems associated with science learning but also in the design of new instructional approaches based on assimilation theory. These included the development of an audio-tutorial elementary science program that served as a foundation for many of our research studies with elementary school students. It was from this research dealing with a 12-year longitudinal study of science concept learning that the technique of concept mapping was developed by our research group (Novak & Musonda, 1991). Since 1974, much of our research and many of our innovative practices in teaching have involved the utilization of the concept mapping as we developed it.

One strength of Ausubel's theory is that it allows integration of many observations on learning into a single, coherent theory. This coherence is a prime source of difficulty in grasping his theory; each part makes most sense when associations with other parts are understood. But how can one initially grasp the meaning of these associations? It is partly because of this difficulty that we have found a variety of diagrams and concept maps to be valuable. Figure 5.1 shows a concept map of the key concepts and principles (propositions) in Ausubel's theory as I now view his theory, together with some key ideas from epistemology. It is apparent from this figure that his theory is not simple at first glance, but as one begins to work through the figure, it can be seen that each part makes sense, and the key problem centers around understanding the six basic principles shown in the center-right of this figure. These principles are discussed later this chapter.

Ausubel's theory addresses primarily cognitive learning, or the acquisition and use of knowledge. Affective learning, or that information that is stored in our lower brain centers, results from internal signals and interacts with and plays a role in cognitive learning. Ausubel's theory relates to affective learning and we have adopted and extended some of his ideas in our work. Throughout this book, I emphasize the interplay between thinking (cognition) feeling (affect) and acting (motor or psychomotor). Although Ausubel's first doctoral degree was in medicine and he studied and practiced psychiatry until his retirement in 1994, his theory of learning centers on cognitive learning, but it also has important implications for affective and motor learning.

MEANINGFUL LEARNING; ROTE LEARNING

The central idea in Ausubel's theory is what he describes as meaningful learning. To Ausubel, meaningful learning is a process in which new information is related to an existing relevant aspect of an individual's knowledge structure. However, the learner must choose to do this. The teacher can encourage this choice by using tools such as concept maps. Although we do not know the biological mechanisms of memory (or the storage of knowledge), we do know that information is stored in regions of the brain and that many brain cells (perhaps tens of thousands) are involved in the storage of a knowledge unit. New learning results in further changes in brain cells, but some cells affected during meaningful learning are the same cells that already store information similar to the new information being acquired. In other words, the neural cells or cell assemblies active in storage during meaningful learning are undergoing further modifications and are probably forming synapses or some functional association with new neurons. With continued learning of new

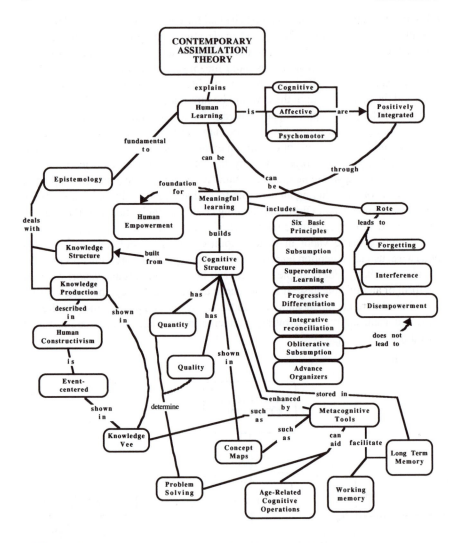

FIG. 5.1. Key ideas in Ausubel's assimilation theory integrated with key ideas from epistemology. These ideas are elaborated further in later sections of this book.

information relevant to information already stored, the nature and extent of neural associations also increase. These ideas are shown in Fig. 5.2.

Throughout this book, I use concept maps to represent the meaning structures that form the conceptual/propositional framework of knowledge. It is into our idiosyncratic knowledge frameworks that new knowledge must be assimilated. To illustrate the process of assimilation using concept maps, consider the knowledge structure of Denny shown in Fig. 5.3. Denny was a 6-year-old student who drew this concept map to show the meanings he had for the words listed on the left. This was the first concept map Denny had made after some 30 minutes of previous instruction in concept mapping. The list of words was provided on the paper.

Notice that Denny's map shows valid meanings for all of the concept labels (words) except *vapor.* All of the words on the list are words discussed in Denny's class and the teacher thought these would be familiar to the students. Denny either overlooked the word vapor, did not recognize it, or did not know its meaning with enough clarity to link it into his concept map. Assuming the latter was the case, Denny could learn the concept of vapor meaningfully. First Denny would need to know what regularity is represented by the label *vapor.* He could learn this by discovery learning where he gradually came to recognize that water can appear in a variety of forms including an invisible form that makes air humid. This form is sometimes called *vapor.* Discovery learning could be highly meaningful to Denny, but it would take considerable time, even if school experiences were provided to help Denny observe vapor in various contexts. Most school learning proceeds otherwise, usually reception learning where meanings of the new concepts (words) are given verbally. For example, a teacher or book could define, "vapor: water in the form of an invisible gas." If Denny chose to learn the concept meaningfully, he would need to relate the meaning of vapor to concepts and propositions he already knows in a substantive, nonarbitrary, nonverbatim manner. This can be illustrated as in Fig. 5.4.

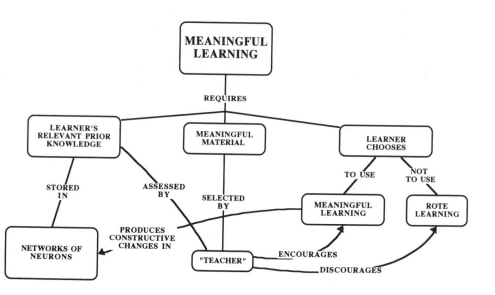

FIG. 5.2. The three requirements for meaningful learning.

54

concepts | concept mapping | name _Denny_

water
solid
liquid
gas
vapor
river
ice
steam

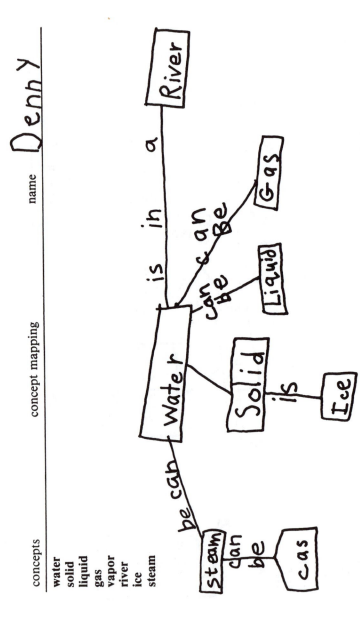

FIG. 5.3. A concept map prepared by Denny, a 6-year-old student, using the words provided on the left. Denny's class had 30 minutes of prior instruction in concept mapping. From Novak and Gowin, 1984 (p. 106). Reprinted with the permission of Cambridge University Press.

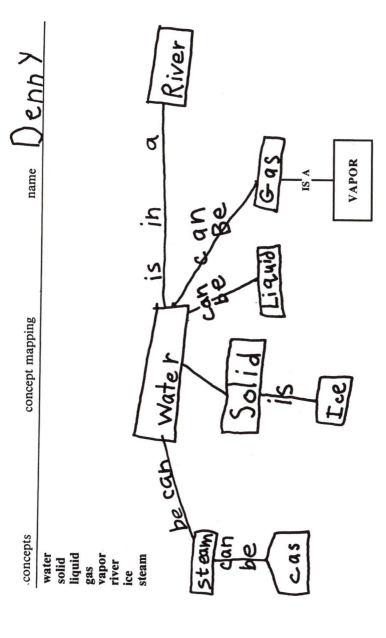

FIG. 5.4. Denny's concept map showing a way in which the concept vapor might have been incorporated following meaningful learning of this concept.

Too often, children in school choose to learn by rote and in this case, the definition of vapor would be learned verbatim and not assimilated substantively and nonarbitrarily into his existing knowledge framework. This is illustrated in Fig. 5.5.

Illustrated also in Fig. 5.5 is a useful relationship that can exist between rote and meaningful learning. A learner can begin learning a new concept by memorizing a definition of the concept, this being representational learning. However, meaningful learning requires further effort; the learner must choose to relate the concepts and proposition(s) of the definition in some substantive way to what relevant knowledge already exists in the learner's cognitive structure. As all of us know from our own experience, this may take more effort, at least initially. As we build up knowledge frameworks in a given domain, learning the definitions and the meanings for concepts becomes easier and easier to acquire. Moreover, concepts learned meaningfully are retained much longer, some for a lifetime. The three basic requirements for meaningful learning were shown in Fig. 5.2. This figure also shows the interplay between three elements essential in any educative event: the learner, teacher, and knowledge or subject matter.

RECEPTION AND DISCOVERY
APPROACHES TO LEARNING

An important contribution in Ausubel's writings has been the distinction he emphasized between the rote—meaningful learning continuum and the reception—discovery continuum for instruction.

After the Russian launch of Sputnik in 1957, there was a national outcry that U.S. education was weak and that we were falling behind the Russians. One of the condemnations of school learning was that too much school instruction, and too much of our testing, emphasized nothing more than rote learning. The alternative that became widely promulgated, especially in science and mathematics, was to move instruction toward greater emphasis on teaching strategies centered on discovery learning. The result was the development of programs where students were provided activities where the answers were not given, and where manipulation of materials or equipment could lead to discovery of concepts. Because it is patently obvious that children in school settings could not discover the concepts and principles constructed by geniuses in various fields over the past few centuries, it was not surprising that the emphasis on learning by discovery soon led to disenchantment with this approach by teachers and the public. Even under the best of circumstances, and with considerable guidance, only the more able students were demonstrating significant achievement. (See, e.g., Shulman & Keislar, 1966.) Instruction emphasizing discovery learning began to disappear in schools, albeit most schools and teachers never embraced this approach.

What was needed in the 1960s, and what I believe is needed today, is not more emphasis on discovery learning, but rather more emphasis on meaningful learning.

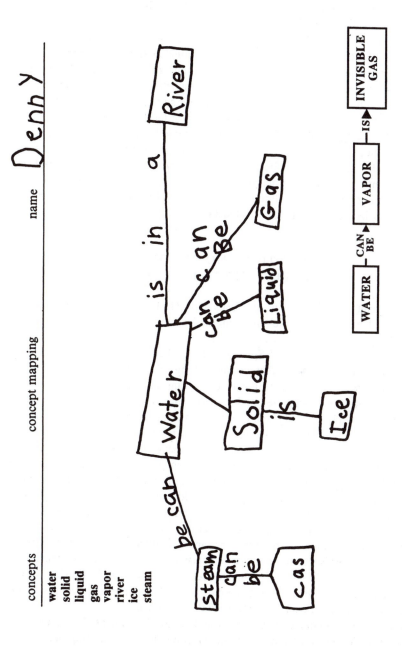

FIG. 5.5. Denny's concept map showing the definition of vapor as learned by rote. The propositions in this definition are not related to, nor incorporated into, his prior conceptual framework.

57

Figure 5.6 illustrates the orthogonal relationship between the rote-meaningful learning continuum and the reception-discovery continuum for instruction. Any instructional strategy can lead to meaningful or rote learning. What Ausubel presented in his 1963 *The Psychology of Meaningful Verbal Learning* was a psychology of learning that defended the role of reception or expository teaching in schools as necessary and efficient and pointed toward instruction and learning approaches that could move school learning from predominantly rote learning toward predominantly meaningful learning. Current preoccupation with setting test standards for students and teachers probably is moving much school learning toward increasingly rote learning, with negative consequences for acquisition of organized knowledge that can function to facilitate new learning and creative problem solving. This book is an effort to offer a comprehensive alternative program.

In the corporate setting as well as in schools, learning is too often by rote. This is especially the case when underlying reasons for rules, practices, and procedures are not explained to workers. Too often, corporate training programs are training almost in the way rats are trained to run a maze. Most of the learning encouraged is rote learning, and evaluation practices often encourage rote, not meaningful, learning. In the simpler work environments before the globalization effects set in, rote learning in training programs was sufficient and generally more economical. With the rapid changes occurring in almost all work environments and the growing

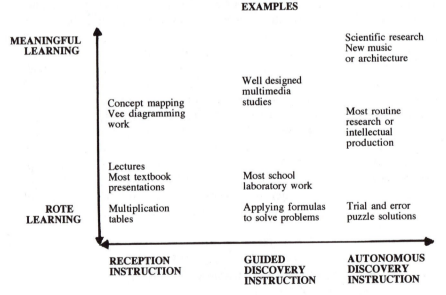

FIG. 5.6. The rote-meaningful learning continuum is distinct from the reception-discovery continuum for instruction. Both reception and discovery instruction can lead to rote learning or meaningful learning. School and corporate learning needs to help move learners toward high levels of meaningful learning, especially in reception instruction that is the most common.

complexity of most jobs, training programs can lead to costly mistakes; what is required are education programs that provide for and foster meaningful learning. The military services, for example, are finding they need a different kind of recruit, one who knows how to think and how to learn meaningfully. Most high school graduates who apply fail to meet their criteria for recruitment.

SUBSUMPTION AND OBLITERATIVE SUBSUMPTION

In the course of meaningful learning, new information is linked with concepts in cognitive structure. Usually this linkage occurs when more specific, less inclusive concepts are linked to more general existing concepts in cognitive structure. In order to place emphasis on this linking phenomenon, Ausubel (1968) introduced the terms *subsuming concept* or *subsumer*. The justification for adding these terms lies in the primary role that subsumers play in the acquisition of new information. A subsuming concept is not a kind of mental fly paper to which information is stuck; the role of a subsuming concept in meaningful learning is an interactive one, facilitating movement of relevant information through the perceptual barriers and providing a base for linkage between newly perceived information and previously acquired knowledge. Furthermore, in the course of this linkage, the subsuming concept becomes slightly modified, and the stored information is also altered somewhat. It is this interactive process between newly learned material and existing concepts (subsumers) that is at the core of Ausubel's assimilation theory of learning.

In my example with Denny, the concept *vapor* was subsumed under the concept *gas* and in turn under the concept *water*. This subsumption process would in small ways change Denny's meaning for the concept *gas* and the concept *water*. Moreover, other concepts in Denny's cognitive framework may also have had their meanings altered somewhat, perhaps in recognition that steam and vapor are both gases. If, at a later date, Denny obliteratively subsumes *vapor* as a concept (that is, he can no longer give a good description of the regularity represented by this label), his concept of water and steam would still be modified and probably enhanced as compared with the meanings Denny had before learning about *vapor*. When you consider the fact that at least tens of thousands of neurons are involved in subsumption of a new concept, there are almost unlimited neurological possibilities for varying degrees of subsumption or obliterative subsumption in the course of meaningful learning and later when knowledge is retrieved.

FORGETTING CONTRASTED WITH
OBLITERATIVE SUBSUMPTION

Most information we learn cannot be recalled at some time in the future. Although the debate continues as to whether the biological mechanisms accounting for forgetting result in physical destruction of stored memory traces, or whether forgetting is purely a psychological phenomenon, for purposes of education the fact that information becomes irretrievable some time after learning is of primary concern. Most careful research on retention has been done in laboratories where subjects are given nonsense syllables or word pairs to memorize and are then tested for later rote recall of information. Some studies have used poetry, story passages, and ordinary school materials for analysis of retention. These studies show that substantial forgetting occurs in a matter of hours for nonsense syllables; for poetry and story passages, much is lost in a matter of days; and for science, history, or other classroom information, retention drops to a fraction of original learning in a matter of weeks. Some information, however, is retained for months or years, especially information that has been rehearsed extensively. Forgetting has both an everyday meaning (i.e., a failure to recall something) and a specific technical meaning (i.e., the kind of failure to recall after rote learning). Figure 5.7 shows the relationships between forgetting and obliterative subsumption.

In Ausubel's theory, variation in amount of recall depends primarily on the degree of meaningfulness associated with the learning process. Information learned by rote (nonsense syllables and meaningless word pairs) cannot be anchored to major elements in cognitive structure and hence form a minimum linkage with it. Unless materials learned by rote are restudied repeatedly to achieve *overlearning* (continued study after error-free recall has been achieved), they cannot be recalled several hours or several days after learning. Information that is learned meaningfully (associated with subsumers in cognitive structure) can usually be recalled for weeks or months after acquisition. The process of subsumption results in some

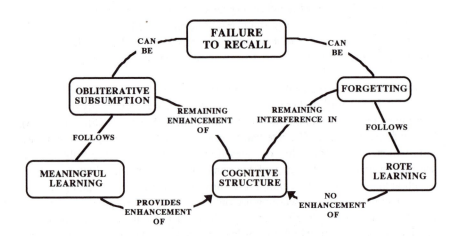

FIG. 5.7. Failure to recall is a different process following meaningful learning of information than that following rote learning. There remains a residual enhancement of cognitive structure with meaningful learning and no interference with future related learning.

modification of the stored information, however. As a result, recalled information may appear in a form slightly different from that originally learned. In time, recalled information may take on more general attributes of the subsuming concept(s) into which it was assimilated, and after obliterative subsumption has occurred, the *specific* messages learned are no longer retrievable. Nevertheless, there remain enhanced ideas in cognitive structure that can facilitate future learning. For example, we found that students who took algebra in ninth grade did substantially better with later studies on vectors in a physics class, even though much of their specific knowledge from algebra was obiteratively subsumed (Gubrud & Novak, 1973).

Rote learning has one important advantage over meaningful learning; I have already noted that sometimes it is useful to recall knowledge learned in precisely the same form as the original message. Phone numbers, for example, cannot be approximate. However, this process is all too frequently required in school testing. When verbatim recall of definitions of concepts or principles is required, meaningful learners can be at a disadvantage. This phenomenon underlies what Hoffman (1962) described as the tyranny of testing. Evaluation problems are discussed further in chapter 9.

Meaningful learning has four important advantages over rote learning. First, knowledge acquired meaningfully is retained longer—much longer in many instances. Second, subsumed information results in increased differentiation of subsumers, thus adding to the capacity for easier subsequent learning of related materials. Third, information that is not recalled after obliterative subsumption has occurred has still left a residual effect on the subsuming concept, and in fact, the whole related framework of concepts. Thus there is facilitation of new related learning even after loss of recall of a specific subordinate element has occurred. Fourth, and perhaps most important, information learned meaningfully can be applied in a wide variety of new problems or contexts; the transferability of knowledge is high. It is this power for transferability that is necessary for creative thinking.

The differences in recall of information after rote or meaningful learning is very important. Laboratory studies have shown that information learned by rote inhibits subsequent learning of additional similar information (Suppes & Ginsberg, 1963). Even information learned by rote that is forgotten inhibits learning of similar new information. The reverse effect operates after meaningful learning. Although it is true that restudy or relearning of the same information is facilitated by prior retention in both rote and meaningful learning, the savings (as psychologists refer to this facilitation) in rote learning are only for relearning of precisely the same material, whereas meaningful learning will result in savings for relearning and facilitation (rather than inhibition) of learning new, similar (relevant to the same subsumer[s]) information.

Many students experience the feeling of being snowed under by the material of a course. Usually this feeling becomes most intense 6 to 8 weeks into a course.

Some studies (see Hagerman, 1966)[2] indicate that most information learned by rote in schools is lost within 6 to 8 weeks. As a result, students recognize that they have forgotten much of the information presented earlier and that their earlier learning is now lost and is interfering with new learning. They must force themselves either into review and meaningfully restudy earlier materials, cram for hours to overlearn earlier material, or give up hope of passing the course. The same phenomenon may occur at the beginning of a course when materials are highly related to similar previous courses, and prior learning was rote in character.

Figure 5.8 illustrates the problem that derives from rote versus meaningful learning. Because rote learning takes relatively little effort on the part of a learner initially, it is relatively efficient; that is, a learner can repeat verbatim some of the key concept definitions and propositions presented in the instruction. However, because the latter are stored arbitrarily and nonsubstantively in cognitive structure, they soon cannot be recalled and confer interference with new, related learning and recall of related information. During interviews on almost any topic, persons who have been learning by rote may recall bits of information but relate these in very inappropriate ways. For example, in a video developed at Harvard University, 21

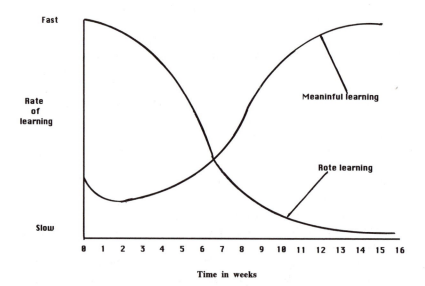

FIG. 5.8. Early in a learning program, rote learning of information can be faster than meaningful learning of the information. However, as forgetting occurs, interference with new related learning occurs, and learning speed is relatively slower than that for meaningful learning where recall is stronger and no interference, but rather learning facilitation, occurs.

---

[2]One might expect that studies of retention of school-taught information would be extensive. Unfortunately, this is not the case, except in more generic form where a variety of studies show school-taught information has little impact on cognitive structure building (cf., Helms & Novak, 1983; Novak, 1987; and Novak & Abrams, 1993).

out of 23 graduates and faculty members knew that the earth's orbit was not a perfect circle (actually, they thought it was much more elliptical than is the case), but they erroneously believed that the seasons on the Earth (at least in the Boston area) were caused by the earth's proximity to the sun (Schneps, 1989; see also Fig. 7.4). In fact, the Earth is actually slightly closer to the sun in the Northern Hemisphere in the winter than in the summer. Even a graduate who had taken a course in Physics of Planetary Motion failed to explain why we have seasons. Obviously, most of his learning had been by rote, but he did graduate from Harvard!

PROGRESSIVE DIFFERENTIATION

As meaningful learning proceeds, development and elaboration of subsuming concepts necessarily occurs. The refinement of concept meanings in cognitive structure giving more precision and specificity to these concepts is called *progressive differentiation* of cognitive structure. Addition of new concepts through meaningful learning, or restructuring existing segments of cognitive structure, also produce progressive differentiation of the learner's cognitive structure.

In Ausubel's (1968) view, concept development proceeds best when the most general, most inclusive concepts are introduced first and then these concept are progressively differentiated in terms of detail and specificity. For example, to introduce the concept of culture, we might begin by explaining that all the knowledge, skills, values, and habits passed on from parents to children constitute the culture of the human race. We could subsequently discuss Samoan or American Indian or urban American cultures, describing the methods and agencies by which the general cultural elements are transmitted.

Determination of what in a body of knowledge are the most general, most inclusive concepts and what are subordinate concepts is not easy. In a later chapter, I argue that good curriculum design requires an analysis first of the concepts in a field of knowledge and second, consideration of some relationships between these concepts that can serve to illustrate which concepts are most general and superordinate and which are most specific and subordinate. One reason school instruction and instruction in corporate training programs has been so ineffective is that curriculum planners rarely sort out the concepts they hope to teach and even more rarely do they try to search for possible hierarchical relationships among these concepts. As stated previously, my premise is that concepts are primarily what we think with, that concept and propositional learning is the principal function of schooling. Therefore, we must sort out from the mass of knowledge those major superordinate and subordinate concepts we wish to teach. Attitudes and skills are necessary and supportive elements for concept learning, but for most education, these are associated or concomitant learning and do not constitute the primary structure of school curriculum. Even in trade schools, in the study of auto mechanics, for example, learning concepts in the field is at least as important as learning skills. Moreover, all skills require a cognitive framework to control the actions, and skills can be acquired better when this cognitive framework is made explicit. Many of the professions require skill learning as well as concept and propositional learning. In nursing, for example, Smith (1992) showed that improving the quality of knowledge learned also led to improved performance of nursing skills.

To illustrate the idea of progressive differentiation I refer again to the concept map made by Denny. If Denny could assimilate the meaning of the definition given for vapor (i.e., vapor is water in the form of an invisible gas), he would subsume several concepts under existing concepts he already has. (See Fig. 5.4.) He might also recognize that water can be small droplets that can float in air as in fog or clouds. He would recognize that these small droplets are droplets of liquid water that float in air. The conscious process Denny would need to engage in during meaningful learning may lead him to wonder: How is vapor different from fog? Why do the small droplets float in air? Is there also vapor in fog or clouds? What is a gas? To get answers to these questions, Denny would need to differentiate his knowledge further (hence the progressive nature of differentiation). Answers to these questions would also lead to new linkages between concepts he already holds and perhaps new discriminations, as for example, what is a gas and what is not a gas. These new meaningful learning experiences would result in integrative reconciliation. (See Fig. 5.9.)

INTEGRATIVE RECONCILIATION AND QUALITATIVE IMPROVEMENT OF CONCEPTUAL HIERARCHIES

Subsumption and progressive differentiation lead to more than quantitative addition of knowledge to a conceptual framework. There are also qualitative changes in that each of the concepts in the relevant structure are modified in meaning to some extent. It is evident that as we subsume concepts into a mapped hierarchy, the meanings of all the concepts are modified at least slightly because there are meaningful connections vertically and horizontally across the structure. Neurologically, at least some new synapses would be forming between the neurons storing the new concept and neurons storing all previously learned, related concepts. Thus we see that both quantitative and qualitative changes in knowledge result from meaningful learning. The same effects do not arise from rote learning, as illustrated in Fig. 5.5.

Another form of cognitive differentiation arises when new interrelationships are seen between concepts in cognitive structure, relationships we can represent as crosslinkages on a concept map. These crosslinkages represent what Ausubel, Novak, and Hanesian (1978) described as integrative reconciliations. They could arise from answers to the questions suggested on page 88. Included in the category of integrative reconciliation of concepts would be understanding when a given concept is similar to but also different from another concept, such as how a vapor

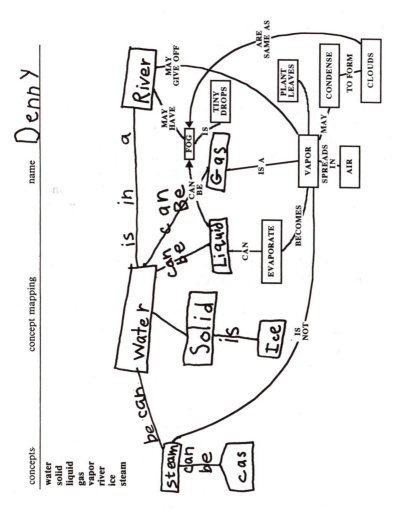

FIG. 5.9. Denny's hypothetical map showing further progressive differentiation and integrative reconciliation of concepts and propositions relevant to water.

is like fog (it drifts about) and different from air (made of water molecules, not oxygen, nitrogen and other molecules). When integrative reconciliation occurs, there is simultaneously some improvement or progressive differentiation of cognitive structure. Figure 5.9 illustrates possible integrative reconciliations in Denny's concept map. In the course of seeking to make integrative reconciliations (resulting from answers to why or how questions), a learner often acquires one or more new concepts and integratively reconciles the meanings of the new and old concepts. There is integration because new concepts or relationships are substantively incorporated into the cognitive structure and there is reconciliation when meanings of similarities and/or differences are incorporated into cognitive structure. When meaningful learning is pursued by a learner in any subject matter over a span of time, subsumption, progressive differentiation, and integrative reconciliation all occur simultaneously, at least to some degree.

To illustrate new concept learning, subsumption, progressive differentiation, and integrative reconciliation, I refer to concept maps prepared from interviews with Paul in second grade and 10 years later in twelfth grade (Novak & Musonda, 1991). In second grade, Paul understood that some substances were made of tiny chunks and these substances could break into tiny chunks, as when sugar is put into water. He also recognized that these tiny chunks would not be seen. (See Fig. 5.10.) After 10 years of schooling, Paul had acquired the concept of *molecule,* and recognized that all substances were made of molecules, separated by space (a new concept). (See Fig. 5.11.) His initial concept of *tiny chunk* now had a new and more explicit meaning and he has also differentiated between atoms and molecules as tiny chunks

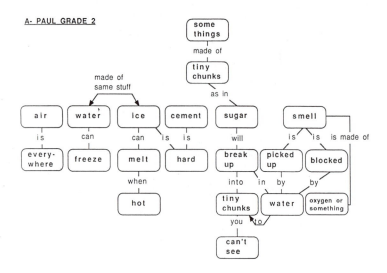

FIG. 5.10. A concept map drawn from an interview with Paul, a second-grade student. From Novak and Musonda, pp. 139–149. Copyright © 1991 by the American Educational Research Association. Reprinted by permission of the publisher.

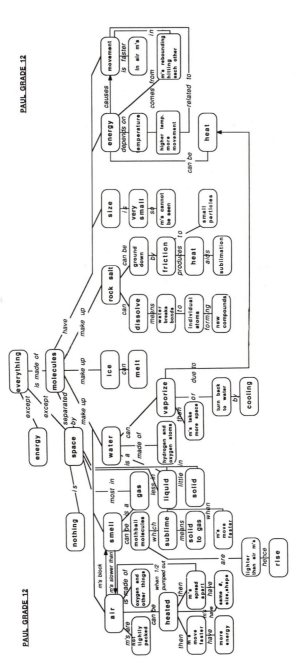

FIG. 5.11. A concept map drawn for Paul from an interview in twelfth grade. Notice the quantitative and qualitative growth in Paul's conceptual/propositional knowledge about forms of matter. From Novak and Musonda, p. 140. Copyright © 1991 by the American Educational Research Association. Reprinted by permission of the publisher.

67

of matter. He has acquired the concept *energy* and has integratively reconciled this concept with atom and molecule to understand why things dissolve, sublime, vaporize, or melt. Concept maps made from interviews in seventh and tenth grades would show intermediate stages of concept development, differentiation reconciliation. What has been conspicuous in our 12-year study of concept learning in science is the remarkable degree to which new learning builds on prior knowledge, including prior misconceptions (faulty propositions), and also the limited extent of cognitive development for those students who have not been learning science meaningfully (Novak & Musonda, 1991).

Piaget's developmental theory presents the concepts of assimilation, accommodation, and equilibration. To Piaget, assimilation occurs when new learning fits into a cognitive operational structure and requires no change in that structure. Accommodation occurs when new learning requires some modification of an operational structure, leading to a new equilibration of the structure. Piaget's cognitive structures are not subject matter specific conceptual/propositional frameworks such as I have been illustrating with Denny's and Paul's concept maps. Instead, they are general or generic cognitive capacities that apply in any subject matter and that progress from sensory motor (ages 0 to 2) to preoperational, concrete operational and finally formal operational thinking (age 11 onwards). (Refer back to pp. 44–48). Thus there are some similarities between Ausubel's ideas of subsumption, progressive differentiation, and integrative reconciliation and Piaget's ideas of assimilation, accommodation, and equilibration—in both cases these take place over time—but there is also one crucial difference. Piaget's cognitive developmental periods refer to general reasoning capacity, whereas my version[3] of Ausubel's assimilation theory holds that reasoning capacity is primarily a function of the adequacy of the relevant conceptual framework a person has in a specific domain of knowledge. This is not to deny that older learners, in general, have better qualitative and quantitative knowledge frameworks for most domains of knowledge as compared with younger learners. However, as Chi (1983), Nussbaum and Novak (1976), Carey (1985), Papalia (1972), and others have demonstrated, young children can acquire large and complex knowledge frameworks in limited areas and their reasoning capacities in these areas may exceed that of many adults. It is the children in many homes who program the VCR machine for their parents. Refer again to the quotation from Flavell (p. 47–48).

There are, of course, generic strategies regarding learning, and older learners may acquire more powerful learning strategies than younger learners possess. In fact, the principal purpose of our work in helping students learn how to learn is to empower learners not only through helping them develop their conceptual frameworks but also through aiding them to gain more competence in acquiring and using strategies to gain qualitatively and quantitatively richer conceptual frameworks,

---

[3]Ausubel and I vary somewhat in our views on cognitive reasoning capacity, with my view being much more optimistic regarding young learners.

and enhanced self-esteem. This idea will be discussed further in later chapters. Also discussed later are genetic or hereditary factors in learning.

SUPERORDINATE LEARNING

Occasionally in the history of any discipline, or in the life span of an individual, new concepts are constructed that pull together and integrate large domains of knowledge that were not previously recognized as intimately related. This was the case when Newton conceived of his law of gravitation that explained not only why objects fall toward the center of the earth, but also why planets follow their orbits around the sun. Newton's concept of universal gravitation brought together domains of knowledge that most people saw as totally unrelated. Similarly, Einstein's concept of relativity led to his ideas on the equivalence of mass and energy and his now famous proposition, "energy is equal to mass times the square of the speed of light" (e = mc^2). Before Einstein, whoever thought that mass and energy could be so related?

In a similar manner, once in a while during the course of a lifetime, a learner may experience the acquisition of a new broad, general concept that then subsumes in powerful new ways the meanings of previously learned concepts and adds new and rich meanings to these concepts. This occurred for me when I began to understand more comprehensively the meaning of meaningful learning. Most of my graduate students have reported similar experiences, leading them to such remarks as, "Meaningful learning is truly the bottom line, isn't it? It ties together everything we know about learning and schooling!" As you study and grasp the ideas in this book, you may experience similar superordinate learning. It is easy to memorize verbatim the theory of education stated in chapter 2: "Meaningful learning underlies the constructive integration of thinking, feeling, and acting leading to human empowerment for commitment and responsibility." It may take months or years for you to grasp the superordinate meaning of this idea or the concept of meaningful learning. I believe that my understanding of the meaning of the concept *meaningful learning* continues to grow with each new research project and with every class I teach.

One of the research projects we have done in the field of chemistry demonstrated the power of learning a superordinate concept for facilitation of other learning in chemistry. Cullen (1983) designed a study guide for freshman chemistry that sought to help students understand the meaning of *entropy* as a major superordinate concept that helps a student understand most of chemistry. Briefly stated, entropy is the degree of disorder in any system, and energy is required to lower entropy (or disorder) in a system. Chemical reactions usually proceed in a direction that increases entropy unless energy is supplied to push the reaction in the direction of less entropy. Now most of us can memorize the last two sentences rather easily, but what do they mean in terms of all the reactions students usually memorize when they study chemistry? To acquire the meaning of the concept *entropy* and to have this concept rise to the level of a superordinate concept in our conceptual framework takes time—and carefully guided instruction. This is what Cullen sought to do, although as a graduate teaching assistant in the course, he was limited in the degree of intervention permitted. His specially prepared laboratory study guide, some audio-tutorial lessons (Postlethwait, Novak, & Murray, 1972) available to experimental students in the library, and his own emphasis on entropy in laboratory sections he supervised were the extent of intervention permitted. The lecture portion of the course, common to all students, also placed considerable emphasis on the entropy concept.

Cullen (1983) found that most of the students in the experimental sections performed no better than students in the control sections on regular course examinations. There was a significantly higher performance for one experimental section on a test for routine problem solving. Also, experimental students did not use the entropy concept to explain answers to problems more frequently than control students. These data are consistent with many of our research findings that most college (and secondary school) students resist moving toward meaningful learning strategies and may show little or no achievement gains on standard course exams. However, when Cullen looked at individual students who gave the best answers to complex, novel problems, all 12 of these (out of 81) used the entropy concept as a major organizing idea. Eleven of these 12 were students in the experimental section. For them, substantial superordinate learning of the concept of entropy had occurred. For most of the others, superordinate learning of the concept of entropy had not occurred; they demonstrated no unusual proficiency in understanding chemistry.

We have found in our work with both secondary school students and university students that the majority would prefer to get by with memorizing information rather than working to build conceptual understanding. Years of school experience with evaluation practices that require little more than rote recall may be at least partly to blame. Perkins (1992) also identified other factors that discourage what he calls *complex cognition*:

> Complex cognition has more intrinsic interest and promises more payoff outside of school and later in life. But consider the cost to learners: complex cognition demands much more effort. It creates greater risk of failure. It introduces the discomforts of disorientation, as learners struggle to get their heads around difficult ideas. Peer status for complex cognition is certainly mixed; who wants to be known as a "brain"? And very commonly, so far as grades and teacher approval go, complex cognition buys students no more than the simpler path of getting the facts straight and the algorithms right. No wonder, then, that students perfectly reasonably do not automatically gravitate toward complex cognition. (pp. 59–60)

After 12 or 16 years of this kind of schooling, it is difficult for individuals to change the patterns of acting when they enter the real world. Waitley (1995) identified 11 action reminders that may help some to achieve this transition, such as, "Invest in developing your knowledge and skills. The only real security in life is inside us" (p. 34).

ADVANCE ORGANIZERS

Ausubel is perhaps best known for his idea of an advance organizer. In order to help learners bridge the gap between knowledge they already possess and new knowledge to be learned, Ausubel suggested that a small segment of instruction should be offered prior to the larger instructional unit that is more general and more abstract than the material in the larger unit. This prior instruction can serve as an advance organizer, helping the learner relate new knowledge to knowledge the learner already has. Advance organizers are easily the most researched idea from Ausubel's work, but this is only a very limited part of his assimilation theory of learning; advance organizers are primarily an instructional strategy. I consider these later and also discuss the design of effective advance organizers.

In the epigraph to his book, *Educational Psychology: A Cognitive View*, Ausubel (1968) made this statement, "If I had to reduce all of educational psychology to just one principle, I would say this: The most important single factor influencing learning is what the learner already knows. Ascertain this and teach him accordingly" (p. iv). What a growing body of cognitive research studies have shown in the last 2 decades is that for the most part, this Ausubelian principle is valid, especially if we consider ascertaining explicit cognitive frameworks relevant to the new concepts we seek to teach. We have found the use of concept maps to be powerful tools to "ascertain what the learner already knows," including faulty knowledge structures or misconceptions, and also to organize the subject matter of new material to be taught, as I illustrate later (cf. Wandersee, Mintzes, & Novak, 1994). However, our research and the research of others is showing that metacognitive knowledge, including knowledge about how to learn meaningfully, is also crucially important.

To be effective, advance organizers must meet two requirements: (1) The learner's specific existing relevant conceptual and propositional knowledge must be identified. And (2) appropriate organization and sequencing of new knowledge to be learned must be planned in such a way as to optimize the learner's ability to relate the new knowledge to the concepts and propositions already held. This is no easy task, partly because of the range of variation in and adequacy of various learners' relevant concepts and propositions. However, we and others have found that for any given population of learners, there is often a common set of concepts and propositions that can serve to anchor the learning of new concepts and propositions. Carefully planned advance organizers can do much to facilitate this anchorage.

Concept maps and Vee diagrams (see chap. 6) can serve as powerful advance organizers, and they can assist in the design of instruction that builds on learner's existing knowledge structures. If students are asked to build the best concept map or Vee diagram for a given topic or activity, they will reveal both their valid and their invalid ideas relevant to this topic or activity. The process of creating concept maps and/or Vees alerts the learner to the fact that he/she does have some relevant knowledge for the new topic, thus adding to motivation to learn meaningfully. Maps and Vees can aid in planning the instruction in such a ways as to build on existing valid ideas and reduce the chances for reinforcing existing invalid ideas.

ASSIMILATION, LEARNING, AND CONSTRUCTIVISM

There is today much discussion about constructivism in educational circles. Descriptions of constructivism are almost as numerous as individuals who seek to describe this. What is most commonly described is the fact that each learner must construct his or her own concepts or knowledge. Often there are no precise definitions of concept or knowledge. Many of the discussions fail to clarify how individuals construct knowledge (the psychology of learning) versus how scholars in disciplines construct new knowledge (the epistemology of knowledge). I deal with constructivism extensively in the next chapter and show how assimilation theory explains both individuals' knowledge construction and the growth of knowledge in discipline.

There are, of course, numerous other theories of learning that have been published since 1968. For example, Anderson's (1990) *Adaptive Character of Thought,* Sternberg's (1986) *The Triarchic Mind,* and Gardner's (1983) *Frames of Mind,* are widely cited in the literature. From my perspective, none of these or other theoretical works possess at once the simplicity of Ausubel's assimilation theory nor the power to explain why learning succeeds or fails in any context: personal, school, university, or corporate. Trained in the sciences early in my career, I am an adamant proponent of theories that at once have simplicity, but explain complexity. In the sciences, this is known as elegance. Moreover, if one looks at recent publications, such as The American Psychological Association's "Learner-Centered Psychological Principles" (Marshall & McCombs, 1995), it is evident that all of these are not only consistent with Ausubel's theory, but also their principles can be explained and understood through his theory.

In the 2½ decades that we have used Ausubel's assimilation theory to guide our research and instructional innovations, we have not obtained any results that refute or cast doubt on the major ideas just described. Most of our studies have been highly supportive of these ideas and have led to some modifications and, we hope, improvements in the theory. For example, in his earlier works (Ausubel, 1963, 1968), progressive differentiation and integrative reconciliation were concepts referred to primarily in instructional design. Our research group has found these important explanatory concepts for explaining cognitive learning, as well as concepts that can be applied in instructional design. In the next chapter, I argue that

concepts from assimilation theory are also powerful explanatory ideas for understanding the process by which humans construct new knowledge. Partly for this
reason, I see the idea of meaningful learning as the bedrock on which creative
knowledge construction rests and the key concept in my theory of education.

CREATIVITY

There are numerous definitions and descriptions of creativity. My view is that
creativity is simply successful integrative reconciliation or superordinate learning
and the emotional desire to do this. As such, it ranges on a scale from relatively
modest creative insights when relatively common integrative reconciliations are
formed by a person to those extraordinary integrative reconciliations and/or superordinate concept constructions that lead to Nobel or Pulitzer prizes. Every one
of us has some creative capacity (i.e., we make our own unique integrative
reconciliations), but only a small fraction of the population appears to have the
capacity and emotional drive to make the creative leaps that advance science, music,
literature, or other fields of human endeavor. Figure 5.12 illustrates the keys factors

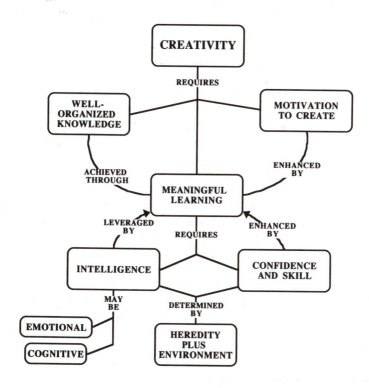

FIG. 5.12. Necessary requirements for creative thinking.

I see operating in creativity.

According to my view, the creative performance of everyone can be enhanced by improving the capacity and desire of people to learn meaningfully. It is retarded or inhibited by inordinate emphasis and rewarded for learning by rote. Because the latter has been so common in most school learning, it is not surprising that the biographies of geniuses often refer pejoratively to their experiences in schools. Schooling can be changed to encourage, reward, and enhance meaningful learning and creativity. I return to this idea in later chapters.

Sternberg (1988) proposed a three-facet model of creativity, suggesting that the creative person has a blend of these three facets and some combinations may be more synergistic than others. The three facets he identifies are: (a) intellectual or intelligence; (b) stylistic, such as legislative (rule-oriented), self-government (varying degrees of drive and tolerance); and (c) a personality facet, such as tolerance for ambiguity, willingness to grow, moderate risk-taking, and work for recognition. These are all traits that most people exhibit from time to time, and hence one must assume that the creative person has more of and a better blend of these traits.

In a more recent book, Sternberg (1996a) distinguished between successful intelligence and inert intelligence. Successful intelligence is required for creative production. Sternberg stated:

> I define creativity not only as the ability to come up with new ideas. I believe it is a process that requires the balance and application of the three essential aspects of intelligence—creative, analytical, and practical—the same aspects that, when used in combination and balance, make for successful intelligence. (p. 191)

Another recent book on creativity is Gardner's (1993) *Creating Minds*. Gardner studied the biographies of recognized geniuses and identified four separate components in the study of genius: (a) organizing themes, such as the relation between the child and the adult creator; (b) organizing frameworks, such as a life-course perspective of creative work; (c) issues for empirical investigation, including individual, domain-specific, and field-related issues; and (d) emerging themes, such as the creative person's cognitive and affective support at the time of breakthrough.

We see in both Sternberg's and Gardner's descriptions of creative performance the richness and complexity of factors that have been associated with creativity. However, I do not believe these and similar descriptions explain creativity. To me, it is much more parsimonious and much more powerful to view creativity as a manifestation in individuals who seek high levels of meaningful learning. Each of the many facets or components of creativity described by Sternberg and Gardner can be viewed as the consequence of determined constant pursuit by the individual to seek high levels of concept and propositional integration into well-structured cognitive frameworks. The intrinsic affective rewards that come from such cognitive development and differentiation drive the individual to seek out settings and supportive individuals that further catalyze the growing complexity and integration of his or her cognitive frameworks. It is the empowerment that comes from successful integration of thinking, feeling, and acting through meaningful learning that underlies and drives the creative process. To understand creativity requires that one understand in a profound way the meaning of meaningful learning.

Gardner (1993) emphasized in his description of creativity that the creative individual produces products (things or ideas) that are, in time, recognized by society as creative products. He also stressed that often creative individuals encounter resistance to, or even ridicule of, their ideas or products, but in time, their ideas or products prevail. Sternberg (1996), in a similar way, emphasized that creativity combines creative, analytical, and practical intelligence that leads to sustained action eventually recognized as creative. Sometimes it may be difficult to distinguish between foolish and creative products, but both Gardner and Steinberg argued that, in time, the creative product will be recognized. In a similar vein, Higgins (1995), in his book, *Innovate or Evaporate* defined creativity as "the process of generating something new that has value," and an innovation is a creation that has significant value (p. 9). In most of the contemporary writing on creativity, we see in current literature this emphasis on the need for recognized value as one criterion for judging an act as a creative act. Unfortunately for some creative people, this judgment may not come until after they are dead.

INTELLIGENCE

When I was an undergraduate student, one of my psychology professors defined intelligence as "the trait that intelligence tests measure." I remember at the time being very unhappy with this definition, for I was not convinced that intelligence tests, or any similar tests such as the one I took for college admission, had a great deal to do with real intelligence. My experience somewhat mirrored that of Sternberg's.

Sternberg (1996a) described what he called "successful intelligence":

Successful intelligence is, in part, what is sometimes called business sense. IQ doesn't measure this business sense at all. Indeed, many people with high IQ's seem not to be aware either that they have customers or that these customers are important. (p. 39)

By contrast:

Inert intelligence is what you show when you take an IQ test, or the Scholastic Assessment (sic) Test, or the American College Test, or any of a large number of similar tests used for college and graduate-school admissions. Many people do well on these tests, thereby showing impressive academic prowess, at least according to those who believe in the tests. But the intelligence measured is inert—it doesn't lead to goal-directed movement or action. As a result, these people's most impressive accomplishments may well be their test scores, or their grades in school. Those who can recall facts, who may even be able to reason with those facts, do not necessarily know how to use them to make a difference, either to themselves or to anyone else. (p. 11)

I find myself strongly in agreement with Sternberg's claims, and I believe his book has much of value to persons seeking a better way to conceptualize intelligence and creativity. And yet there is blind acceptance of measures of inert intelligence in both schools and business. As Sternberg observed:

> Yet many businesses—deceived into believing that inert intelligence makes a difference in job performance—use tests in much the same manner as do colleges. The goal is to find people who will perform well in particular jobs. The military uses tests as well. The testing game itself is big business, and tests are used to sort out those who are given better jobs and access routes to better jobs from those who are not. But it sorts them on IQ-type measures rather than on successful intelligence, which is what will truly determine who succeeds. (p. 39)

More recently, there is a growing concern with the use of test for selecting graduate students. Georgi (1996) reported that at Harvard University, Graduate Record Exam (GRE) scores in physics showed no correlation with graduate course grades. Moreover, Georgi observed that some of his most brilliant women students did very poorly on the physics GRE test. In general, women scored 100 points lower (out of a possible 990) than men, thus leading to serious gender bias against women in selection for graduate study in physics. At Cornell University, our dean of the graduate school did an informal study of correlation of GRE scores with professors' rating of Ph.D. students. He found a correlation of 0.02, about as close to zero as you can get. I have not been able to find similar data for business schools, but I'm sure such data will be reported in the future, if it is not out there now.

Over the years, my research work has supported the position taken by Sternberg, but very few scholars working in education or psychology have voiced the kind of concerns he has expressed, to say nothing about the vehemence with which he makes his assertions. Early in my career, I thought things would change and the limited value of IQ and other similar measures would be recognized.

What I underestimated was the depth of entrenchment of the mental measurements crowd and their enormous ability to prevail over the years. Although there are a growing number of scholars such as Sternberg (1996), who regard IQ tests, scholastic aptitude tests and similar tests as measures of at best inert intelligence, what I refer to as the *psychometric gang* remains dominant in the field of psychological and educational testing, both in school and in corporate settings. In part, this derives from an unwarranted reverence for precise numbers, as in IQ of 121 or SAT scores of 760 and 540. The people who design and administer these tests are not quacks or charletans; they really believe in the validity and reliability of their tests. The reliability of the tests is relatively good; that is, these tests tend to produce similar scores for the same individual on repeated testing. It is the validity issue that is the problem. When one correlates IQ, SAT, or similar test scores with measures of real world job performance, the correlations are near zero! This problem is discussed further in chapter 9. What IQ tests measure may be useful for creative thinking, but it is not the same aptitude as creativity (Getzels & Jackson, 1962; Guilford & Christensen, 1973).

EMOTIONAL INTELLIGENCE

The idea that intelligence is not a unitary, one-dimensional thing has been around for many years. Guilford (1959) suggested that intelligence can be factored into 120 separate components, and more recently we have the seven different intelligences suggested by Gardner (1983). A somewhat novel idea has been put forward by Goleman (1995) in his book, *Emotional Intelligence.* There is no simple definition for emotional intelligence, nor a test that will yield a emotional intelligence score. Instead, Goleman described characteristics such as social poise, cheerfulness, sympathetic, sensitivity to other's feelings, empathy, outgoing, confident, low anxiety, and similar traits as typical of emotionally intelligent people. He presents numerous examples of successes by people high in emotional intelligence and failures by people low in emotional intelligence. In general, the data he gives shows little or no correlation between characteristics of emotional intelligence and IQ or similar measures of cognitive ability.

Both the biological foundations and the psychological implications of emotions have been studied with increasing intensity in the past 20 years. We know much more about how and why emotional responses are generated and expressed. There is also a growing body of literature on how to develop positive emotional intelligence in children, and actions that have deleterious effects on development. Unfortunately, bad parenting can lead to poor emotional intelligence and more bad parenting as these children become parents. The cycle is not easy to break, but there are educational approaches that have had positive results. Goleman's work and the work of many others interested in emotional intelligence needs more attention in schools and corporations. I would expect to see growing awareness and concern with these ideas in the next few decades.

So what is the bottom line on intelligence? That depends, in part, on the game you're playing. If you want to predict SAT scores or grade point averages, IQ scores will have reasonable reliability and validity. Unfortunately, they are also likely to predict your chances of admission to better colleges and universities because admission policies often emphasize performance on such tests. If you want to predict the number of patents a person will achieve, grade point averages or achievement test scores have almost no predictive value; and in some cases, these would severely penalize the most productive, most creative individuals (Novak, 1977a).

So how should we define intelligence and how should we measure intellectual achievement? As with most complex, desirable things, there are no easy answers.

We need to assess both the quantity and the quality of knowledge a person has in those domains of knowledge that are pertinent to the field of work. Of course, it is not easy to define what is pertinent. Many creative achievements have come about precisely because the creator brought to bear some knowledge outside of the usual domain and saw new ways to connect it with domain knowledge well known by most persons competent in the field. These are the kind of connections I refer to as major *integrative reconciliations,* in that the creative person sees how to make the right connections between concepts in two domains of knowledge that were previously regarded as unrelated, or in some cases even contradictory. There may still remain the task of demonstrating to skeptics the power and validity of the new connection(s), but in due course, the dogged persistence of the creative person and his or her adherents is recognized and sometimes rewarded. This kind of intelligence is obviously precious to society at large and to corporations in their quest for competitive advantage. Attention to criteria that indicate emotional intelligence also need to be given more time and effort. Too few of the recruitment criteria used by corporations at the present time recognize that they may be doing a great job of selecting for inert intelligence, but a poor or counterproductive job of selecting for successful intelligence. The latter, from my perspective, is the person who has a history of seeking high levels of meaningful learning and a tenacity to persevere until his/her hunches begin to gain acceptance. Measurement and evaluation issues are discussed further in chapter 9.

   It should be evident from the text and figures I presented that I seek to facilitate your subsumption, progressive differentiation, and integrative reconciliation of concepts regarding human learning. This process will be aided if you construct your own concept maps, both of subsets of concepts, and ones for the large groups of concepts. Try to build your own composite maps—and also add illustrative examples from your own experiences. Then refer for comparisons to Fig. 5.1 that shows a composite map for the key ideas of Ausubel's assimilation theory that I have constructed. As you gain in your understanding of assimilation theory, it should be possible for you to gain in your capacity to engage in high levels of meaningful learning. This, I predict, will permit you to be more creative in those domains you choose to pursue.

6

The Nature of Knowledge and How Humans Create Knowledge

THE NATURE AND SOURCES OF KNOWLEDGE

That humans learn is self-evident. It is also self-evident that humans organize and communicate knowledge to one another. What is not obvious is the origin of knowledge. Where does knowledge come from? This has been a question pondered by some of the best minds for centuries. Most of the great philosophers throughout history have spoken and written on this question.

It is not my purpose to review the long history of philosophical ideas about the nature of knowledge and knowing, but it is necessary to deal with some of the ideas that have been dominant in the past 300 years because they continue to influence teaching, learning, schools, businesses, and society today. First, however, I try to make clear the philosophical ideas that now guide our work and my answer to the question: Where does knowledge come from? The branch of philosophy that deals with the structure and origins of knowledge is called *epistemology*, and I shall try to make clear my epistemological ideas.

All knowledge is comprised of concepts and propositions, including concepts and propositions that deal with learning strategies and methods of conducting inquiries and also including the affective dimension of experience associated with those concepts and propositions. Meaningful learning underlies the constructive integration of thinking, feeling, and acting that occurs in human learning and in new knowledge construction. This interplay is unique to human beings and hence I choose to label it *human constructivism* (Novak, 1993). Human constructivism is a label I see as appropriate both for the way in which humans learn their usable

79

knowledge and also for the way in which they construct new knowledge. The nature and process of meaningful learning underlies both human learning and human knowledge creation.

I next discuss some older ideas about the nature of knowledge and origins of knowledge and reasons why I believe these ideas are in error, less powerful, or less relevant to education and knowledge creation. In this chapter I seek to present a view of epistemology that I believe has power for improving both. Whether it has power for the advance of the field of philosophy dealing with epistemology is for others to decide. It will be seen that ideas of human constructivism are complementary to or congruent with emerging ideas on epistemology being advanced by contemporary philosophers and historians interested in the process of knowledge production.

Gowin's Epistemological Vee

My colleague, D. Bob Gowin (now retired), has been interested in the study of philosophy and epistemology as it applies to education, beginning with his Master's degree work 4 decades ago. His interests and expertise in philosophy have been valuable to our research program in science education, especially in research studies that have focused on science laboratory learning. In general, most students experience considerable anxiety and confusion in science laboratory work, especially when this work involves experimental or quasi-experimental studies. College students also find the reading of research reports frustrating or confusing, and sometimes completely opaque.

To aid students in understanding research reports, Gowin (1970) devised five questions, the answers to which could provide the student with a better understanding of the research. These five questions were:

1. What are the telling questions? These are questions that tell what the inquiry seeks to find out.
2. What are the key concepts? These are the dozen or so disciplinary concepts that are needed to understand the inquiry.
3. What methods of inquiry (procedural commitments) are used? These are the data gathering or data interpreting methods used.
4. What are the major knowledge claims? These are the answers claimed by the researcher as valid answers to the telling questions.
5. What are the value claims? These are claims, explicit or implied, about the worth or value of the inquiry and the answers found in the inquiry.

Gowin and I found the use of these questions to be helpful to students not only in the analysis of research reports but also in laboratory work, for the design of research, and as a tool for discussions on the meaning and value of research studies. However, many students found it difficult to relate key concepts to the telling questions or the events or objects being investigated. In pondering the problems experienced, Gowin came up with the idea of the Knowledge Vee heuristic in early 1977. Figure 6.1 shows the general form of the Vee.

We have found it is relatively easy to teach persons to construct Vee diagrams once they are familiar with concept mapping and the ideas that underlie concept maps. Appendix 2 shows a set of procedures we have found to be effective. The ideas presented in this chapter will aid in understanding both the concept map

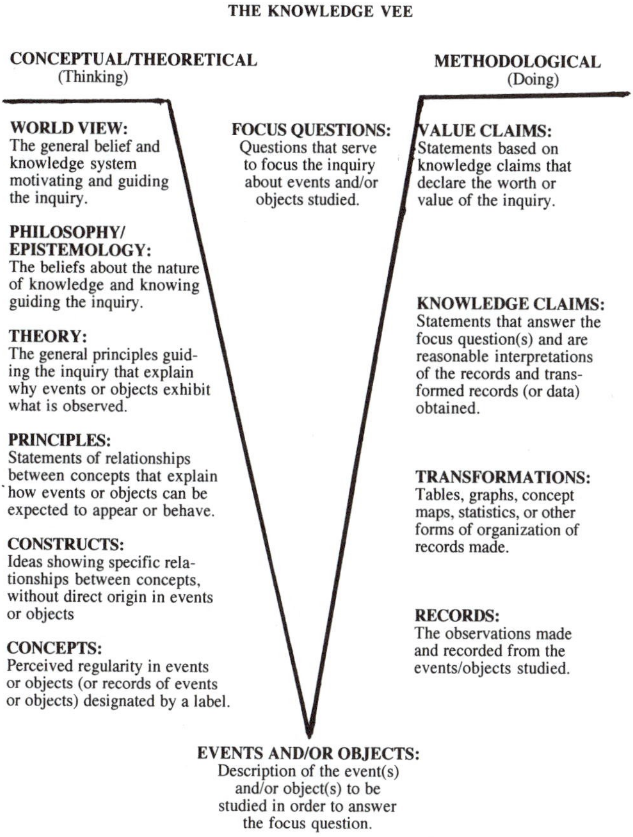

THE KNOWLEDGE VEE

CONCEPTUAL/THEORETICAL
(Thinking)

METHODOLOGICAL
(Doing)

WORLD VIEW:
The general belief and knowledge system motivating and guiding the inquiry.

FOCUS QUESTIONS:
Questions that serve to focus the inquiry about events and/or objects studied.

VALUE CLAIMS:
Statements based on knowledge claims that declare the worth or value of the inquiry.

PHILOSOPHY/ EPISTEMOLOGY:
The beliefs about the nature of knowledge and knowing guiding the inquiry.

THEORY:
The general principles guiding the inquiry that explain why events or objects exhibit what is observed.

KNOWLEDGE CLAIMS:
Statements that answer the focus question(s) and are reasonable interpretations of the records and transformed records (or data) obtained.

PRINCIPLES:
Statements of relationships between concepts that explain how events or objects can be expected to appear or behave.

TRANSFORMATIONS:
Tables, graphs, concept maps, statistics, or other forms of organization of records made.

CONSTRUCTS:
Ideas showing specific relationships between concepts, without direct origin in events or objects

CONCEPTS:
Perceived regularity in events or objects (or records of events or objects) designated by a label.

RECORDS:
The observations made and recorded from the events/objects studied.

EVENTS AND/OR OBJECTS:
Description of the event(s) and/or object(s) to be studied in order to answer the focus question.

FIG. 6.1. The Knowledge Vee, showing the relationships between epistemological elements involved. All elements interact with each other in knowledge creation. The conceptual/ theoretical elements play a central role in selecting events and/or objects to observe, developing focus questions and guiding the methodological activities to construct knowledge and value claims.

tool and the Knowledge Vee tool.

The beauty of the Vee heuristic is its comprehensiveness and also simplicity. It serves to illustrate that there are a dozen or so epistemic elements that are involved in constructing or examining a piece of knowledge, and yet it places these elements into a simple structure that helps to illustrate how each of these elements function. Although a variety of shapes for an epistemological heuristic could have been used, Gowin chose the Vee shape because it points to events/objects, that segment of the universe we are trying to understand. It also serves to distinguish the fact that both thinking (conceptual/theoretical) elements and doing (methodological) elements are involved in knowledge construction. Each element on the Vee interacts with every other element as our minds, hearts, and bodies work to construct new knowledge, or rather knowledge claims. However, those elements shown on the left side are in our head and help to guide the actions on the right side that produce the knowledge and value claims. The Vee heuristic is a heuristic based on a constructivist view of knowledge wherein we recognize that the way a piece of universe we choose to study appears to look or behave depends on other elements of the Vee. If we choose different questions, use different concepts, principles or theories, make different records or transform records differently, we can legitimately arrive at different knowledge claims about the same events or objects. In short, how we see events or objects in the world depends on how we personally construct our vision of these events or objects.

For example, early chemists saw burning as the loss of phlogiston, whereas the new chemical theory and principles we now follow sees burning as the oxidation of carbon, hydrogen or other elements. Modern ideas explain why wood disappears (except for a small amount of ash) when it burns and why iron and mercury become heavier when they are burned. The theory of phlogiston could not explain the latter two events and was contradicted by the weight records for iron and mercury before and after burning. No chemist or physicist claims to know exactly how atoms and molecules behave when substances are burned, but our current theories and principles certainly have far more explanatory and predictive power than earlier theories. The radical constructivist (see von Glasersfeld, 1984) holds that we will never know the right theories or principles, but we can make progress toward constructing principles and theories that have greater explanatory power. There is no apology by the constructivist for the fact that we can make only claims about how we believe some piece of the universe looks or behaves. Truth or absolute certainty is not the goal of the constructivist thinker. It has been the goal of positivist/empiricist philosophy for hundreds of years, and positivistic views abound in textbooks, lectures, and schooling in general. I return to this issue later in this chapter. Figure 6.2 shows some of the distinctions between constructivist and positivist or empirical epistemologies.

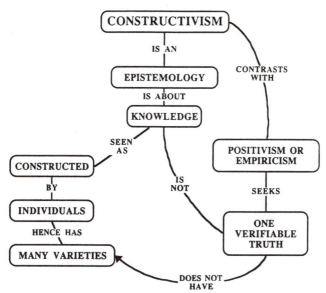

FIG. 6.2. Some of the key concepts of constructivism contrasted with positivism/empiricism.

Elements of the Knowledge Vee

There are 12 epistemic elements shown on the Knowledge Vee in Fig. 6.1. Each of these elements functions in the construction of meanings and also in the construction of knowledge, although we are often not conscious of their roles, nor do we consider how each element is operating for a given learning experience. It is possible to begin the discussion with any element on the Vee, but for convenience, I begin at the top with the focus question(s).

Often new learning begins with a question. It may be a simple question such as, "what is that thing called?" Or it may be a more complex question such as, "how does that event take place?" For example, Rachel, my 3¾-year-old granddaughter, while weeding flowers with my wife, asked, "Is this a weed?" pointing to a small grass seedling. Soon she was skillful at discriminating young flowers from weeds. As the weeding progressed, Rachel asked, "Do flowers eat dirt?" My wife explained that flowers do use some of the dirt to grow, but mostly they used water, air, and energy from the sun. Rachel then asked, "When the flowers get big, will there be less dirt?" to which my wife responded, "Yes, but only a very tiny bit less." What is evident in Rachel's questions was that she was not operating in a conceptual/theoretical vacuum; she had some concepts, principles, and theories about what plants are and how they grow, acquired over the last 2 or 3 years of her short life. I will use this example to illustrate the knowledge elements of the Vee and how they interrelate. Figure 6.3 shows the concepts and relationships for the left side of the Vee, and Fig. 6.4 shows a concept map representing ideas on the right side of the Vee.

First we see that Rachel had a curiosity about flowers and how they grow. It was evident that her world view indicated a concern for flowers and a belief that there are reasons why things are the way they appear to be. Our world view is that constellation of beliefs and values that shapes the way we see events and objects in the world, and also what we choose to care about and learn about. Our world view is shaped by our values and the emotional commitments we have regarding happenings in our universe. It is shaped over our lifetime of experiences and influenced by our culture, religion, family, and personal relationships.

Rachel's manifest philosophy was a rationalist/constructivist view that happenings in the universe should make sense, that there are reasons for how and why plants grow, and that these reasons are understandable. Philosophy and world view are not easily distinguished, in part because they are interdependent. However, we have found it useful to make a distinction, with world view representing the more global, value-laden ideas a person holds about the universe. In terms of the Vee, it

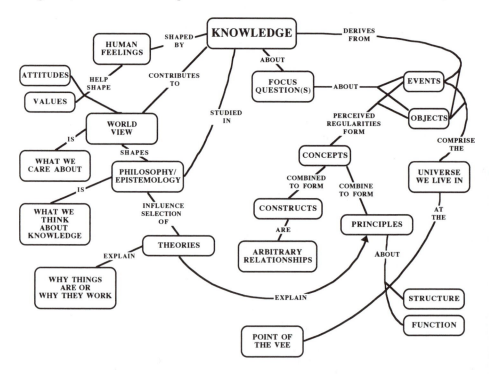

FIG. 6.3. A concept map representing the ideas involved in the elements on the "left side" of the Knowledge Vee.

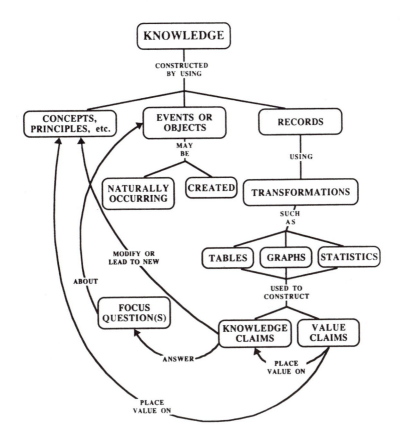

FIG. 6.4. A concept map representing the ideas involved on the "right side" of the Knowledge Vee.

is best to think of philosophy in terms of our epistemological beliefs, that is, where do we believe knowledge comes from?

Matthews (1980, 1984) did an analysis of interviews where young children (6- to 8-years old) raised some of the same questions and issues and presented similar arguments as those recorded in the writings of some of the greatest Western philosophers. Even very young children have already established philosophical ideas about how people behave and how the world works. In this respect, Matthews (1980) rejected outright Piaget's claim that philosophical reasoning does not develop until the teenage years.

Our world view motivates us to act, to construct questions, and to find answers. We have chosen to place focus question(s) at the top center of the Vee because these, in many ways, are what drive the inquiry that leads eventually to new knowledge.

Rachel's question, "When flowers get big, will there be less dirt there (in the garden)?" was her focus question.

Moving down the left side of the Vee to theory, we see that Rachel is manifesting and trying to refine some theories about plants and nutrients. She recognizes that plants, like animals, need to eat to grow. This is also reflective of her emerging theory of conservation of substance or matter: The stuff in the large plant must come from somewhere, and if some dirt is used to grow, there should be less dirt in the flower garden when plants get big. Theories are defined as explanations for why and how things appear the way they do. Rachel was developing her theories for how living things grow (particularly plants) and where the stuff comes from that they need to grow. This curiosity may have been stimulated by Rachel's mother, who is a nutritionist, but the ideas where expressly Rachel's. She had a theory about dirt and correctly hypothesized that if plants use dirt to grow, there should be less dirt in the ground when the plants get big. Rachel is not unique in this regard. Any 3- or 4-year-old could develop such a theory and use it for abstract reasoning if they had a sequence of learning experiences similar to those of Rachel.

Principles describe how things work or how they appear to be structured. Rachel manifested several operating principles: (a) weeds look different from flowers (i.e., weeds were grass-like in our garden of marigolds and zinnias); (b) plants use dirt to grow; (c) when dirt goes into plants, the soil has less dirt. The learning experience with her grandmother helped Rachel to consolidate and refine the meanings of these principles (propositions). The experience also helped Rachel to differentiate and integrate her concept meanings for plants, dirt, flowers, weeds, growing, and maybe also water, air, and energy. Rachel was engaged in meaningful learning.

Constructs are ideas that represent regularities nor directly observable in events or objects. Often they represent two or more concepts that are connected in some arbitrary way. For example, if Rachel were to suggest that her grandmother's flowers were growing in healthy air or healthy dirt, she would be using constructs. If Rachel had concepts of healthy and some concept of air and dirt, she could combine these to suggest the conditions under which the flowers were growing. Halpern (1989) defined *hypothetical constructs* as concepts having no external reality, giving learning and memory as examples. This could also be said of atoms, love, and photosynthesis, but it seems much more coherent to label these as concepts, representing specific regularities in events or objects, albeit they may be observed indirectly. Constructs such as IQ are arbitrary relationships between concepts—there is no necessary reason to divide mental age by chronological age. Arbitrary constructs are more common in the social sciences. Constructs differ from principles because they do not explain how some aspects of the universe functions or is structured.

I have defined *concept* as a perceived regularity in events or objects, or records of events or objects, designated by a label. Clearly Rachel had established meanings for the concept labels just noted, and was refining these meanings; that is, she was becoming more discriminating as regards the regularities represented by each of the concept labels. Rachel did not work from records to build her concepts, as Van Helmont did with his willow tree experiment,[1] but she will undoubtedly do so in the future in other experiences that relate to the concepts cited.

Events are things that happen such as growing, eating, running, wars, and so on. Objects are some unit of stuff or matter, such as plant, dirt, or weed. Everything in the universe is either an event or object, and all events involve objects; even changes in forms of energy involve objects in some way. Thus, at the bottom point of the Vee we anchor our experience to some piece of the universe. All meanings that humans construct are anchored in events or objects they have experienced, or metaphors drawn from events or objects. Our concepts help us to perceive regularities in the events or objects we observe, and in some cases we construct new labels to designate new regularities. But without a functioning framework of relevant concepts and principles, it is more difficult to construct new knowledge. This is one reason children's acquisition of language from birth to 3 years old is such an incredible learning accomplishment!

It is very important to help learners become clear and specific about the events or objects they are trying to understand. We find repeatedly in science laboratory work that many students have at best only a fuzzy idea of the objects or events they are trying to understand and for which they are trying to seek out the regularities. The same can be said for elements of events in sports, dance, music, or literature. Literature can be especially troublesome to learners because most good literature relies on metaphor to structure the story. Similarly, mathematics is difficult for most of us because the concepts and principles of mathematics are usually not specified and/or not related to real world events or objects for which we already have relevant knowledge. We see later that lack of clear conceptualization of events in organizations is also a problem.

Rachel's questions signaled clearly what events and objects she was trying to understand. Rachel was engaged in a relatively high level of meaningful learning. We could follow through with examples of how elements on the right side of the Vee could function in the construction of knowledge and value claims, but the limited context of Rachel's learning did not include making records or transforming records. Examples of this will come later in her life.

Experiments

Emerging in the 17th century, Galileo and others we now called scientists (they saw themselves as natural philosophers) developed the experiment. Experiments are

---

[1]In 1650, Van Helmont inquired into the source of materials needed for plant growth. He grew a willow twig in a tub of soil and concluded (erroneously) that all the substance used to grow came from water. He did not know about the composition of air, and carbon dioxide as a gas in the air was not known until much later. His scales could not detect the small amount of nutrient minerals absorbed from the soil.

events created by researchers, and the conventional experiment requires that we observe both experimental events and control events. The requirement includes that all elements we are observing should be identical, except the one experimental variable. Differences in records we obtain from the events permit us to test hypotheses regarding the influence of the experimental variable on the event being studied. How we record and transform the records is determined, in part, by the hypotheses we seek to test. Hypotheses could also be called "anticipated knowledge claims." In the 20th century, new statistical tools were developed that permit experiments to be done with multiple variables or experimental conditions, thus also permitting construction of hypotheses about how two or more variables interact to produce the records we obtain.

The success of experimental procedures in the natural or hard sciences as ways of producing useful knowledge has led to widespread efforts to apply this methodology to the social or soft sciences, including education. The two major difficulties in the social sciences are that we can seldom truly control events that involve people, and secondly, our methods of making records have serious problems of validity and reliability (see later this chapter and chapter 9). However, used with sufficient caution and guided by theory and principles that have reasonable validity, experiments can prove useful for knowledge creation in the social sciences as well.

Records

These are literally the records we gather about events or objects (see also chapter 9). They can be simple descriptions of observations, such as the number of each kind of object observed, or they may be meter readings, computer print-outs, or other records made by complex instruments. In the latter cases, there is always the issue of reliability and validity of the records. Faulty equipment or the improper selection of equipment can produce faulty records. *Fact* is a label I use for accurate, valid records, and many records gathered in research are not facts, especially in educational research where the data gathering instruments (e.g., tests) are never highly reliable and highly valid record-making tools. Unfortunately, it is not always easy to know when our records are truly facts, acceptable but containing some error, or biased and distorted. Learners need to be helped in ways to make validity checks and reliability checks on their data. In work settings, workers often know better than their managers the limitations on records gathered. Corporations that respect and use this knowledge enhance their productivity.

Many advances in the sciences have come from the invention of new ways to make records of events. The telescope and the oscilloscope are two examples. Telescopes have led to enormous advances in astronomy, and oscilloscopes have advanced our understanding of electricity and electromagnetic waves. Much of what we call technological advances results from modifying instruments developed for basic research to practical uses. Oscilloscopes laid the groundwork for television, and concept maps are central to our programs to help learners to learn and to create knowledge. Some research groups become so successful creating events or in refining record-making tools that they lead the world in new knowledge creation in their specialty. For example, this is so true for the research group Darmstaat, who have become so skillful in creating new elements that they are credited with creating elements, 107, 108, 109, and most recently, element 110 (Clery, 1994).

The records we choose to make depend on the question(s) we hope to answer, and all of the elements on the left side of the Vee. Usually we focus our attention on the principles guiding our inquiry because these describe regularities or relationships we may find in the objects or events we are studying. We need to be sure that we are gathering records that are consistent with our principles and may allow us to confirm or deny the validity of the principles guiding our inquiry.

Artifacts

Artifacts are the records of human activity. The implements, pottery, and jewelry studied by archaeologists are products that are used to reconstruct the life of prehistoric people. Artifacts do not occur naturally in the universe but depend on human thinking and activity. Because humans have an infinite capacity to change their minds, artifacts as records can give different messages from different people or from different times. There are regularities in artifacts, and reliable predictions can be made using this kind of record. Much that we deal with in education and all of the social sciences is basically artifactual records such as test scores, interview data, and opinions or feelings about things. Although it is always a slippery business to interpret records of events or objects, it is especially difficult to interpret artifactual records. This is one of the reasons the social sciences are less advanced than the natural sciences. It is also a reason why viable theory may be even more powerful in the social sciences as a tool for guiding action. Theory helps us make judgments as to whether or not the artifactual records we used and the claims we constructed have a reasonable chance of being valid.

Record Transformations

Usually we do not try to construct knowledge claims from raw data or records as they are gathered from our observations. It is common to do some kind of transformation of the new data. Simple groupings, tables, charts, and graphs are some of the common record transformations we use. *Data* is a term usually used for any records or transformed records. Although Rachel did not record in writing her observations of flowers, she was making mental records of her observations and using previous records she had observed.

Record transformations we make should be guided by our concepts, principles, and theories. The transformations are also determined by the focus question(s) we hope to answer. Principles help us to organize our data to show patterns or relationships anticipated by applying our principles. For example, there is a principle of economics that holds that interest rates are dependent on the money supply in an economy. Thus, applying this principle, we would have gathered records on money supply (as reported from federal sources) each week or month for some period of time, and also records on the interest rates for each week or month. We could place these records into a table showing dates in one column, money supply in another column, and interest rates in a third. However, a better view of the relationship would be a graph showing money supply on one axis and interest rates on the other. A nice line graph showing steady increase in interest rates with a regular decline in money supply would confirm or support our economic principle. Alas, if this did not occur in our record transformation, we might question the validity of the principle. More commonly, we begin to recognize that something else must be happening, and we may reach into our store of economic principles to see if any other principles can explain our graph. We may find the principle that consumer buying is related to interest rates, and now we must go back and gather more records, records on consumer spending over the time interval we are studying. Then we construct new transformations of our records. Of course, it is always possible that our principles may be faulty, and economics is a good example of a field where there is considerable dispute among experts as to which principles are valid or which are most important. For one thing, we are dealing with events (e.g., consumer willingness to buy or to borrow money) that are choices people make. The records of interest rates are therefore artifacts, not facts.

Statistical record transformations are very common in many fields, especially in educational research. Unfortunately, statistical transformations will not improve biased or invalid records, and these are all too common in the social sciences. Statistics will not make facts out of records that are artifacts. Statistical tests and their interpretation are also subject to sets of concepts and principles, and too often these are not known or ignored by the researcher. For a good critique of statistics in education, especially the common use of factor analysis and similar tools, see Gould (1981).

Knowledge Claims

These are the answers to the focus questions that we claim our records and record transformations lead us to. Or we may simply make a knowledge claim from our observations of events without the precision that may come from good records and record transformations. Rachel's conjecture that there would be less dirt in the garden when the plants got large would be an example of this. The commonly used term, *hypothesis,* is an anticipated knowledge claim. However, hypotheses are statements we are trying to prove or falsify. From a constructivist perspective, hypotheses have only limited value. Gathering different records or using different record transformations could lead to very different answers to the same questions about the same events. Moreover, we can never be certain about the validity or reliability of our records, and at least to some degree, deficiencies in our records could lead to faulty knowledge claims. As we noted earlier, applying different concepts, principles, or theories could change entirely the knowledge claims that emerge in any inquiry. Constructing knowledge claims is indeed a slippery business. There are so many ways to go wrong, so many ways to be in error. This is especially true in any field where principles and theories are either lacking or of dubious validity. This has been the case in much educational research (as well as research in other social sciences), so there is good reason why teachers and the general public are skeptical about so called educational research findings. Moreover, with poor or nonexistent theory, questionable principles, and limited record making tools so common in educational research, it is no wonder that research findings are often contradictory. The most common finding when alternative teaching or learning strategies are compared is: "There were no statistically significant differences between groups (or methods)." Kaestle (1993) commented on the awful reputation of educational research. He noted a lack of influence of research on practitioners, the disarray of the educational community, and the politicization of the field. He failed to note the theoretical poverty of the field.

Value Claims

These are claims about the value or worth of the inquiry for achieving the goal(s) that motivated the study. For example, some of our studies were designed to ascertain whether or not concept maps and Vee diagrams could be helpful to students, both in terms of knowledge achievement and in terms of gains in self confidence or interest in the field of study. Our data generally support the knowledge claim that concepts maps and Vee diagrams help learners to learn and to gain in confidence and interest. (See, e.g., Novak, Gowin, & Johansen, 1983.) Therefore we make the value claim that these are useful tools that should be used by teachers and learners. Value claims are always linked to knowledge claims, but they are not the same thing. We have found it helpful to students and teachers to make deliberate efforts to identify and record value claims for every inquiry. This also helps both students and teachers to recognize that knowledge construction is a very value-laden endeavor! If Rachel had exclaimed that it was wonderful that beautiful flowers could grow from air, water, and dirt, she would have stated a value claim about flowers. I believe most of us would agree with such a value claim.

Our world view and our philosophy will, in many ways, influence the fields we choose to study and the kinds of questions we seek to answer. There is a strong relationship between the value claims we seek to construct and our philosophy and world view. An important component of my world view is that I believe human beings have the power to reduce the degree of human suffering in the world, and that improved education, based on theory, is an important endeavor to reduce human suffering. That is why I have chosen education as a field of work, and why I have been striving to develop a theory and related principles to guide our research and practice. I may not live long enough to see convincing evidence that theory-based improvement in education can reduce human suffering, but some of our more recent work, and the work of others, makes me optimistic.

There is an important difference between schools or universities and the business world. Today every large business faces fierce competitive pressures, not only from other businesses in this country, but also from businesses located all over the world. The globalization of business, as so many writers are pointing out, means that survival of the business requires rapid, effective, and efficient new learning and new knowledge creation. Nonaka and Takeuchi's (1995) assertion that all businesses must become knowledge creating organizations suggests to me that the ideas and tools I am presenting in this chapter may find more rapid acceptance and application in the business world than in the academic world. They do not have the luxury of continually increasing taxpayers' support to sustain their ineffective approaches.

There are other epistemic elements that could be discussed; however, this is not a book on epistemology. Nevertheless, I regard an understanding of epistemology as essential to understanding the nature of the knowledge we seek to teach or to learn. It is essential for teachers, learners, and managers to acquire *metaknowledge,* that is, knowledge about knowledge. Of course, one could argue that teachers have taught and learners have learned and managers have managed for centuries without understanding the nature of knowledge and the processes involved in knowledge construction. The point is, if we want to improve the educative process by a quantum leap, teachers, learners, and managers need to learn more, not only about how humans learn but also about how they create knowledge. This is the central goal in our book, *Learning How To Learn* (Novak & Gowin, 1984).

We have found the Vee heuristic to be helpful to students in our research group for designing their own research projects, and also to serve as a vehicle for dialogue between individuals. On a single page, it is possible to present the key elements that are guiding the inquiry, the objects or events to be studied, the focus questions to be pursued, and the elements that will be used to construct knowledge and value claims. Figure 6.5 shows an example of a Vee constructed by one of my former PhD students for her thesis work in nutrition education. She has gone on to achieve a worldwide leadership position in the field, partly as a result of the power of her theory-driven research program.

The Interrelationship of Learning and Knowledge Creation

Throughout the last chapter and in this chapter, I have tried to show how I see meaningful learning and knowledge construction as highly related. In fact, in my view all knowledge construction is only an extension of the human capacity to construct new meanings (new concepts and concept relationships in cognitive structure). Thus, the psychology of meaningful learning underlies and gives rise to the epistemological process of knowledge construction. Human Constructivism is

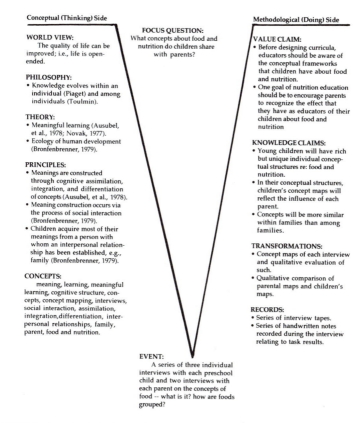

FIG. 6.5. A vee heuristic that (a) defines each element involved in the process of knowledge construction (in italics) and (b) illustrates the plan for a theory-driven inquiry in nutrition education. "Theory Driven Research as a Means to Improve Nutrition Education," by C. L. Achterberg, J. D. Novak, and A. H. Gillespie. Reprinted with permission, *Journal of Nutrition Education*, *17*(5), p. 180, 1985, Society for Nutrition Education.

both a psychological and an epistemological phenomenon. This view is illustrated in the concept map in Fig. 6.6.

Figure 6.6 is an exceedingly complex figure. Do not expect to understand all of the concepts and relationships represented in it with a single reading. Instead, use it as a reference map to see how ideas presented in this chapter and chapter 5 interrelate with one another. Most of my graduate students find it takes them 1 to 3 years to feel comfortable with the ideas of human constructivism, including some time to shake off old ideas and attitudes that are positivistic in character. Our society is permeated with positivistic thinking, and it is not easy for one to move away from this. Behaviorist theories of learning may be almost dead in the world of psychology, but they are alive and well in schools and corporations. Neither positivist

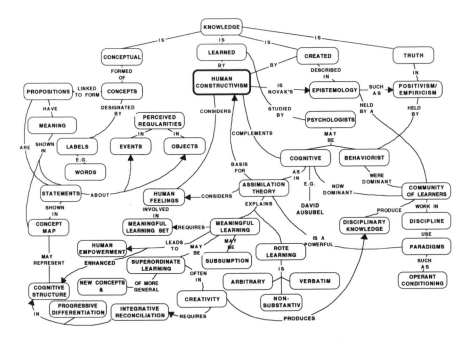

FIG. 6.6. A comprehensive map of ideas involved in Human Constructivism. This conceptual road map requires frequent references as you progress through this chapter and seek to understand my views on how humans create knowledge. It combines elements from both the psychology of learning (chap. 5) and epistemology, or the study of the nature of and creation of knowledge.

epistemology nor behaviorist psychology that is rooted in positivist epistemology will be expunged from society in the foreseeable future.

Illustrated in Fig. 6.6 is the idea that knowledge may be learned during the life span of an individual and that new knowledge is created by scholars or communities of learners in disciplines. Increasingly, I expect that new knowledge creation will occur in business organizations. Piaget (1972) hinted at the idea that the ontogeny of knowledge acquired by an individual is constructed in a way that is similar to the phylogeny of knowledge produced by generations of scholars. However, Piaget did not see learning as principally the acquisition of complex frameworks of concepts and propositions and hence his constructivist parallel between learning and knowledge creation was very different from what is illustrated in Fig. 6.6. Moreover, Piaget tended to play down the roles that affect or human feelings play in both learning and knowledge production, possibly in part as a result of his early training as a scientist, which was then, and often is today, explicitly positivistic in character (see Kitchener, 1986).

One of the ideas that grows out of the work of Toulmin (1972) is that knowledge is constantly evolving. We use current knowledge to design new inquiries and the product of these inquiries leads in time to new or modified concepts or principles, and more rarely, new theoretical or philosophical ideas. We can illustrate the evolving nature of knowledge with a parade of Vees as shown in Fig. 6.7. For both the individual researcher, who is undergoing meaningful learning through the research, and for the discipline undergoing gradual modification through collective inquiries, the relevant left side of the Vee becomes modified over time. New knowledge and value claims modify old ideas and the process of knowledge construction continues. Bush (1945) characterized science as the endless frontier because new knowledge leads to new questions, and there is no endpoint where all the answers will be known. Collectively, and as individuals, scientists and scholars in every field will keep on learning—and modifying their theoretical/conceptual frameworks.

In some of our studies we used questionnaires and interviews to compare the learning approaches used by students who held constructivist as opposed to positivistic views on the nature of science. We found a strong trend toward meaningful learning for those students who held constructivist ideas and an inclination to prefer rote learning for those students who held positivistic ideas (Edmondson & Novak, 1993). Songer and Linn (1991) reported similar findings. One of the reasons I believe it is difficult to move some students toward meaningful learning strategies is the deterrent effect of their positivistic thinking. This is one reason I believe learning tools such as concept maps are needed to help move students to higher levels of meaningful learning.

The idea that new knowledge construction is nothing more than an extension of the meaningful learning process of those who create the knowledge has at once a

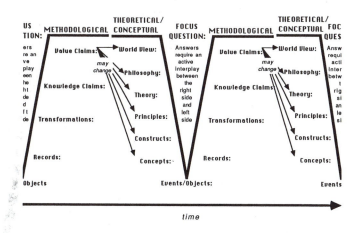

FIG. 6.7. The Parade of Vees illustrating the constructivist view that we build new knowledge about events or objects based on what we now know, and this process goes on and on, evolving our ideas shown on the left side of the Knowledge Vee. Modified from Novak and Gowin, 1984 (pp. 152–157). Reproduced with permission from Cambridge University Press.

great simplicity but also great complexity. It gives a simple explanation for how new knowledge is created, but it also necessitates an understanding of the psychological complexity of meaningful learning. There is in the view of human constructivism at once a simplicity and also a comprehensiveness that conforms to the principle of parsimony that has guided knowledge creators for several centuries.

The Principle of Parsimony

One other major influence on western scientific thought was William of Occam. Writing in 1340, Occam stressed that explanations should be economical and simple, with no more constructions than are needed to explain an event or phenomenon; all unnecessary causes and explanations should be scrupulously removed. This principle of excising unnecessary causes became known as Occam's razor. Sir William Hamilton (1853) stressed again the importance of Occam's canon and termed it the law of parsimony. Hamilton rephrased the law this way: "Neither more nor more onerous causes are to be assumed than are necessary to account for the phenomena" (p. 22).

The history of physics and biology illustrates the power of parsimonious thinking. In biology, a half-dozen or so major principles serve to give meaning to an almost infinite variety of observations. Evolution, gene theory, and complementarity of structure and function are a few of the constructions that meet Occam's criterion and that have served to advance our understanding of living systems. In contrast to physics and biology, psychology and education have been characterized by innumerable principles and theories, each of which has at best a dubious interpretive value over a very narrow range of phenomena. The field of education has been strikingly devoid of parsimonious explanations. One reason for this, in my view, is that educators have relied too heavily on psychologists for principles and theories. Most of the research done by psychologists has been what Niesser (personal communication) called white lab coat psychology, done in the laboratory, usually with animals, and of almost no relevance to human learning in school settings. Educators must build their own education principles and theories that apply to humans in educational settings. And educators must seek to construct principles and theories that have wide-ranging power and relevance to educational events. Parsimony in theory building should always be a focal concern.

My enthusiasm for Ausubel's (1968) assimilation theory of cognitive learning has grown over the past 3 decades, partly because my research group sees increasing power and relevance of the theory for innumerable educational events in every domain of subject matter and for all age groups. In short, we observe enormous parsimony both in the relative simplicity of the theory and also in the enormous range of educative events to which it can be applied. The most important principle in Ausubel's cognitive learning theory is meaningful learning, that is, the principle that meaningful learning occurs when the learner chooses to relate new knowledge to prior knowledge, nonarbitrarily and substantively. Principles of subsumption, progressive differentiation, integrative reconciliation, and superordinate learning further explain how assimilation of new knowledge occurs in meaningful learning in any educational setting. In our work in research and instructional innovation, we have found the principle of meaningful learning to be fundamental to understanding a wide range of phenomena occurring in educative events, which this book seeks to illustrate. Our research group has also seen growing power and parsimony in *A Theory of Education* (Novak, 1977a) as it has been applied and modified over the past two decades and evolved to the form presented here. It will, we hope, continue to evolve as it is used. I expect the evolution and application of the theory will accelerate rapidly as businesses seek to apply and adapt the ideas.

Improving Research Productivity

As an outgrowth of university faculty development seminars in which participants were taught how to use concept maps and the Vee heuristic to improve their teaching, with the suggestion that they try also to apply these tools to their research work, we found the tools to show marked success in facilitating new knowledge construction. More recently, my colleagues and I have been applying these tools in corporate settings with striking success. For example, in seminars with research directors at a very large consumer products company, we used concept maps and Vees to help groups design new products and to pinpoint gaps in knowledge available that needed to be filled through new, targeted research. The manager in charge of this program remarked, "You led the team to see better the nature of the new product and research that needs to be done in four hours than usually occurs in four months." Unfortunately, proprietary rights do not permit me to show examples of concept maps and Vees created with this and other companies.

One of our current research projects involves a research team at Cornell University led by Professor Zobel. Concept maps and Vees are being used to help the group see the global structure of the total research effort as well as to sharpen the definition of research work of individual team members. Figures 6.8 and 6.9 show examples from this project.

Although the application of concept maps and the Vee heuristic to facilitation of research work is still in its infancy, we already see evidence of high promise of these tools for aiding in the creation of new knowledge, both in academic and in for-profit corporations. As we see in chapter 10, facilitating knowledge creation may be the key to economic survival of any nation.

FORMS OF KNOWLEDGE

Knowledge Versus Information

There is currently much discussion about various forms of knowledge. Nonaka and Takeuchi (1995) distinguished between knowledge and information:

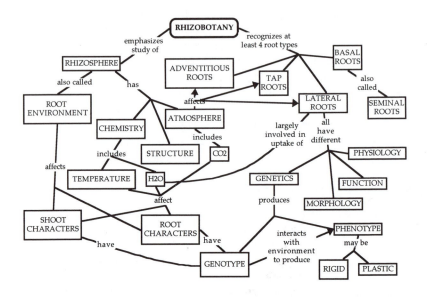

FIG. 6.8. A concept map showing key concepts involved in a Ph.D. study that is part of the Rhizobotany research group at Cornell University. Reproduced with permission from Matthews, 1995.

First, knowledge, unlike information, is about *beliefs* and *commitments*. Knowledge is a function of a particular stance, perspective, or intention. Second, knowledge, unlike information, is about *action*. It is always knowledge "to some end." And third, knowledge, like information, is about *meaning*. It is context-specific and relational. (p. 58)

If one looks at Nonaka and Takeuchi's descriptions from the perspective of the Vee heuristic, it is evident that what they describe as information is essentially records, and knowledge is much more complex. Their description would be similar to what is shown on the Vee as knowledge claims and value claims. Viewed from the perspective of the Vee heuristic, however, knowledge is really much more complex than they describe. Moreover, the Vee helps us to see more explicitly the processes involved in knowledge creation.

Tacit and Explicit Knowledge

Another distinction Nonaka and Takeuchi (1995) discussed at some length is tacit contrasted with explicit knowledge. They built on the earlier work of Polyani (1966) and characterized tacit knowledge as subjective knowledge and explicit knowledge as objective knowledge. The latter is the product of rational thought and may result from empirical studies. Explicit knowledge is knowledge we can easily show or

FOCUS QUESTIONS

What can I understand about plant gravitropic responses, specifically the interaction with temperature and carbon dioxide?

WORLD VIEW & PHILOSOPHY

•understanding the effects of gravity on life is a fundamental question of substantial, inherent scientific value and provides a unique environmental tool in our search to understand life • plants are an integral part of the world as we know it, so understanding them is important • we can construct knowledge about plant gravitropic responses

THEORY

• life on Earth has been exposed to the constant force of gravity • gravity helped shape and continues to influence the structure, function, and on-going evolution of all living organisms, including plants • plants use gravity to effect "normal" growth

PRINCIPLES

• gravitropic responses are not seen when plants are subjected to microgravity conditions • on Earth, plants use a geotropic response to send roots "down" and shoots "up" • plants must have within them 1) gravity sensors 2) a means of action 3) a means of translation between the sensors and the action • plants use gravity to produce "normal" growth, but sometimes we see abnormal growth in gravity situations and we must be able to explain this • gravity sensing involves a pressure gradient created by both starch granules and Golgi bodies • the translated signal begins with the cell producing ethylene, which then regulates the transport of auxin; the signal may also be affected by calcium • the mechanism of action is based on auxin movement • I will integrate new knowledge based on my previous congnitive framework

CONCEPTS

• concept map • Vee diagram • pressure gradient • gravitropic response • auxin • ethylene • carbon dioxide • plant hormones • gravity • gravity sensors • Golgi bodies • starch granules • endoplasmic reticulum • auxin sensitivity • hybrid

VALUE CLAIMS

• temperature and carbon dioxide are two environmental stimuli that affect plant gravitropic responses • since different hybrids respond in different manners to both temperature and carbon dioxide, then there may be a genetic component that is somehow regulating or directing these responses

KNOWLEDGE CLAIMS

• some areas of the gravitropic response are still under consideration • ethylene, auxin, and calcium all play a role (and there may be others) in a gravitropic response, but the roles are not well understood • carbon dioxide is a competitive inhibitor of ethylene, so in high CO2 a gravitropic response may be inhibited • temperature affects the gravitropic responses of some hybrids more than others • carbon dioxide affects the gravitropic responses of some hybrids more than others • there are no significant differences in seed angles between treatments; therefore the only variable in this experiment is temperature or carbon dioxide • some significant differences between temperatures and carbon dioxide level exist for initial shoot angle, final shoot angle, initial root angle, and final root angle

TRANSFORMATIONS

• averages and standard deviation for all reps for each hybrid • AMMI analysis for genotype by environment interaction

RECORDS

• 12 replications of 5 seeds each for each of 5 hybrids (Cargill 4327, DeKalb 524, Eastland 541, HyTest 474, Pioneer 3751) • Measurements are: seed angle, initial shoot angle, final shoot angle, initial root angle, final root angle

EVENT

Evaluation of maize seedling gravitropic response at various temperatures (17.5, 20, 25, 30°C) and at various carbon dioxide levels (.035%,0.15%,1.5%)

FIG. 6.9. A Vee diagram constructed in tabular form to show epistemological elements involved in a Ph.D. study of plant gravitropic responses. Reproduced with permission from Matthews, 1995.

explain to others, whereas tacit knowledge is knowledge we build up over our lifetime, and often we are at a loss to explain what we believe to others. For example, a skilled driver or golfer can have a difficult time explaining to another person how to drive or golf skillfully, as he or she does. Experts in any field have a good deal of tacit knowledge that they do not know how to impart to others. We found this to be the case in dealing with an expert cardiologist (Dr. Andrews) when we tried to capture his knowledge to design an Artificial Intelligence (AI) Program to train other cardiologists in a new diagnostic technique (Ford, Canas, Jones, Stahl, Novak, & Adams–Weber, 1991).

The principal challenge Nonaka and Takeuchi (1995) saw facing corporations was how to capture, preserve, and exchange tacit knowledge and how to transform tacit into explicit knowledge. We have found concept maps to be a powerful tool in these processes. For example, once we captured Dr. Andrews' tacit knowledge of "first pass functional imaging" for diagnosis of coronary problems, it was relatively easy to design the AI Program for training, and even lab technicians were achieving 93% correct diagnosis (on cases in the files) using the AI Program. Figure 6.10 shows the concept map prepared in this work.

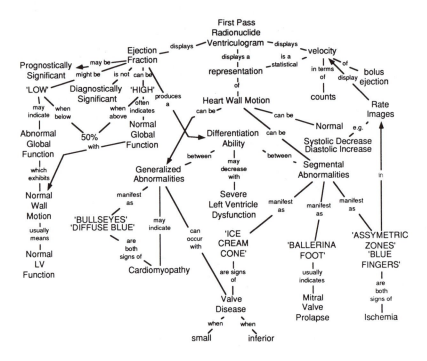

FIG. 6.10. A segment of a concept map from the domain of nuclear cardiology. This map served as the foundation for planning a highly successful artificial intelligence training program for cardiologists. Reproduced with permission from Ford et al., 1991.

Declarative, Procedural, and Structural Knowledge

Declarative knowledge is usually described as knowledge or awareness of some object, event, or idea. Ryle (1949) described this kind of knowledge as knowing that, and contrasts it with procedural knowledge or knowing how. Declarative knowledge is needed to construct procedural knowledge. Jonassen, Beissner, and Yacci (1993) described structural knowledge as that knowledge "that mediates the translation of declarative into procedural knowledge and facilitates the application of procedural knowledge" (p. 4). Their book goes on to describe various methods for representing, conveying, and acquiring structural knowledge, including discussion of our work on concept mapping.

Although the declarative/procedural knowledge distinction is currently popular in psychological writings, I see this as of relatively little value. For one thing, it is more parsimonious to recognize that all knowledge is fundamentally concept-propositional in nature. Furthermore, the distinction between declarative and procedural knowledge is often ambiguous and at times purely arbitrary. As previously noted, information may lack structure, but I regard all knowledge as possessing structure. In the 2½ decades we have been working with knowledge representation tools, we have not found any subject matter or field of inquiry where the structure of the knowledge has not been important. Certainly when it comes to knowledge creation, the quality of the structure of knowledge we possess is the critical variable.

APPROACHES TO KNOWLEDGE CAPTURE AND UTILIZATION

The Personal Interview

Across the years, we have found the personal interview to be the most powerful tool for capturing the knowledge held by an individual or groups of individuals. Personal interviews involve a one-on-one conversation between the interviewer and the interviewee. The key to successfully probing and capturing how the interviewee thinks, feels, and acts toward an idea, thing, or experience is for the interviewer to ask the type of questions that reveal as spontaneously as possible the interviewee's thoughts, feelings, and actions. This requires some experience and skill on the part of the interviewer. Numerous books and articles have been written on interviewing, including Piaget's prodigious works and writings that contributed enormously to the popularization of interviewing. None of these works, however, were based on a specific theory of knowledge and complementary theory of learning, combined with knowledge representation tools based on these theories. Since the early 1970s, we have used concept maps to design and interpret personal interviews. Since the late 1970s, we have used both concept maps and Vee diagrams to design and interpret personal interviews. See Fig. 6.5 for an example of a Vee design for a research project dealing with nutrition.

We must be careful not to underestimate the complexity of ideas younger interviewees can deal with. Matthews (1980) found that, in interviews with children 3- to 9-years-old, some remarkably profound philosophical ideas were expressed. These ideas rated favorably with similar ideas expressed by great philosophers. For example, the question of the constancy of objects in different frames of reference has a long philosophical history. Matthews observed:

> One day John Edgar (four years), who had often seen airplanes take off, rise, and gradually disappear into the distance, took his first plane ride. When the plane stopped ascending and the seat-belt sign went out, John Edgar turned to his father and said in a rather relieved, but still troubled, tone of voice, "things don't really get smaller up here." (p. 6)

This and many other examples led Matthews to conclude that although young children may have less language sophistication and fewer relevant experiences, they are capable of profound philosophical thinking. We found, in interviews with preschool children and their parents, that, in terms of the number and variety of nutrition concepts expressed by the children, they were comparable to their parents, and in some cases, even more sophisticated than their fathers (Achterberg, 1986).

Market researchers seldom consider children's ideas regarding products other than toys or breakfast cereals, even though it is recognized that young children can influence parent product or service choices. Woodruff and Gardials (1996) recent book, *Know Your Customer,* has no discussion on interviews with children, although they do give strong endorsement and preference to personal interviews over other research techniques.

The design of good personal interviews involves several steps. First is the clear definition of a question or set of questions we hope the interviews will answer. From the perspective of the Knowledge Vee, these are the focus questions. We must consider all of the elements on the left side of the Vee that are pertinent to our focus questions and relevant for our target population. For example, the concepts and principles relevant to interviewees of ages 3 to 6 or 7 might be quite different than those for interviewees of ages 18 to 30.

A concept map should be prepared to organize the structure of knowledge the interviewer anticipates will be relevant to the focus questions and that will represent a good composite of the concepts and principles that may be expressed by the interviewees. For knowledge domains where the pertinent knowledge is clearly defined, this map may represent the knowledge structure held by experts, with the degree of sophistication dependent on that of our target population. For example, a concept map for interviews on the question: Why do things float? is shown in Fig. 6.11. Although this would be too simplistic for interviews with physicists, it served very well as a template for interviewing school children and adults of all ages.

For domains of knowledge where there are no right concepts or principles, the task may be initially more difficult. If we want to know why people choose to buy or not buy a certain beverage most often, we can start with a preliminary concept

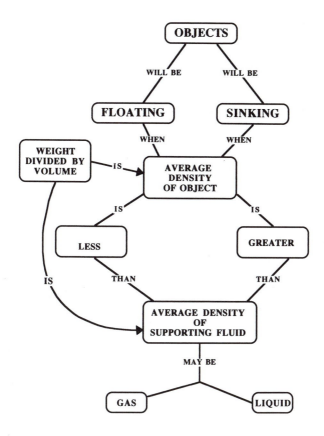

FIG. 6.11. A concept map showing the knowledge required to understand why things float. The concept of density and the role it plays in floating or sinking is usually not understood.

map based on our own experiences, but it will very likely be necessary to modify this map substantially. In any case, this includes an interactive process where we design interview questions based on a first approximation map, revision after an interview or two, a redesign of the interview, two or three more interviews, and, a repeat of the process. My experience, based on teaching several thousand students, teachers, and professors how to interview, is that three to five cycles of design-try-out-redesign are needed to achieve highly effective interviews. We have found that interviews with 6 to 10 subjects from a given population provide essentially all of the concepts and principles that will be expressed and can serve as a basis for understanding the belief structure of that population on the questions posed. Zaltman and Higie (1993) reported that 90% of the ideas held by consumers were captured in 3 to 10 consumer interviews, with the number required varying with the product or service. In general, they conclude that there is little new insight to be gained after 8 to 10 customer interviews. Our interview strategies are only recently being applied in corporate settings.

Interviews should be conducted in a friendly, cordial manner. They should not be interrogations where questions are fired at the interviewee in rapid succession. Interviewees need some time to think, to scan their memories, and to formulate answers. In classroom settings it has been found that on average, teachers wait only 0.7 seconds before firing another question or moving to question another student. Rowe (1974) found that students give no answers or superficial replies when wait time is 0.7 seconds or less. A wait time of 3 to 4 seconds is minimal, and questions that require some introspective thinking by the interviewee might best be followed with a wait time of 10 to 15 seconds or more. This will appear to be an eternity to the interviewer, so novice interviewers need to watch a clock during interviews. If you want to uncover what some people call customer's unarticulated concerns or desires, you need to use sufficient wait time and good follow-up questions to get this kind of deep reflection.

There is always the question, "Will my interviews only reveal what I designed them to reveal and miss large and important segments of the interviewee's beliefs?" Our experience has been that this is unlikely if interviewers use good techniques and if sufficient iterations of interview design and redesign are employed. The latter process will show a gradual reduction in interview modifications needed and a growing confidence that a relatively complete set of interviewee beliefs are being recorded. Detailed instruction on design, execution, and interpretation of interviews can be found in Novak and Gowin (1984).

Questionnaires

The principal advantage of using questionnaire or survey forms is that they can be administered to much larger samples than is usually possible or feasible for interviews. Another major advantage is that numbers can be extracted from the response forms, and these can be used in various statistical transformations, tables, graphs, and so forth. There is, in the general population, the idea that if you have large numbers and maybe two or three numbers after the decimal point, then the results must be right. Sometimes this belief is strongly held by managers. The problem is that the individual's responses to each question and the totals of various combinations of responses may mean very little if we don't understand why the respondent chose to respond as he or she did! There can be significant validity problems in that the respondent's choices may not represent his or her real thoughts, feelings, or actions. And neither the respondent nor the researcher can ask, "What do you mean by that (question or response)?" The questionnaire may also miss important topics, ideas, or feelings, further contributing to validity problems.

Looked at from the perspective of the Knowledge Vee, many sources of validity problems are possible. Was adequate consideration given to questionnaire respondent's world view, philosophy, theories, concepts, and principles? Were the focus questions the right foundation for design of the questionnaire? There may be high reliability for the records obtained from the questionnaire, but how valid are the records? No amount of statistical manipulation will add validity to the raw records. Even worse, there is always the danger of reification, that is, we may extract factors or correlation coefficients from our statistical transformations, but it is not easy to decide whether these are real or valid, and even more difficult at times to determine what they mean. For all of these reasons, my bias leans toward the power and cost-effectiveness of personal interviews when we want to understand a population's beliefs about anything.

All of this notwithstanding, questionnaires can be used effectively in conjunction with personal interviews. In fact, the best way to design a questionnaire or survey form is to begin with a series of interviews as described. Using the knowledge claims from the interviews as a starting point, questionnaire items can be designed. When this approach is used, much more valid results can be obtained. Furthermore, the Vees and concept maps generated from the interview process can help to interpret the meaning of the qualitative data extracted from the questionnaire responses. Another benefit of this approach is that the response rate from mailed questionnaires or other forms of distribution can be much better. Because the survey instrument was designed from actual statements of the sample population's thoughts, feelings, and actions, the items of the survey make sense to most of the respondents and may even intrigue the respondents. Whereas typical response rates to mailed questionnaires are 20 to 30%, we obtained a 61% response rate to a mailed, very complex questionnaire sent to a random sample of a city's water customers (Hughes, 1986). The questionnaire revealed a surprisingly good understanding of factors influencing ground water contamination and toxicity, as was also true in the interviews done to design the questionnaire. Probably every reader has had the experience of receiving a questionnaire to complete where the items or choices just didn't make sense. Your response was probably the same as mine—into the rubbish it goes!

Focus Groups

A common practice in business is to gather a group of 15 to 20 consumers together and ask them as a group to express their thoughts, feelings, and actions regarding some product or service. Too often the results of these focus groups are difficult to interpret, and they have serious validity problems. For example, they are typically conducted during the working day; thus most participants are people (usually female) who do not have jobs during the day. It also takes a very knowledgeable, skillful leader, knowledgeable regarding the topics of the focus group discussion as well as skillful in leading such groups. The generic focus group leader many companies employ are often limited in both pertinent knowledge and leadership skills. There are also the technical problems associated with video or audio recording of the sessions.

For focus groups, as for questionnaire studies, results can be improved by applying the personal interview strategies in preparation for the focus groups. However, it is likely that the focus group findings will be largely redundant with the interview findings. They can serve, nevertheless, as a kind of cross-check on the interviews to see if patterns are similar.

Team Concept Mapping

One of the most useful roles concept mapping can play is to aid a group or team to capture and come to consensus on their collective knowledge regarding some question or set of questions of interest to the team. This process may proceed in several ways.

In one of our early applications of the process, each staff member of a state school for girls was asked to concept map how they perceived their role in the school. The school was faced with significant budget reductions necessitating some redeployment and reduction in staff. There was a need to become more efficient and to raise the morale of the staff. After staff members completed the concept maps, the maps, with no names or other identification, were taped to the walls of a large meeting room. The staff then spent an hour reviewing all of the concept maps and taking notes. The subsequent discussion led to very productive suggestions on how operations and staff activities could be made more efficient. This led, in time, to substantial improvement in staff morale, student morale, and effectiveness of the school.

A different approach was used with a research team, the Rhizobotany Group at Cornell University, studying plant roots. After an orientation to concept mapping and opportunities for individual team members to construct a concept map dealing with their segment of the research program, the whole research team assembled to construct a global map for their area of plant science research. The professor in charge of the research group led the discussion with one of my graduate students helping to facilitate the discussion and recording the ideas in the form of a concept map on the blackboard. The team used this map to help orient each team member as to where, in the larger domain of knowledge, did each individual's research project fit. From time to time, revisions were made to the global map, and individuals continued to refine their own maps as the research program progressed. Figure 6.12 shows the global map as it was at the time we discontinued our work with the team. The professor in charge and most of the individual team members found the use of concept maps to be very helpful in guiding their research. Interestingly, a technician and a visiting foreign researcher made no effort to produce their own concept maps, and they saw little or no value in them. On the other hand, a new graduate student joining the research team saw immediately how the maps helped her to understand the research in progress with the Rhizobotany group and to see how her own research questions could be designed to fit into and extend the knowledge structure the research team was developing (Novak & Iuli,

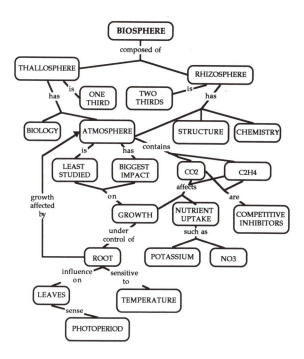

FIG. 6.12. A map of the major ideas involved in Zobel's research program in Rhizobotany. Compare with Fig. 4.2.

1995). She reported that she had a better understanding of the research work being done by the team after a 1-month association with the group than she had for the work of an entomology team she had worked with for 2 years.

A third method we have employed extensively in the corporate setting involves a somewhat different approach. We first work with a team leader who has responsibility for some area of technological or market development to define the key question or questions that are of most pressing concern, for example, how can we double sales in 5 years of X products in the Japanese market? The team leader also works with one or more of our facilitators to develop a preliminary global concept map containing perhaps 10 to 12 concepts that he or she believes are the most general or most inclusive, and linking words to form some of the key propositions on the global map. This prework helps the team leader become oriented to the process of concept mapping and also builds confidence in the person for leading the whole team in the process of concept mapping.

We have found that it is useful to provide all team members some orientation to the theory of learning and theory of knowledge underlying concept mapping early in the process of team concept map building, or preferably in advance through readings or technologically mediated orientation materials. We are currently working on a CD-ROM orientation program for a very large consumer products company that will include specific examples from some of the concept mapping projects completed with that company.

Our experience has been that the optimal size for knowledge capture and mapping teams is usually 12 to 20 members. The team needs to be large enough that most of the relevant knowledge and/or experience is represented in the group, but not so large as to make whole-team discussions difficult. As with all teamwork, optimal size of the team is not always easy to determine in advance. Moreover, the team leader may not have recognized the need for a member with a certain area of expertise until after the mapping process gets well along and the team knowledge map begins to show knowledge gaps that are now obviously pertinent but were not recognized earlier.

Subsequent to orientation of the team members, which may occur during the final half of the first morning, the whole team discusses the focus question(s) and the tentative global map created by the team leader. We usually work with Post-its^{TM} of various sizes, using larger Post-its™ for the large general concepts of the global maps and smaller Post-its™ for specific concepts. These are often mounted on large sheets of butcher paper, permitting the finished maps to be rolled up and saved, either for later review and modification or for transfer to electronic files via computer. It usually takes about an hour for the team as a whole to discuss, debate, and reach consensus on one or two good focus questions and the 8 to 12 concepts representing the top concepts of a global map. Usually this global map will contain a top concept and three to five second-level concepts. The team is now divided into subteams, and a leader is selected for each subteam. These subteams now proceed to develop a concept map for their sub domain of the global map. This process usually takes 2 to 4 hours. Ideally, a facilitator skilled in leading groups in concept mapping is available for each subteam.

After the subteams have developed a prototype concept map for their subdomain, a whole-team review of each of the subdomain maps is conducted, with the subdomain leader walking the whole team through his or her subdomain map. Each subdomain map is discussed, questions are raised, and suggestions for revisions are made. After all of the subdomain maps are reviewed, each subdomain team returns to extend, modify, correct, or in other ways, improve their map. This process may take 1 or 2 hours, depending on the difficulties encountered.

The next step is for the whole team to reassemble, either to review again each of the subdomain concept maps or to continue the development of a global map for the team. Suggestions are proffered as to how each subdomain map could be incorporated into a global map, and how modifications of the original global map might lead to better inclusion of all of the knowledge captured up to this point. This process may be continued to the end of the first working day, or extend to a second day. Alternatively, the team may work over a period of weeks, exchanging ideas on how each subteam map can be improved and how the global map might be improved. Electronic communication of maps, revised maps, and suggestions can greatly facilitate this process.

Another step in the process is for the team to work both individually and as groups to see better and novel ways to integrate knowledge in each of the sub domains of the global map. In short, the team is doing a creative exercise in searching for better ways to organize the knowledge of their field and to seek new integrative reconciliations between segments of the global map. These are the processes that lead to new creative insights, new ways to break out of the box, to express an idea common in business (cf, Vance & Deacon, 1995). Here we come back to the significance of each team member recognizing and considering the important theoretical foundations underlying concept maps and their role in facilitating learning and creativity.

To date, we have found the approach just described to be enormously helpful. The necessity for confidentiality with private corporation concept maps prevents me from showing any of the maps developed at this date. Sometime in the future, the whole story can be told. I can say this, however, compared to the global concept maps we have developed in the academic world, the concept maps we have developed in the business world are enormously more complex, frequently containing 100 to 200 concepts. Contrast this with the 10 concepts required to understand "Why do things float?" Is it any wonder that corporations frequently stumble along, making poor decisions and moving ahead very inefficiently at best? Figure 6.13 shows an example of the kind of concept map we developed while working with a major corporation. I cannot show the details of this map, but the figure illustrates the complexity of the global map constructed. Furthermore, in terms of complexity, this is only an average map that we have developed in our work. Others contain

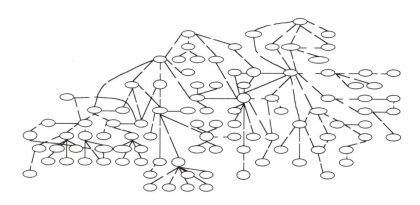

FIG. 6.13. The complex knowledge structure required to understand ideas relevant to a product domain. Specific concepts and propositions cannot be shown due to confidentiality, but the complexity of this knowledge structure is obvious.

two to three times this number of concepts.

Concept maps can be used to capture and display knowledge a company has in core competencies. These can be very helpful both in achieving and making available to all employees the knowledge the company has in core competency areas and in identifying new core competencies that are needed and new market opportunities. Hamel and Prahalad (1994) presented a four-section grid, with new and existing core competencies combined with new and existing markets. Gaps in knowledge that could be useful often become obvious to teams constructing core competency concept maps, leading to suggestions for new core competencies that might be developed. The ease with which new cross links on core-competency concept maps can be constructed permits identification on new market opportunities.

The process of knowledge capture by teams is likely to be greatly facilitated by new technological developments. For example, electronic white boards are now available that transfer concept maps directly to a computer and then to other computers controlling white boards. This permits construction of concept maps by teams whose members are scattered all over the globe. Moreover, the work can be done in real time or team members can interact over days or weeks using either their personal computers or electronic white boards in their locations.

Other Approaches to Knowledge Capture

The Knowledge Vee has also been used very successfully as a tool to help individuals or teams capture, organize, and utilize knowledge more effectively. Some examples have been presented earlier. Compared with concept maps, using the Vee requires significantly more training, incubation time, and reorientation in the way most people think about knowledge and knowledge creation. My guess is that it will take 2 or 3 decades before the power and utility of using the Knowledge Vee for knowledge capture and facilitation of thinking takes hold, even in the business community where management motivation may be high, but probably not understanding of the nature of knowledge and knowledge creation.

There are, of course, other approaches to knowledge capture, representation, and utilization. Some of these, in my opinion, are little more than gimmicks to stimulate discussions among group members and schemes to record information in pictorial ways. They obviously have some value because some schools and companies spend thousands of dollars in staff time, materials, consulting fees, and other costs to employ these strategies. It has been my experience, and the experience of many with whom I have worked in schools and businesses, that the value of most other knowledge tools pale in comparison to the value experienced using concept maps.

If the last decade belonged to the businesses that were successful in utilizing Total Quality Management (TQM) and reengineering their operations, I believe the decade ahead will be dominated by those corporations who become most effective in using tools such as concept maps to help them organize, create, store, and access knowledge more effectively. TQM brought with it ideas such as benchmarking best practices and just-in-time inventory systems, but most of these activities were centered on processes of corporate functioning and not on knowledge creation. Similarly, reengineering also places emphasis on processes utilized, although there is also concern with mechanisms for providing leadership for process improvements (Hammer & Champy, 1993).

By comparison with the change in corporate practices, change in schools has been very modest at best, as we discuss in later chapters. My hope is that schools and universities will eventually follow their lead.

7

The Effective Teacher/Manager

INTEGRATING THINKING, FEELING, AND ACTING CONSTRUCTIVELY

As stated in chapter 2, human beings experience concomitantly thinking, feeling, and acting. This is true for learners and workers as well as for teachers and managers. I consider workers as a learners in a work context and view both as learners. The challenge is how to help students and workers integrate in a constructive manner these concomitant experiences. When learners do this successfully, the teacher's or the manager's experience is also positive, constructive, and rewarding. I also see managers as teachers in a work context and call them both teachers. When learners fail to achieve a constructive integration of their thinking, feeling, and acting, both teacher and learners lose, although the loss can be more serious for the learner. In the worst case, the bedlam that can result in the classroom or in the workplace can lead to great teacher or manager frustration or even dismissal from the job.

Teaching is a complex activity. This is evident in the thousands of research studies, such as those summarized in *The Handbook of Research on Teacher Education* (Houston, 1990). Rowan (1994) compared teachers' work with work in other occupations and found that, "Teaching children and adolescents is complex work compared with other professions, and successful performance of this work requires high levels of general educational development and specific vocational preparation" (p. 13). As a complex activity, I believe it is imperative that teaching be guided by a comprehensive theory of education. However, in a study of foundations courses for teacher education, Bauer and Borman (1988) found no such courses listed in 508 courses from 100 college catalogs. The idea that teachers need a theory of education to guide their work is clearly an idea whose time has not come, at least in the United States.

The same, unfortunately, is true for management. This, too, is a complex activity, and although books abound on how to manage, theory-based ideas of management are hard to find. Those books that do deal with theoretical issues, such as the classic works of Argyris and Schön (1978) and Schön (1983), do not deal with a theory of learning or a theory of knowledge. Schön, for example, argued that effective practitioners must base practice on theory, but he did not describe the theory that is relevant nor give examples of the relationship between specific theories and specific practices in teaching or management.

My theory is that meaningful learning must underlie the constructive integration of thinking, feeling, and acting if learners are to be successful and achieve a sense of empowerment—and also a sense of commitment and responsibility. The responsibility is to themselves as learners, to peers, and to the learning environment. I have discussed at length in earlier chapters what is required to effect meaningful learning, and this chapter focuses on the challenges the teacher must face in order to achieve what I like to refer to as *successful negotiation of meanings*. Although learning is an activity that cannot be shared, but is rather the responsibility of the learner, it is the teacher's responsibility to seek the best possible negotiation of meanings and an emotional climate that is conducive to learn meaningfully. Teachers must also recognize their role in negotiating meanings and for creating a favorable emotional climate to encourage such negotiation.

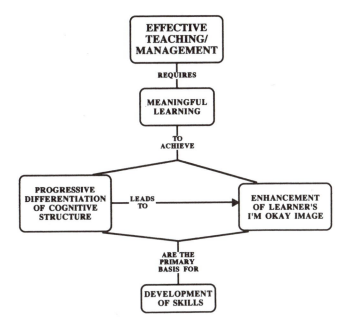

FIG. 7.1. Effective teaching and management requires skill in achieving progressive differentiation of cognitive structure in a manner that leads to ego enhancement.

First and foremost, effective teaching requires that we constantly remain cognizant of the fact that only meaningful learning can lead to progressive differentiation and integration of cognitive structure and concomitant enhancement of an individual's ego. This is shown in Fig. 7.1. Second, and also exceedingly important, we must recognize that every teaching event should seek to achieve two purposes: (a) to enhance further differentiation of the learner's cognitive structure, and (b) to enhance the learner's sense of "I'm okay." These two attributes also underlie development of skills when combined with practice of the skill. I do not believe that there is ever an occasion when teaching or managing that deliberately assaults a learner's ego is justified, although this is commonly observed in schools and in job settings.

One can never overestimate the amount of knowledge and the extent of emotional sensitivity required to teach or manage effectively. Moreover, knowledge and emotional sensitivities must be brought together to achieve effective teaching and management skills, and mastery in teaching or management takes time and constant effort. Although people vary in their innate talents to effect constructive integration of thinking, feeling, and acting, as with all human talents, my thesis is that any person can become a much more effective teacher or manager through theory-guided efforts. Some of the key ideas I address to help in this effort are shown in Fig. 7.2.

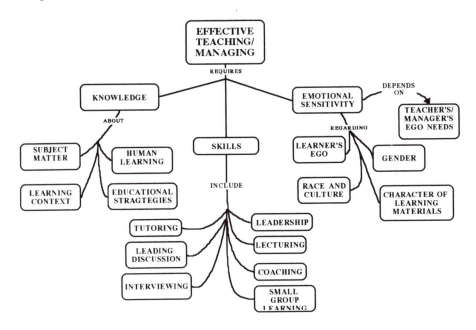

FIG. 7.2. Necessary conditions for effective teaching/management.

Teachers and Managers Need Knowledge and Emotional Sensitivity

Knowledge, as discussed earlier, is a well-organized framework of concepts and propositions. For effective teaching or managing, these frameworks must include knowledge of the subject matter to be learned, knowledge of alternative contexts for learning (even in the constraints of a poorly equipped shop, classroom, office, or school), knowledge about how humans learn, and knowledge about alternative evaluation and other educational strategies that can facilitate meaningful learning while recognizing the limitations the learners may possess and the context of the learning. In short, university programs in education and programs in business need to include instruction in a theory of education (Fig. 7.3).

Perhaps even more important, effective teaching and managing requires emotional sensitivity on the part of the teacher, a sensitivity to the emotional status and needs of the learner and a consciousness of his or her own emotional status and needs. Harris (1969), in his book, *I'm OK, You're OK,* showed in a practical way how all of us, to some extent, feel "not okay," because this feeling derives, in part, from early childhood experiences in the normal course of growing up. In the most deleterious early environments, the "I'm not okay" feelings can be so deeply rooted that a lifetime of antisocial actions, or actions that are personally destructive such as drug abuse, eating disorders, and so forth may result. Because humans live in societies that are not ideally suited to engendering "I'm okay" feelings, where ethnic, cultural, racial, or gender biases may aggravate early "I'm not okay" feelings, the challenge to the teacher is how to deal with the multiple ego needs of learners in constructive ways, constructive both to the learners and to the teacher.

Sternberg (1996a), now a distinguished professor at Yale University, related his experience as a child growing up in schools that put inordinate emphasis on IQ scores:

> I was lucky, damn lucky, in a way few students are. In fourth grade, when I was nine years old, I ended up in Mrs. Alexa's class. Whereas my teachers in the early primary grades had all been older and deeply dug into the trenches of the testing field, Mrs. Alexa was fresh out of college and either didn't know or didn't care much about IQ test scores. She believed I could do much better than I was doing, and she expected more of me. No, she demanded more of me. And she got it. Why? Because I wanted to please her, even more than I had wanted to please my teachers in the first three grades. (In fact, I would have proposed marriage to her on the spot if she hadn't been just a little too old and, inconveniently, already married.) (p. 18)

My wife and I can relate to this. Our oldest son was also not the best on tests given in school, although he tested highly on IQ tests given privately by a psychologist. Combined with the fact that he was left-handed, he had numerous difficulties in elementary grades, and we were advised by his fourth grade teacher that we had to face the fact that he was "a bit retarded." Mostly, he was incredibly bored with school tasks that required him to do simple, repetitive tasks when his

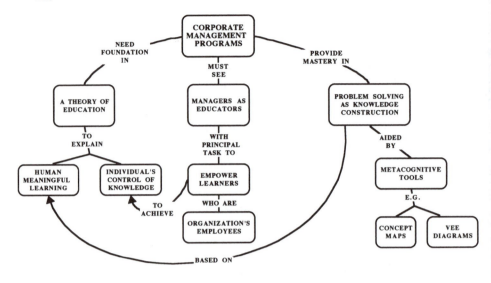

FIG. 7.3. Effective management should be viewed the same as effective teaching, both of which require integration of knowledge, skills and emotional sensitivity.

activities at home involved much more complex tasks. He did go on to complete a BS degree in architecture, an MBA degree at Cornell University, and in his early 40s, an MS degree in computer science. Alas, our grandson showed the same proclivities! Fortunately for him, his parents recognized his unusual abilities and also could afford to send him to an exceptionally good private school. The most outstanding feature of this school, his parents and we agree, is that they have great concern for variation in individual aptitudes and in the positive ego development for their students. We are experiencing once again, as our grandchildren progress through school, the enormous positive or negative effect teachers can have on children's ego development.

Knowledge relevant to teaching and managing becomes merged with emotional sensitivity in the skillfully guided educative event. For example, in conducting a discussion, still the most common educative event in most schools and corporate settings, an enormous set of ideas and feelings must be brought together. To illustrate, let us consider a relatively simple topic: Why do we have seasons?

The first consideration is, "What are the relevant concepts and principles needed to understand an answer to this question?" I have found that the preparation of a concept map for any topic to be taught is an enormously helpful way to begin, albeit at first this is time-consuming. But the time invested early in one's career, both to gain skill in constructing concept maps and in gathering the information needed for each topic, can pay off handsomely in a few years. Even very experienced teachers are often surprised at the fuzziness of their own ideas about a topic they may have taught for years when they take the time to concept map the topic (Novak, 1991). So I begin my example with a concept map on seasons (see Fig. 7.4).

Although some regions of the earth have essentially no seasons, that is, no major climate variations from month to month during the year, some regions experience wet and dry seasons. Most of us, however, think of seasons as colder or warmer—a bias that comes from living in a geographic area where this occurs. We might ask if any our learners come from a region (or have relatives in a region) where temperature is not the major factor in seasons—a nice way to help foreign-born students feel participatory in our class, especially if they are encouraged to share their knowledge or experiences. We may also forget that it is summer in the Northern hemisphere when it is winter in the Southern hemisphere because we live

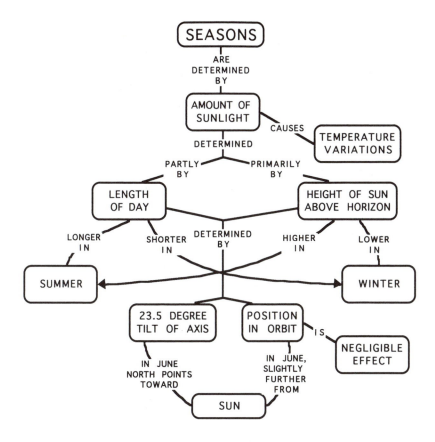

FIG. 7.4. A concept map showing the key ideas needed to understand why we have seasons. Many people fail to understand the effect of the inclination of the earth on its axis as the primary cause for summer and winter in both hemispheres.

in the Northern hemisphere. Again, sharing what New Year's Day may be like in the home or their relatives' home can be culturally sensitive and educative in terms of our knowledge goals.

Some of the knowledge about learning that should be brought to bear on this topic is that most of us develop misconceptions or limited conceptions about events in our lives. For example, most people believe that seasons are caused by how close the Earth is to the sun. This belief may arise from the common experience that we feel warmer when we are close to a fire or a light bulb and less heat when we are further away. If we have also learned that the Earth's orbit is not a perfect circle, this may reinforce our faulty belief because we now know that the Earth will be closer to the sun sometimes during the year and further away at other times. We may not know, or have obliteratively subsumed, the factual details that the variation in the distance to the sun is only about 3 million miles from the average distance of about 93 million miles (or about 3%). Furthermore, the Earth is actually closer to the sun when it is winter in the Northern hemisphere, and summer in the Southern hemisphere. One might ask, "How would you expect the temperatures in summers to compare at the same latitudes in the Northern and Southern hemispheres?"

The effective teacher or manager will know that people do not change their minds easily. The literature on faulty conceptions is enormous (see, e.g., Novak & Abrams, 1993), and most of it points to one stark reality: Giving learners the correct information does not displace their faulty conceptions! It takes a lot of negotiation of meanings, a lot of shared experience to help learners reconstruct their internal concept maps to be congruent with the expert's knowledge. We have found, however, that engaging students in building their own concept maps, showing (and negotiating) these in small groups, and reflecting on the teacher's map can be effective in helping learners reconstruct their knowledge frameworks (Feldsine,1987).

Knowledgeable teachers and managers know that it is not sufficient to just give students the facts. Yes, they can memorize these if they are motivated to do so but, for most, it will not alter their understanding of seasons. For example, a videotape produced by the Harvard Smithsonian Center for Astrophysics, A Private Universe, shows that most (21 out of 23 interviewed) Harvard graduates could not give an adequate explanation of why we have seasons, including a new graduate who had recently completed a course in The Physics of Planetary Motion! You can get a Harvard B.S. degree largely by memorizing facts presented (and tested for), but you may not get much education. Students need opportunities to act on ideas, to pretend they are the planet Earth and orbit the sun (or maybe a bright light) tilted 23° from the North Pole, and pretend first they are in the Northern hemisphere and then in the Southern hemisphere. It takes a lot of acting out ideas to reconstruct faulty ideas, but what else is worth doing? Moreover, there can be some joy, humor, and excitement when learners are engaged in helping to come up with ways to act out ideas.

We see in this example the potential for merging much of the knowledge, emotional sensitivity, and skill that is necessary for helping learners take responsibility for their own meaningful learning. I refer back to this from time to time as one of my paradigm cases.

Recently I had my car towed to the Nissan garage because it would not start. It was a Saturday morning, and a full crew of mechanics was not available. The mechanic who worked on my car was "almost positive the problem was an ignition module, since 95% of the time, cars with this problem had a faulty ignition module." I took his advice and replaced this part at a cost of $165. Unfortunately, my car would not start the next morning or Monday morning and was towed to the garage again. A more experienced mechanic looked at the car on Monday and replaced a simple plug in relay that controls the fuel injection motor (at $19). No more starting problems. Was I liable for the misdiagnosis of my problem? Technically, probably yes, but there is a lesson to be learned here. Inadequately educated mechanics can cost customers and/or the management problems and money and frustrations for all concerned. In this case, the dealer refunded the first charge and suffered some losses, but he also gained a customer. I will give preference to this Nissan dealer when I choose to buy another car.

In some 4 decades of work with teachers and managers, I have become very familiar with the limited conceptual understanding many teachers and managers (in school, university, and corporate settings) have regarding the subject matter they are charged to teach. This is not due to any intellectual shortcomings on their part, but is primarily a product of poor educational opportunities and little guidance for professional growth. For example, Fedock, Zambo, and Cobern (1996) found that college science teachers involved in a special program for K through 12 teachers not only gained new instructional strategies and skills, but also new insights about their subject matter. As one professor commented, "I never saw science as integrating with other facets of life. I had a very narrow perspective of science, being a cell biologist, but my perspective has broadened greatly, and I am amazed" (p. 17).

One of our studies (Kerr, 1988), based on intensive interviews with female scientists at Cornell University, illustrates the problem even outstanding students have had in acquiring subject matter knowledge.

> In her early education, it was the effort she put into these [science] projects that provided the meaning of learning. . . . The social institution, the school provided the meaning for those projects. . . . But it was not *her* meaning for learning that compelled her effort, only what the performance meant. At some point, *her* understanding of the meaning of science replaced performance. This did not occur until she was a senior undergraduate. What caused the switch?

> The first experience was discovering the conceptual foundation of evolution.

> ". . . it really is a passion . . . [it] sort of made everything fall into place." (pp. 61–62)

Contrasting learning in biology with learning in physics, another scientist reported in Kerr's study commented, "I had a tendency to over-learn; over-study, because I probably never *did* know when I knew for certain" (p. 74). Kerr also reported that:

> Biology was simple for her, but physics was not, and she got through physics by cramming it all into my head and hoping on exams, but without coming to an intuitive feeling of what was involved. It was years before she had any intuitive feeling for some of those topics. . . . She admits that there was always the beginning memorizing . . . and "then there is something that clicks. Or all of a sudden it fits. And you are not having to go back to proposition one to get to proposition ten." (pp. 74–75)

What Kerr described is the very difficult process of constructing a powerful conceptual framework for any domain of science when the teacher(s) fail to help bring clarity to the concept and propositional structure necessary to have a feeling for the subject. Although admittedly each learner must construct his or her own conceptual frameworks, teachers can do much to facilitate this process.

In my experience, most teachers, especially novice teachers, focus on teaching activities and tend to ignore learning activities. They center attention on how to teach a given topic, rather than on what is required for a learner to learn the topic. This stems, in part, from teachers' limited knowledge of the learning process and implications for the teaching process. The long-term consequence for many teachers (especially professors in tertiary schools) is a growing cynicism toward learners and a manifest lack of empathy and emotional support for the struggle learners face in constructing and reconstructing their knowledge frameworks.

Problems in Organizational Settings

What I did not anticipate when I began working with corporations a decade ago was that most administrators and managers have a surprisingly poor conceptual understanding of their organizations. Oh, they may know well the organizational chart showing who reports to whom. What they grasp only with fuzzy vision is how each member of the organization contributes to the overall operation of the organization. For example, when we interviewed and then concept-mapped how various members of the Cornell University Theory Center viewed and how they felt about their jobs, we found some striking differences in perceptions of the organization between various individuals' perceptions and those of senior administrators. Figure 7.5 shows an example of one of these concept maps and describes some of the complexity of the organization's mission and functions. Prior to preparing this map, Martyne was not clearly aware of some of the factors that were impacting her work as a manager of networking functions.

Shown in Fig. 7.6 is the view of the Cornell University Theory Center held by the Director of the Center. This map was made by a class member in a course on Application of Educational Theory and Methods to Corporations from a lecture

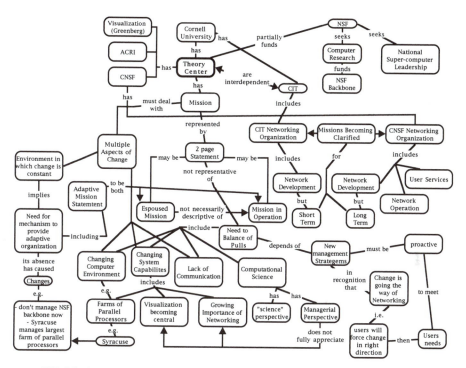

FIG. 7.5. A concept map prepared from interviews with one of the Theory Center staff members after modifications by the staff member.

given by the Director to a local Rotary Club meeting. It was later reviewed and corroborated by the Director. Other class members interviewed individuals involved in the administration in various subordinate positions. What we found is that their perceptions of the Theory Center, and their views on their work, were significantly at variance with that of the Director.

Our findings that managers do not understand what they are managing is not a new idea. Many years ago, Crosby (1992) tried to figure out operations at a missile plant where he was employed. He created a flow chart to help himself and observed:

I spent about two weeks on the chart doing that in between chasing problems. I got all involved with laying it out on a long sheet of paper, using different shaped blocks for different missile and supply systems. It was a lot of fun. When the chart was about complete, I had one aspect I couldn't figure out, so I took it to my boss and asked him for guidance. "Where did you get this?" he asked. He was astounded that such a piece of paper existed. Everyone wanted copies, and I was an instant hero. (A little later my chart was classified "Top secret" which was one level above my clearance—so I never saw it again.) That is when I began to realize that hardly anyone knew anything about what was happening except in his or her own area of work. (pp. 5–6)

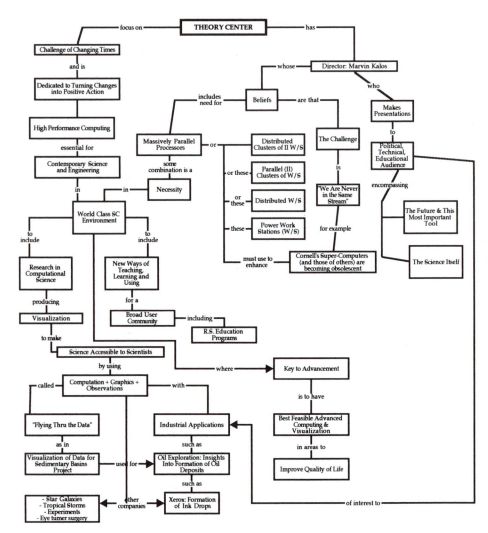

FIG. 7.6. View of the Cornell University Theory Center held by the Director of the Center.

My work and the work of my students in recent years has shown examples similar to Crosby's in every organization where we have worked. We learned something else, too. The low-cost (not no-cost!) student interviewer(s) may be very intimidating and embarrassing to the person who hired the expensive consulting firm. The student interviewer can learn more about the organization and organizational problems by interviewing and concept-mapping persons from line workers to the chief executive officer than may be revealed by very expensive consultants.

Therefore, whoever contracted with the consulting firm does not want to be embarrassed and will try to have the student interviewer(s) removed or counsel based on their concept maps silenced. As Senge (1990) pointed out:

> It is no accident that most organizations learn poorly. The way they are designed and managed, the way people's jobs are defined, and most importantly, the way they have all been taught to think and interact (not only in organizations, but more broadly) create fundamental learning disabilities. Learning disabilities are tragic in children . . . they are no less tragic in organizations. . . . (p. 18)

KNOWLEDGE OF A THEORY OF EDUCATION

Nobel Laureate Kenneth Wilson (Wilson & Davis, 1994) asserted in his recent book, *Redesigning Education,* that teacher training "requires them to know more about theories of teaching than about the subjects they teach, and whose training imparts those theories without giving them a chance to learn how to practice them effectively" (p. 83). Although I agree with the latter assertion, my experience is that teachers learn almost nothing about a theory of education—at least not a theory that meets the criteria of a theory, namely that it has explanatory and predictive power for educative events. What teachers too often learn in conventional teacher education programs is a collection of rules or procedures, many of them called theories, none of which have the necessary comprehensiveness, explanatory power, and predictive power to guide the teacher in the hundreds of decisions that must be made in a single day of teaching. The combination of the invalid, unworkable, and nonparsimonious character of the theories usually presented lead experienced teachers to advise novice teachers to "forget all that theory stuff you learned in college." None of the award-winning elementary school teachers we recently interviewed in depth to ascertain why they were so successful found their preservice teacher-education programs of value (Gerber, 1992). Partly this reflected the uselessness of many of the teaching methods courses that were taught 2 decades ago and remain all too common today. However, these teachers do attend professional meetings, take selectively further university in-service education courses, and seek out conversations with experienced colleagues on theoretical issues. We found very high congruence between their theoretical beliefs and the ideas put forward in this book.

As noted repeatedly, teaching and managing are very complex activities. To illustrate this again, refer to Table 7.1 to see how teaching practices under the traditional paradigm differ from teaching practices under contemporary constructivist ideas.

In my work with preservice and in-service teachers, I have seen my own work move from emphasis on procedures that are effective or ineffective, plus heavy emphasis on the need to understand the subject matter of the discipline (see, e.g., Novak, 1963), to instruction that begins with basic ideas of *A Theory of Education*

TABLE 7.1

Traditional Patterns in Education of Teachers in Relation to Five Elements[a]

Learner	Teacher	Curriculum	Context	Evaluation
Task is to acquire information (usually by rote learning).	Management and class control emphasized.	Fixed, textbook centered.	Schooling is good. Minor improvements may be needed.	"Objective" tests are the key to evaluation, with grades assigned "on a curve".
Emphasis on lesson planning focused on discipline, not learner's prior knowledge.	View that teachers cause learning.	Emphasis on coverage techniques.	Children should do as they are told.	Frequent testing helps students meet course objectives.
Failure regarded as lack of aptitude or motivation.	Motivation strategies emphasize clear statement of rewards and punishments.	View that knowledge is truth to be learned (i.e., memorized).	School curriculum is generally okay, but more emphasis on "basics" is needed.	Scores on standardized state publishers' tests are good criteria of success.
Use of "objective" tests validates view of learner as "empty vessel" to be filled with information.	Teacher charisma is a desired goal.	Little planning or regard for student's feelings.	Teachers should be rewarded according to standardized test scores received by their pupils.	Time-consuming evaluation methods are not worth the effort (e.g., essay exams, group project reports).
Group instruction validates view that failure is due to lack of aptitude.	Audiovisual aids, computers seen as information givers rather than as tools to help in meaning making.	Subject matter taught and testing should show close to one-to-one correspondence.	Years of service and college credits/degrees earned are primary basis for salary levels.	"Test item banks"—collections of test questions "covering" various subject matters—are a primary resource for teacher made tests, together with tests prepared by book publishers.
Rewards and punishments are principal motivators for learning.	Lecturing, test writing skills emphasized.	School, state, or university exams set the criteria for what is covered.	Educational theory and research is of little relevance and value to teachers or program planners.	Facts must be learned before understanding can develop; hence, tests should stress knowledge of facts.
	Little concern for curriculum development by teachers.	Publishers are responsible curriculum developers.	Administration should run the schools.	

[a]These five elements are my modification of Schwab's (1973) "commonplaces": (1) learner, (2) teacher, (3) subject matter, and (4) social milieu. I have added (5) evaluation, because it plays a dominant, indeed, often an controlling role in schooling.

TABLE 7.1 continued

Constructivist Patterns In Education of Teachers in Relation to Five Elements

Learner	Teacher	Curriculum	Context	Evaluation
Learner must make new meanings based on his/her prior knowledge.	Emphasis on finding out what the learner already knows.	Emphasis on major conceptual ideas and skills.	Schooling emphasizing rote learning is "domesticating."	Progress of students should be monitored with files containing a broad range of performance indicators.
Meaningful learning is primary basis for positive motivation and sense of empowerment.	Research and theory guide practice.	Recognition of diversity of learners and need for variety in learning resources.	Schooling emphasizing meaningful learning and creativity is empowering.	A broad range of evaluation measures is needed.
Teacher skills needed for appraising student's prior knowledge (e.g., pretests, concept maps, occasional interviews).	Clear distinction between topical or "logical" organization of subject matter and "psychological" organization. Use of concept maps to help with latter.	Efforts in student involvement in planning and executing instructional program.	Much of the school curriculum is anachronistic, and major revisions in curricula are needed.	Objective tests measure only a small percentage (about 10%) of aptitudes and achievement relevant to real-life application.
Learners need help to learn how to learn.	Techniques needed for helping students learn how to learn.	Emphasis on evolving nature of knowledge.	Teacher preparation should be viewed as lifelong with continuing efforts for appraisal and "renewal."	Evaluation measures should help students and teachers identify conceptual problems and work toward their resolution (e.g., concept maps).
Human potential is much greater than usually manifest.	Optimistic view of human potential.	Wide variety of learning approaches, with flexible evaluation.	"Career ladders" are needed to keep the most talented teachers in classrooms and help them to help their peers.	Evaluation should help students take responsibility for their own learning (e.g., use of journals, self-report measures, concept maps, etc.).
Feelings are important.	Lack of motivation seen as derived in large part from lack of meaning/under-standing.	Confidence in meaningful learning as preparation for standardized exams.	Teaching practice should be theory and research based and evaluated.	Teachers should conduct occasional in-depth interviews with students.
Learning is the responsibility of the learner.	Teacher is responsible for sharing meanings with/between learners.	Emphasis on empowering learners rather than "coverage" of material.	Major decisions should involve teachers, parents, and administration.	
	Gaining skills is lifelong process.			

and combines tools and ideas from this work with subject matter. The response from my students has been increasingly positive. With experience in applying the theory and tools, they become strong proponents of these ideas and tools. Many go on to publish papers, textbooks, and other materials, in various languages, to help spread the word. Some of the tools, such as concept mapping, are becoming common in science textbooks, with Vee diagrams and applications in other disciplines progressing more slowly. Change in education is indeed a slow process.

An Illustrative Case

Although I deal more extensively with the context element of educating in the next chapter, it is important to recognize the role that the teacher or manager plays is setting the context. A primary responsibility of the teacher is to set the agenda for learning. This can be done as thoughtlessly as proceeding with the next section of a highly prescriptive syllabus, which in the worst school settings is almost the only option for the teacher, or as part of a thoughtful sequence of experiences growing out of the needs of the learners, the opportunities in the physical and cultural setting, and the vehicle provided by the knowledge or subject to be studied.

We saw in the example of Rachel's inquiry about flowers using dirt an ideal context for learning, where Rachel raised the questions arising out of a context of experience she chose to engage in that was also emotionally comfortable to her. Although my wife set the learning agenda by inviting Rachel to weed flowers with her, she did not predetermine questions to be raised or the subject matter to be covered. The result was a highly successful learning experience for Rachel (and for her grandmother as regards Rachel's interests), and one that laid a foundation for future learning.

The power of this kind of contextualized learning was illustrated 6 months later when, after watching logs burn in the fireplace, Rachel asked, "Where does wood go when it is burned?" Rachel, just past her fourth birthday, again illustrated her developing concept of conservation of substance, namely that wood cannot just disappear; it must go somewhere. I began to address her inquiry by reminding her of the question she asked her grandmother last summer, "Do flowers eat dirt?" Rachel recalled the question and also the answer that flowers and other plants used a little bit of the earth, but most of the plant comes from air and water. Although it is possible that Rachel had occasion to ask her question again and to review again this relationship of plant growth with dirt and air, her mother could not recall Rachel repeating this experience. The remarkable recall, by usual school standards, Rachel exhibited is actually not remarkable when children have the opportunity to learn answers to their questions in a context that makes sense to them. It was now easy to build on this framework of concepts and propositions and to suggest that when wood burns, the wood turns back into water and air (actually carbon dioxide) and some of the energy from the sun used to form the wood is now released as heat (and light) from the fire. The ash that remains is that little bit of dirt the tree needed to grow. "Do you understand now where the wood goes when it burns?" I asked. "Yes," Rachel replied confidently. "Can you explain it to me?" I asked. Rachel proceeded in her own words to give an accurate description of where wood goes when it burns, albeit she left out the bit about the stored energy from the sun being released as heat and light. Clearly, energy was a concept that was not integrated well into her knowledge framework at that time. However, the idea that the volume of a substance must come and go somewhere, the idea of conservation of volume in this context seemed to be solidly established in Rachel's method. Contrast this with the poor performance of 7th and 12th grade students shown in Fig. 4.6.

A 12-Year Longitudinal Study of Concept Learning

During the 1960s, there was a widely proclaimed view that young children could not learn abstract concepts. Part of the argument was based on Piagetian ideas that only formal operational students could learn ideas that required a kind of inferential reasoning. In chapter 5, I discussed the difference between what Ausubel called primary abstractions and secondary abstractions. The former are concepts that derive directly from experience with concrete objects or particular events, whereas the latter derive recognizing relationships between other concepts. Although it is true that primary concepts must be formed before secondary abstractions are possible, I saw no inherent reason for this to be the case in a strictly age-related fashion, but rather more dependent on the quality and the sequence of those learning experiences. My own experience with young children, including my own children, indicated that with proper conceptual preparation, even 5- and 6-year-old children could demonstrate a remarkable understanding of abstract concepts, or secondary abstractions. Although this is no longer an idea that goes against conventional wisdom, it was very much opposed by conventional wisdom in the 1960s.

It was my view that to understand science, children must very early on begin to build concepts of the particulate nature of matter, the nature of energy, and the role of energy and energy transformations as they relate to changes in matter. My experience with young children suggested that a reasonable understanding of these concepts was attainable with carefully developed instructional sequences. The problem was how to test this hypothesis in a wider school setting, recognizing that most adults, including primary-grade school teachers, are very limited in their understanding of these ideas. I therefore chose to utilize a context for educating that we had developed with college botany students, namely audio-tutorial instruction (Postlethwait, Novak, & Murray, 1969, 1972).

In audio-tutorial instruction, audiotape is used to guide the learner through a set of observations and manipulations of materials to explore ideas dealing with phenomena associated with these materials. For example, in the lessons designed for first-and second-grade children that we developed, children were guided in using batteries, wires, and light bulbs to explore the idea that electrical energy can be produced in the batteries, transmitted through wires, and transformed into heat and light in the light bulb. A series of some 60 lessons was developed, each requiring 15 to 20 minutes of hands-on activity on the part of the learner while guided through observations with audiotape, pictures, photographs, and, in some cases, 8-millimeter loop films. Figure 7.7 shows a photograph of a child in a carrel with one of our audio-tutorial lessons. Carrel units were placed in individual classrooms and teachers were asked to have their students, working one at a time, proceed through the lesson at least once during a 2-week interval. In practice, many children performed each lesson more than once, and, in a few cases, as many as five or six times.

Although this represents a rather unusual context for teaching, it was a financially feasible method for organizing experience for learners without undue disruption of other classroom activities and the ordinary protocols of school operation. I discuss in chapter 8 some of the problems associated with school organization and the context for learning it normally creates, but it is important to note that even in those constraints, high quality instructional segments can be incorporated into the

FIG. 7.7. A 6-year-old child studying an audio-tutorial science lesson in a carrel unit.

student's experience. The lessons were highly popular with both students and teachers, although a few students did fail to study every lesson.

After some 2 years in design and development of our audio-tutorial lessons, we were prepared to conduct a study to test whether these lessons could produce learning at a sufficient level of meaningfulness that there would be facilitation of future science learning. Although preliminary studies suggested that the lessons were successful in effecting student learning (Hibbard & Novak, 1975; Nussbaum & Novak, 1976), the real test of meaningful learning is long-term transfer in facilitation of future learning, even when the context for learning is changed.

Twenty-six lessons that we had developed were placed in a number of classrooms in Ithaca Public Schools, and every 2 weeks a new lesson was introduced into the carrel units. Depending on the pace at which the students proceeded through the lessons, classrooms continued working with these lessons throughout grades 1 and 2 (ages 6 to 8). Following a sequence of lessons, students were interviewed by project staff and subsequent transcripts of interviews, and later, concept maps were prepared. As mentioned earlier, it was from this research study that the tool of concept mapping was developed as a method of representing changes in student knowledge structures. The students receiving the audio-tutorial science lessons in grades 1 and 2 were called instructed students, because they received special instruction in basic concepts of science. There were 191 students in the latter group, and we followed them with occasional interviews throughout their tenure in Ithaca Public Schools.

In the second year of the study, operating in the same classrooms with the same teachers, we interviewed students who did not receive the audio-tutorial science lessons but were members of the same general population of students. This group of 48 students was followed throughout their tenure in Ithaca Schools. Students received science instruction sporadically through the remainder of the elementary grades, and as organized classes in grades 7, 8, 9, and 10, with smaller numbers continuing in chemistry and physics in grades 11 and 12.

By 1984, we had completed all of the data gathering for the study and began to analyze the results by comparing changes in conceptual understanding in one domain of science, namely the understanding of the particulate nature and behavior of matter. Although early instruction included other conceptual domains, it was impossible with the staff resources and funding that we had to continue interviewing in all of these conceptual domains. Furthermore, this would have required such extensive interviewing that logistic and other practical problems would have resulted, as well as contamination of the initial learning experience by the extensive interview experience.

The findings of the study are summarized in Table 7.2 and Fig. 7.8. What was remarkable is that the impact of this high quality early science instruction, in the special education context we had created, had highly substantial effect on learners early in their school experience (that is, in grades 1 and 2) and the facilitative effect of this learning experience persisted for the next 10 years. These findings are so remarkable that I had considerable difficulty in getting the paper describing the research published, having it returned three times prior to publication. It is not uncommon, of course, to have difficulty with editorial review boards when research results challenge the conventional wisdom that prevails. These results were indeed challenging much of the conventional wisdom, even though the rigid constraints in cognitive functioning that was initially suggested by Piaget's work were now questioned by many researchers, as indicated in chapter 4.

One might ask, "Why is it that there is no more research that explores the effect of early instruction on later achievement of the same students?" The obvious answer is that such studies are exceedingly difficult to execute and require a long-term commitment on the part of the researcher. From the initial conception of the study that involved the design of the audio-tutorial lessons to the final publication of the study results in 1991 was a span of more than 20 years. As much as I would like to repeat such a study, it would not be possible during my active professional life. It should also be noted that this kind of study need not cost millions of dollars. The total investment in this research project, including graduate student stipends that provided support for their graduate study, would total less than $200,000. Funds were patched together from various sources, but the most useful continuing funding was from Shell Companys Foundation in small ($5,000–$10,000) unrestricted grants made to me over most of the years of the study.

Let us examine for the moment the meaning of the use of audio-tutorial instruction as a context for learning in conventional classrooms in conventional

TABLE 7.2

Analysis of Variance for Valid and Invalid Notions by Method of Instruction
(A-T Versus No A-T In Grades 1 and 2) and by Grades.[*]

Source	df	Sum of squares	Mean square	F-ratio	Prob.
For Valid Notions					
Grade	3	143.938	47.979	3.6	0.015
Method	1	553.521	553.521	41.0	0.000
Interaction	3	75.187	25.062	1.9	0.138
Error	184	2480.83	13.482		
Total	191	3253.48			
For Invalid Notions					
Grade	3	90.729	30.243	16.0	0.000
Method	1	198.725	198.725	107.0	0.000
Interaction	3	23.636	7.878	4.3	0.006
Error	424	784.352	1.849		
Total	431	1097.44			

[*]From Novak and Musonda, p. 148. Copyright © 1991 by the American Educational Research Association. Reprinted by permission of the publisher.

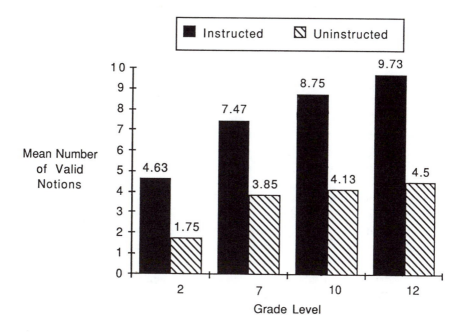

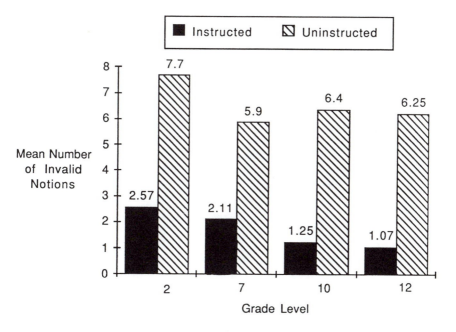

FIG. 7.8a & b. Bar graphs showing the frequencies with which instructed students (dark bars) and uninstructed (striped bars) evidenced valid notions (top figure) about the structure of matter and invalid notions (lower figure). Note that only the instructed students show continuous improvement over the years.

131

schools. First, the data clearly show that very substantial learning of highly abstract ideas was not only possible but achieved to a significant level. By the end of grade 2 when the audio-tutorial science instruction was completed, the majority of students had developed at least rudimentary ideas regarding the particulate nature of matter and the fact that as energy is added to the molecules of matter, we can move from a solid to a liquid to a gaseous state. These ideas appeared to be firmly established in their cognitive structures and some of the evidence for this was the persistence of key concepts and relationships throughout the remaining ten years of schooling. The data shown in Table 7.2 and Fig. 7.8 indicate that students receiving the early instruction had more than twice as many valid conceptions of the particulate nature of matter, and less than half of the invalid conceptions, when compared with their uninstructed counterparts. These are highly significant differences, both from the perspective of practical consequence and in terms of statistical significance. These are differences that exceeded my own expectations and certainly fly in the face of the conventional wisdom prevailing in the 1960s and 1970s. As pointed out in chapter 4, there have been more recent studies by others that point to the underexploited learning capabilities of young children, but this was not the case when the study was designed and executed. Partly for this reason, I was unsuccessful in repeated efforts to obtain federal funding for the study. Wilshire (1990) addressed the problem that scholars who take positions that challenge conventional wisdom are often met with incredulity at best and banishment at worst. This has been true over the millennia and is likely to continue in the future. This may be one of the reasons why students of creative productivity identify the necessity for tenacity and the creative drive to persist in pursuing an idea even in the face of numerous obstacles (Gardner, 1993).

There is another message in the study cited here and that is that technology-mediated instruction, even of the more primitive nature of audio-tutorial instruction, can be effective in a conventional teaching context in a conventional school district. The potential of newly emerging hypermedia systems as a teaching context has yet to be explored and exploited, but I believe the results above suggest that well-designed hypermedia systems can have a profound effect on the facilitation of meaningful learning, whether in school settings, corporate education, home schooling, or independent study. I discuss this further in later chapters.

Teaching in the Context of Counseling Environment

One of my graduate students, Joan Mazur (1989), worked in a drug rehabilitation program near Ithaca, New York. She was intrigued with the ideas we were presenting on obstacles to educating individuals; in her case, a problem of educating drug users to understand the deleterious effect of drug use to themselves and to society, and the motivations that lead them to persistence in drug abuse. The persons with whom she worked were repeat drug offenders who were assigned to the

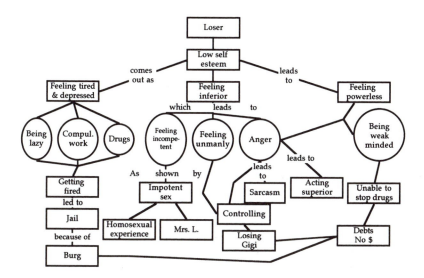

FIG. 7.9. A concept map prepared by John to show his perception of why he used drugs. Reproduced with permission from Mazur, 1989.

treatment center as an alternative to prison. They were cognizant of the fact that they were in a situation of last resort, but nevertheless often remained uncooperative and difficult to reach.

Mazur decided to try to teach concept mapping to her clients to see if this would be a way of creating both a cognitive and an emotional recognition of the reasons for their drug habits. Although she met with resistance in acquiring this technique on the part of some of her subjects, she eventually was successful in getting all nine of her clients to develop concept maps of their drug habits and motivation for using drugs. A sample of one of these maps is shown in Fig. 7.9.

These concept maps served as a basis for one-on-one counseling and also for group discussions on individuals' view of their habit. What Mazur found was that the concept maps were an important tool in facilitating the treatment of these patients and their discharge from the drug treatment facility. Ordinarily, the recidivism rate (reincarceration rate) for drug abusers is about 94% nationwide. In the case of Mazur's clients, none of her nine subjects were readmitted for drug treatment 3 years after discharge, although one was imprisoned for other reasons. Clearly, the concept mapping that Mazur chose to use as a context for expressing thoughts and feelings about drug use was highly successful with her clients. Her colleagues at the drug treatment center have subsequently incorporated the use of concept maps in their treatment programs, but on a more limited basis.

There have been other counseling settings in which my students have employed concept mapping, but the data I have from these students is largely anecdotal. It is my hope that this book and other writings will stimulate more research studies on the role that concept maps may play in counseling settings.

EMOTIONAL SENSITIVITY

When I was enrolled in teacher education courses, I cannot recall ever discussing the issue of the emotional needs of teachers and how these impact on their effectiveness. But what has become increasingly apparent to me over the years, both through experiences with my own children and in my efforts at teaching, is the exceedingly important role that teachers' and manager's ego needs play in how they organize the context for learning and how they operate in it. Those teachers and managers who do not have a strong ego perception of "I'm okay" often in subtle or explicit ways attack the ego of their students or workers.

The research on teacher education is almost devoid of citations of studies explicitly dealing with teacher ego needs and corresponding effects on their teaching activities. For example, a recently published book reviewing research on science teaching and learning, with some 575 large pages of reviews of research, has no entries in the index on ego or ego needs, nor even on emotional needs of teachers and learners (Gabel, 1994). Similarly, an earlier review (Houston, 1990) of research on teacher education also fails to cite any work that deals with the recognition of teachers' ego needs and how they relate to effective or ineffective teaching practices.

Our parents and older siblings are our first teachers. As we see in John's map (Fig. 7.9), his dad's (Burg) ego needs led him to hold high expectations for John, and also to competition with him. John has a Master's Degree in Social Work and was successful in this work for a time. He has an older brother and a younger sister whose successful lives contributed to his feelings of inadequacy. His escape was drugs, which led to crime, imprisonment, and subsequently, a treatment center and work with Mazur. John's concept map shows clearly the "I'm not okay" feelings he had about himself. Counseling with Mazur and others at the clinic helped him to see that his feelings were his creation, and he could act to overcome these feelings, and in fact, had done so for a time as a successful counselor working with cases assigned to him. The starkness of his map made it possible to confront John with the reality and his perceived reality, and in time, to successful discharge from the program.

John's case, and thousands similar to him, show how destructive the ego needs of parents can be to their children. All of us, as parents, fail on occasion to give our children the ego support they need and instead, act to gratify our own ego needs. Probably every reader of this book can recall one or more incidents of this with one or both parents. Those of us who have seen our children move on successfully into adulthood, and perhaps their own successful parenting, have the satisfaction of knowing that we probably succeeded much more often than we failed to help our children achieve a sense of "I'm okay; You're okay."

Trust

In his book, *On Caring,* Mayeroff (1972) identified a number of requirements for successful caring. He pointed out that caring is a process directed at helping others grow. It can apply to people, ideals, or ideas. The major ingredients of caring identified by Mayeroff include; (a) knowing, (b) alternating rhythms, (c) patience, (d) honesty, (e) trust, (f) humility, (g) hope, and (h) courage. All play a role, and all support each other in the caring process. Across the years, I have felt the emotions associated with all eight of these ingredients as I have sought to construct and care for the idea that a theory of education can guide and lead to improvement of education. My many students and visiting scholars have often and in many ways shared in this caring process. In turn, we have also cared for each other, employing all eight of Meyeroff's ingredients.

Perhaps most important, and often times most difficult, is trust. But, in many ways, trust is the fundamental process; the process that is required for all other processes to proceed. Mayeroff wrote:

Trusting the other is to let go; it includes an element of risk and a leap into the unknown, both of which take courage.

The father (or mother) who "cares" too much and "overprotects" his child, does not trust the child, and whatever he may think he is doing, he is responding more to his own needs than to the needs of the child to grow. (p. 21)

This may indeed have been the case with Andrew's parents, and much of his good fortune may have been the true caring of Michelle Lucia who participated in and wrote *Andrew's Story* presented next. Michelle may have helped his parents move toward a more positive caring for Andrew.

What we saw in the case of John was a father who was too competitive and a mother who was too protective. We shall see a similar situation in the case of Andrew that follows:

ANDREW'S STORY:[1]
THE FACE OF A LEARNING DISABILITY

This is the study of one boy, one beautiful little boy who has been hurt by a system and by a society which accepts nothing less that perfection. His story, unfortunate though I believe this to be, will revolve in large part around his learning disability

---

[1]Quoted, with permission, from a paper by Michelle Lucia, who did the study and wrote *Andrew's Story* [abridged by me].

and the treatment he received in school, but this will remain, first and foremost, the story of this very real little boy.

Even more than Andrew's story, this will be my story as well; the story of a student who believed that she had the power and the insight to find answers that no one else had been able to.

For as long as can be remembered, Andrew has had trouble in school. It was said many times, with true confusion, that it was impossible that the boy we all knew outside of school was the same one said to be so "bad" inside school. In first grade, he was labeled as having attention deficit disorder and barely escaped undergoing an intensive treatment of ritalin. When in class, the teacher said he would refuse to read aloud and would rarely complete assignments. At home, he and his parents would fight bitterly over his misbehavior in school and over his "refusal and excuses" about doing work. He was "socially passed" to the second grade. His teacher said she decided to pass him because of his "innate intelligence" and his ability to reason and problem solve orally.

[In a new private school,] the second grade teacher somehow came to the disastrous conclusion that Andrew was simply a "nonstudent;" one of those students who would struggle through school and amount to little later in life. Her comments on one report card of Andrew's read, "[Andrew] is a good boy deep down. He will never be a reader or a stellar student, but he will undoubtedly be a good person." It is hard to say on what actual evidence she based these opinions, but is seems clear from what is now known that she had not at any time sat down and talked to, listened to, or individually worked with Andrew. Again, Andrew received a "social pass" and, again, at a new public school, he struggled painfully through third grade only to receive a "social pass" to fourth grade. What this means is that, at fourth grade, Andrew was still a nonreader. What this also means is that, by fourth grade, Andrew had been to three schools and had missed out on any chance to develop lasting friendships. Always being the new kid and "bad" in class, Andrew was usually the subject of ridicule and ostracization. This means that not only was this little boy dealing with the frustration and pain of being a poor performer in school and the pain of his parents' disappointment in him, but he was also suffering the pain of being shut out socially.

In fourth grade, someone finally took notice of Andrew. His fourth grade teacher saw and questioned the pain and the frustration Andrew suffered and the energy he exerted trying to keep up with the class. This, she said, was not a lazy child, but in fact, this was a child who worked very hard and struggled greatly. Why? Such a simple question, and yet it took four years and myriads of consulted teachers to ask it. Why? Why was this little boy not learning? Why were his eyes tearing when he did his work? Why was this little boy suffering at school?

And that was quite literally all it took; just one question to change Andrew from a lazy and undedicated student to a wonderful child who was likely suffering from a learning disability. A series of unending, prolonged, and stressful tests and evaluations was immediately begun. Andrew was first tested for dyslexia and other well-known disabilities. When those tests came back negative, it was as if the sky had fallen, again. The school board said things like, "See, it's not our fault. Your child is just not a good student . . ." And, Andrew was saying things like, "I don't try to be bad" and "I'm sorry." Andrew's parents were struggling to contain their disappointment at not having found an "easy explanation" and trying to decide how to go on, trying to learn what was left to do that hadn't been tried. The one person who refused absolutely to accept those results was Andrew's teacher. Taking quite a risk, she explained to Andrew's parents that it was likely that Andrew was, in fact, suffering from a learning disability and that the school had chosen to not identify or pursue it further as they would then be obligated, under the rights guaranteed students in New York State, to teach to his unique needs. She referred them to a psychoeducational consultant for private testing and recommended Andrew be tutored with a new reading method known as Orton-Gillingham.

Andrew's parents, again at great monetary sacrifice, sought out both the tutor and the consultant. Thirteen months after testing began, Andrew's parents, armed with the psychoeducational consultant and her report and an attorney, appeared before the school board and stated what were Andrew's needs and rights as a child diagnosed with scotopic sensitivity. (See Fig. 7.10.)

In the presentation before the school board then, a list of requests was set fourth: (1) Andrew should be labeled: Learning Disabled, but for emotional reasons, should continue to be mainstreamed; (2) He should receive individual assistance within the school in the areas of reading and cursive writing; (3) His workload should be reduced through the prioritization of assignments, and he should be excused from "heavy writing assignments;" and (4) The school should support and see that he see a scotopic sensitivity screener. It is important to note that not a single request, but for the last one made by the consultant or the parents, dealt specifically with the fact that Andrew does not see things correctly. Instead, the belief seemed to persist that Andrew just needed to "work harder."

The school board, just prior to Andrew's fifth grade year, agreed to every request except the subsidizing of the screening. Andrew would be sent to a resource room for private help during desk work times and the staff would monitor and guide him in whatever ways possible. His work load would be lightened, and effort would be made to reduce the stress he now feels to get everything done "on time." Aside from the fact that Andrew's physical needs were not being addressed, hopes were high that the individual attention would help Andrew learn to read.

This is the point at which I [Michelle Lucia] came in as a researcher, the beginning of Andrew's fifth-grade year, following what was believed to be a victory with the school board and at a time when things seemed as if they would improve. What I had initially hoped to do in this study was to chronicle the struggle of a learning disabled child in this society, to spend time on the inadequate screening methods in detecting learning disabilities, and devise ways to improve them; to illustrate the inadequate training received by many of today's teachers in that it took four long years for a learning disability to be even suspected in this case, to construct ways to improve the competence of future teachers, and to close with the happy ending of Andrew's present success and well-being. I think it was maybe ten days before I realized that that would not be the story to be told; that in fact, Andrew's struggles are far from over and are of sufficient magnitude even today that just understanding them and their basis and magnitude would occupy the whole of my focus.

For even that early into the school year and into my study, it was evident that Andrew was not improving and was not being helped. What really happened and what is

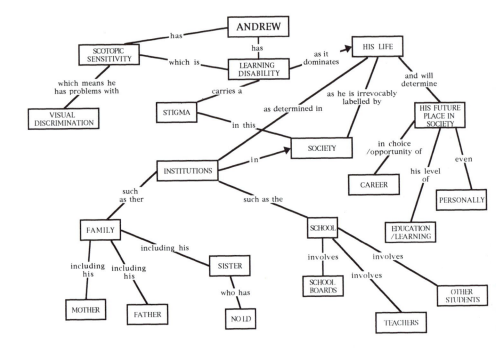

FIG. 7.10. Michelle Lucia's concept map showing characteristics of Andrew's disability.

continuing to happen since the school board meeting is that Andrew is sent to this windowless room in the basement of the building a few times a day where he sits with three or four other children, usually kids who have been sent out of class for behavior problems, and a teacher or monitor who reads the paper and answers only questions asked of her. It is far from private tutoring, and it is anything but helpful. Andrew then returns to his classroom and sits in confusion because the teacher had started a new lesson while he was out of the room. Seeing what they believe is special treatment, Andrew is ridiculed and exiled from his peers, only to be left to suffer in the same way as 5 years before.

In the last 2 years, this woman [Andrew's mother] has championed and sometimes outright battled for her son with everyone from the principal and the school board to the parents of the kids who have teased him. She has watched her firstborn child suffer, seen him come home from school hungry because another child stole his lunch, cleansed his cuts from fights in school, and listened to him weep alone in his room. She has spent most of her free time at the library or on the phone and is, at this point, just about out of energy. She has pursued every lead she could find to the brink of bankruptcy and breakdown. The few options that are left for Andrew now, which will be discussed below are too unknown, not to mention expensive, for her to risk raising her hopes again.

The problem is not that Andrew cannot be taught to read by conventional methods, but that he cannot learn to read because he cannot discriminate between the letters of words.

One need not look very long at the rights of a child in Andrew's school district to know that Andrew has been denied many of his rights. Perhaps most crucial, Andrew's parents were denied the "Right to be Fully Informed." When the school pronounced Andrew as a "normal" student following the first set of tests, they did so with knowledge that this was not true, with knowledge that the erratic test scores and urgings of Andrew's teacher were signaling a disability. While this is not grounds for a history-making lawsuit, had the school board been up front in the meanings and possible interpretations of the test scores, Andrew and his parents may have been spared a bit of the disappointment and pain they suffered during the time when there were no explanations for Andrew's poor academic performance. It seems as if the school board had wanted Andrew's parents to internalize his difficulties, with the effect that responsibility would then be shifted away from the school.

There were other instances in which the school and/or the officials involved could be cited as denying rights, but this one sticks out most in that it is an example of bureaucracy at work, of an institution having forgotten its reason for being. Must we struggle to recall why we have schools at all? From their inception, we have had schools primarily to teach and educate children. In this instance, though, the school was not trying to teach and educate Andrew, but was trying to save itself the money, time, and effort it would be forced to expend in having and teaching a child with an uncommon learning disability.

The final information Bonnie (Andrew's mother) sent to me were two articles on scotopic sensitivity and a new, experimental way to treat those suffering from it. In essence, these articles explain the treatments Bonnie referred to as being too risky and expensive to try. I am not in a position to judge her for I have not suffered as she had, but in reading the information that she sent to me, I couldn't help but become hopeful and excited. The articles explain that research is necessary and continuing, but that the researchers at the Irlen Institute, a clinic committed to the treatment of perception-based learning disabilities, have so far found that by selectively reducing the input of certain light wavelengths, a specially designed filter allows the scotopic sensitive person to more effectively process information.

It is only fair to concede that, along with the potential for disappointment and the extensive testing involved, 10 to 19 hundred dollars is a lot to invest in such an experimental treatment.

After having evaluated the information sent to me [from the Irlen Institute], I did what any researcher must. I went to the libraries to gather information of my own. All in all, the libraries did nothing to further this study, except make very clear to me that Andrew had indeed been diagnosed with a newly recognized and unknown disability.

I next went to the Special Children's Center. Having previously been a volunteer there, many people knew me and were willing to talk with me about Andrew. Unfortunately, the results I obtained in terms of information were much the same as I had from the libraries, meaning the teachers and specialists at the Special Children's Center had little knowledge of or experience with scotopic sensitivity.

What I did gain from my visit to the Special Children's Center was an interview with Kelly, a 5-year-old child diagnosed with dyslexia. What was so interesting in speaking with Kelly was the contrast between her and Andrew in terms of self-esteem, having adapted to a disability, and in prospects for the future. Kelly was diagnosed as dyslexic at age 3, as soon as she was learning to read. Having been diagnosed so early, Kelly's parents were able to obtain for her the best possible education with the best trained staff and save her from the pain and embarrassment of having failed and suffered in school, which is a common way for a disability to be detected. As a result, Kelly is already reading at a second grade level. She is expected to steadily progress as she has been labeled dyslexic and will be treated and taught to as such. She is aware and accepting of the fact that she "reads different," and she is expected to be able to do and read and be anything that she hopes to. As is and will be further seen, Andrew, having been diagnosed later in life and having an uncommon disability, lives a life almost opposite to Kelly's.

Because of a restructuring within the school, Andrew's teacher in fifth grade is the same one who first suspected his disability in fourth grade. She was hesitant to meet with me, saying she'd already "become too involved," but agreed to talk with me on the phone. The two statements she kept repeating were, "Then why are we here? . . . Why am I here? . . . If not for each individual child, then why is there a school system?" She told me of the risk she was warned she was taking, by who she would not say, in voicing her "disgust with the bureaucracy and the 'evil' of the system," but says, at this point, she does not care. As I had been thinking, she says her termination would be, to her, a sign that she should speak out and confront a system which is willing to "so shamelessly sacrifice the individual for the majority."

From his mother, to his teacher, to the consultant, to his sister, we have seen how Andrew is viewed and treated by those around him, but where does Andrew fit in? How does Andrew see himself, his disability, his "future prospects?"

My bias should be apparent by this time, but Andrew truly is a beautiful and intelligent little boy. Speaking with him, one would never once think, "This child can't read. This child is dumb . . ." But, in listening to what Andrew says, one can see that is indeed what he thinks when he thinks of himself and school. Andrew does not understand that his performance in school is, in a sense, out of control, that no matter how hard he tries or how much effort he makes, he will not be able to learn and perform as well or as quickly as the other kids do. He has internalized 5 years of Fs and detentions, and ridicule so much so that it has, as it was inevitable that it would, become a part of who he is today. In the area of intelligence, it is clear that Andrew thinks himself a disappointment and a failure. When I would try to press him or urge him to express himself on this, on general issues concerning himself and school, he would say that he couldn't read, he was dumb, he was bad in school, and then he would get upset and refuse to say anymore.

I asked Andrew's parents if anyone had ever explained to him what was known of his disability, and their initial response was not much more than to stare at me blankly. "Of course, he knows it isn't his fault." "Does he?" More blank stares. At this point,

I saw my first opportunity to help Andrew. Andrew's parents and I talked some more, and I was able to persuade them to talk with their son about exactly what was going on, while doing their sincere best to offer him the complete benefit of the doubt that he could understand what they were telling him. I retreated to the background and watched as, for 2 hours, Andrew and his parents really, and possibly for the first time, communicated with one another. His mother, in an already shaky voice, asked Andrew if he knew what a learning disability was and that he had one and what that meant. As was my suspicion, Andrew sat quietly and, after a long pause, shook his head no. While the meaning of this sunk in to Bonnie, that her son had been blaming himself for not learning to read, that he had been suffering and taking the blame for something which was and is out of his control, Andrew's father did his best to explain scotopic sensitivity and what it means to be learning disabled to Andrew. While speaking, he made a comparison between Andrew's situation and that of his uncle who is paralyzed, and a flicker of understanding and then pain passed over Andrew's face. "I can't be smart?" was the first question he asked. The communication continued, and Andrew was finally told why he was seeing the consultant and having so many tests done and going to the resource room and what they were trying to do, things which should have been explained all along, but which were at least being said now. For two hours, I watched this family come together and mend. I saw a rollercoaster of emotions, from guilt to pain to joy, and I left as Andrew hugged and, in his own way, thanked his parents for giving him so much of themselves that day. Since that time, I have not seen or spoken with Andrew, but Bonnie has told me repeatedly of the breakthrough that was made that day. She cried for the pain that had been needlessly caused Andrew and which is now mending, told me of the questions Andrew is now asking, of his seemingly increased confidence in, for example, admitting and accepting his need for help. While this will not make everything "all better," while it will not make Andrew see correctly, it will allow him the confidence to ask questions, and it will give him some peace of mind in knowing and learning that there is justification and understanding as to his performance in school.

While things are still improving for Andrew at home, they remain much the same in school. [I wondered if there was something I could do to help.] For 4 days, I tried endlessly to get someone—anyone—from the Irlen Institute, as referred to above, to speak with me. Finally, after having spoken so often with me that she was able to recognize my voice, the receptionist concluded that I was not going to stop calling and put me through to one of the researchers. I wanted to know, as my advisor (Novak) and I had discussed, if there was a side of the spectrum or a certain color filter more likely to work or with which they had had a higher success rate. I wanted to know why it was necessary to spend thousands of dollars, why Andrew and his parents could not just sit down with a sample of colored overlays and ask Andrew if any of them were easier to read through. After a further test of my persistence, the researcher admitted the possibility of something as simple as a blue or purple overlay helping to ease Andrew's visual difficulties. He said the only way to find which color was suited for Andrew would be to test the full range of colors. The next day, the day before Thanksgiving, I found colored overlays and went home in anxious anticipation of meeting with Andrew, of him looking through one of the overlays and smiling because it did not hurt and the letters did not move. In fact, I went straight to Andrew's house when I got to town, rushed in, and related to Bonnie the details of my phone call to the Institute and spread the assorted overlays on the table. "No," she said. "No." She was sorry, but she would not allow me to try this. Too many times she had seen Andrew's hopes dashed and this, she did not believe, would be able to help Andrew to read, it was too easy. With my hopes crushed, as I knew that I could not push and that I had to respect whatever and all decisions Bonnie made in regard to her son, I left the overlays on her table and returned to Cornell, intending to tell the added story of a mother defeated by the system her son would now be left to battle alone.

Two days ago (December 8, 1993), I received a message on my answering machine: "Michelle," Bonnie said, "Green. We think that the green one was easier for Andrew. He read to us, Michelle. I'm sorry. I called today, the Institute. Tuesday, Andrew starts the official process then. I'm sorry. You should have been the one to see the smile on his face. We're thinking of you. Thank you." That is what Bonnie said.

There is a satisfying postscript to *Andrew's Story*. Andrew did get the help he needed for his vision, and with continuing support from his parents who helped him recognize his physical handicap and gave encouragement, Andrew began to progress well. By seventh grade, he had made the school honor role! His energy, enthusiasm, and joyful manner returned to that of his childhood.

We see in *Andrew's Story* the tragedy of a system that was both incompetent and insensitive. Except for Andrew's fourth grade teacher, a pattern of blame-the-victim is all too common in schools everywhere. I'm not sure what would have been Andrew's fate if he had not had the love, support, and wisdom of his former babysitter. Michelle took on this project as a means of applying ideas she learned in my course, Learning to Learn, but she went beyond the requirements for credit—she pursued Andrew's case with vigor, competence, and compassion. Michelle, I predict, will be a strong positive influence in the lives of many people in the future.

Andrew's Story is not unique. In *Learning Denied* (Taylor, 1991), the author related a similar struggle of a child struggling to survive in schools where too much incompetence and too much insensitivity persists. There are probably few graduates from any school system, especially males, who have not faced the ego assault that derives from such incompetence or insensitivity. Although the majority of teachers work hard to help their students learn and help them to feel good about themselves, most schools have too many teachers who fail on both accounts. We need to make greater efforts to help those teachers who struggled with the challenges they face, partly by improving the system. Although it is not easy to remove the incompetent teacher, more effort is needed to do this for the sake of our children and to improve the environment for other teachers (Bridges, 1986, 1992). We also need to set a higher standard for learning, for such standards are achievable if we effectively help students build their cognitive structures and skills—and contribute to their ego enhancement. Too often, schools, as Sedlak, Wheeler, Pullin, and Cusick document (1986), are *Selling Students Short*.

TRUST AND HONESTY IN THE CORPORATE SETTING

It is often stated, "business is business, and you can't let personal feelings or friendship interfere." There is some truth in this, especially when it comes to dealing with poor performance, and even then, there may be extenuating circumstances that require special consideration. Apart from shared interests and enthusiasms, the characteristics that are fundamental in close friendships are unqualified trust and honesty between friends. If corporations wish to engender the strongest possible support from employees and customers, they, too, must create a relationship of unqualified trust and honesty.

In a conversation with a senior staff person in a large national accounting firm, I asked what role trust played in his company. He said:

> I think there are people in our firm that clients really trust and turn to for advice; they truly believe them to be trustworthy business advisors. Then there are clients who will look at another professional in our firm and say that person is just a bag of hot air—and we have plenty of bags of hot air in our firm. They can "talk the talk," but they cannot deliver; they cannot "walk the walk." They can be successful as long as they've got people beneath them that *can* deliver, at least most of the time. (Personal communication, December 28, 1996)

I asked what kinds of relationships resulted between subordinates and senior people who could not walk the walk. My interviewee responded:

> It can create some tension, but you have to recognize the fact that, let's say Partner A is very good at "talking the talk," and he can assure a client that Manager A is going to be engaged in doing the day-to-day work, and Manager A is recognized by the client as very competent, then Partner A can sell the work to the client. Manager A may not be full enough of himself nor have a large enough ego to walk into a room and *sell* the client, but in the end, it is Manager A who is responsible to see that the job is done right. (Ibid, 1996)

The situation described here is common in many organizations, not just accounting firms or other business settings, but also in academic and governmental settings. Yes, there is trust and respect in this situation, but there is also exploitation. Sometimes a fine line may exist between mutually beneficial collaborations and those that lopsidedly benefit only one individual or set of individuals. When the prevailing relationships in any organization become too lopsided and subordinates can no longer cover for their superiors, unfortunate consequences can ensue. Hamel and Prahalad (1994) described a situation that developed at Motorola when top management lost the confidence of subordinates. They concluded:

> The lesson here is that setting corporate challenges requires great honesty and humility on the part of top management; honesty in portraying the magnitude of the task ahead; humility in admitting that it must bear its share of the responsibility for

poor performance. Motorola is one of the most self-critical firms we know. Motorola's refusal to every be satisfied with "good enough" shows up in its results. Unfortunately, in some companies, honest criticism is, particularly when it comes from subordinates, more likely to raise hackles than standards. (p. 142)

In an interview with a senior executive in the construction industry, a somewhat different picture on trust emerged (personal communication, December 27, 1996):

Novak: How much trust is involved between you and your customers? Is this a big issue?

Exec.:   Well, it depends; with some customers, trust is an important factor; with other customers—in the construction industry, it's a boom-and-bust industry, here today, gone tomorrow—so, I'm not sure that trust is a wide component. I'm not sure that a lot of entities necessarily expect long-term relationships.

Novak: How about between you and the employees and the other people that you deal with?

Exec.:   There's a lot of different philosophies and styles, the kind of philosophy that trust is a very important factor, that you can't be very successful without developing a high degree of trust. There are a lot of people in the world that don't subscribe to that theory.

Novak: Yes, but I—it seems to me from what I've read, that the drift is where you get further with being trustworthy than seeing what you can get away with?

Exec.:   That's the drift in the literature, but not in practice.

Novak: But, not in practice?

Exec.:   In practice, you see all styles.

Novak: So, when you have an employee where the operating rule seems to be only do that that you have to and get away with everything you can get away with, how do you deal with that?

Exec.:   You terminate them. If that's their core belief, you terminate them.

Novak: You do run into that?

Exec.:   Yes, and—but, that's rare, because most people do want to do a good job, and they want to be successful.

One of the problems in the construction industry is that it is so often boom or bust. When business is booming, hiring more and effective personnel is critical, but when business wanes, employees may be seen as expendable. The interview with this executive continued (Ibid, 1996):

Novak: Do they want to develop a sense of confidence—that you have confidence in them?

Exec.:   Yes, you know they want to do a good job, and they want to be recognized for doing good work.

Novak: Well, it would seem like that would call for building trust on the part of management and other important employees, but you don't see that happening in your company?

Exec.:   Well, you see all types of styles, so that's why those books are written—because there are all types of styles, and they try to describe them. Amazing, isn't it? Some of the styles are highly discredited in the literature, but are very successful in industry.

Novak: What is a good example of "do anything you can get away with" type?

Exec.:   Well, it's not so much "doing anything you can get away with," it's that the autocratic approaches are very prevalent in industry.

Novak: I read about Bill Gates—he doesn't operate that way?

Exec.:   That's a different management style, but I believe the literature will tend to lead you to believe that the most effective style is the participatory, consensus-building, empowering style.

Novak: Team building?

Exec.:   Team building, but in the real world, you see all styles; you see a lot of them that say they use autocratic approaches.

Novak: How would you characterize the president of your company?

Exec.:   He's very old-school-management style. He believes that, on a regular and routine basis, go around and kick everybody in the ass.

Novak: That's his idea on how you motivate them?

Exec.:   Yeah, you go in there and, you know, beat on them.

Novak: I would think that a lot of people wouldn't respond well to that?

Exec.:   Well, it's—that's one reason why the company has about a 70% turnover rate.

Novak: You mean per year?

Exec.:   Per year.

Novak: Holy Smoke! Isn't that expensive?

Exec.:   You would think so [chuckle].

Novak: Not only terms of recruiting and getting people up to speed, but in lost momentum?

Exec.:   I would say very expensive, but those expenses are all soft costs.

Novak: And, your president is not going to change?

Exec.:   No, that's the way he learned the craft; that's the way that he learned management, the style he uses. You know, as I mentioned, people typically don't change.

Novak: With over 70% turnover rate, that indicates there's not a lot of trust there in anything he says.

Exec.:   Yep. The thing that amazes me, there's these couple of long-term employees—been here 10–12 years—one employee has been here longer than anybody else at least, probably because he's not competent to go anywhere else, but the other one is very competent.

Novak: Why does he live with it?

Exec.:   I think it's inertia. It would be easier to stay on than to make a move.

Novak: How do you see honesty and trust related in the work you do?

Exec.:   I guess I have a different management style, and I think, clearly, honesty is no longer presumed. Trust is no longer presumed in any relationship, and it has to be developed. In the past, it may have been presumed. I certainly wouldn't presume anything until I had some evidence.

Novak: The old Texas handshake is not the operating reality.

Exec.:   Yeah, and if you haven't got trust, I don't think you'll have efficiency and effectiveness, and when you don't, you don't, so, unfortunately, the lack of trust and honesty assumes there's a quick fix, short-term perspective. Although many, many organizations operate strictly with a lot of short cuts, short quick fix, and it's hard to invest in them over a long-term perspective. On a long-term, I wouldn't say they have effectiveness.

Novak: Given the growing competitiveness in all markets, do you see a greater and greater problem with that style, or you still won't find a niche?

Exec.:   Well, the literature would certainly lead you to believe that that is a problematic style, but it's so prevalent that you have to wonder, how can it be so prevalent if it's so ineffective?

Novak: Yes, and still stay in business. Is there any data that you know of on the styles that are represented by companies most likely to go belly up versus those that survive? Well, in terms of trying to build trust and a sense in honest relationships, what are some of the things that you have to do to do that?

Exec.:   My own value is you have to be trustworthy, but be worthy of trust, to develop trust and, as I was saying, you've got to be consistent in your practice. You can't be "average." You have to establish a certain degree of predictability so people understand what you're trying to accomplish, and you're consistent with your approach—you're not changing directions every minute.

We see a glimpse of the real world context for business through this executive's eyes. Obviously, contexts for educating and managing that may deviate from the textbook ideal can succeed, at least for a time. It should be noted that the executive quoted plans to leave the company as soon as a suitable replacement can be recruited (and recruitment has been difficult), and there is a real question as to whether or not this company can stave off bankruptcy for another year. This executive did confirm something that is common in the literature: to quote Peters (1994) who quotes Secretary of War Henry Stimson, "The only way to make a man trustworthy is to trust him" (p. 78). And now the same must be true for women. I believe that increasingly the global, competitive environment we are in shall require trust and honesty on the part of both management and employees, for this is the best context for creating and using knowledge.

FACILITATING TEAM WORK

In recent years, there has been much publicity regarding the importance of teams in industry. The Ford Taurus and the Saturn automobiles are heralded as evidence of the payoff that comes from team efforts in industry. Driven, in part, by competition from Japanese auto companies, where team planning has been used extensively, American auto companies found that similar strategies can pay off.

Teams can be as small as two members or number into the hundreds. For example, Team Mustang, which produced a new 1994 model, had 400 members, with chunk teams responsible for parts of the car, coordinating efforts through the larger team (White & Suris, 1993).

In school settings, team learning has become popularized under the label *cooperative learning*. David and Richard Johnson and their associate Qin (1995) have done much to help teachers and administrators understand and apply cooperative learning strategies. Their recommendations stress the importance of structuring group work in such a way that every student has a clear and defined role to play, assuring that all members of a learning group are actively engaged. Cooperative learning in school settings has been shown to facilitate learning and can also have positive effects on ego enhancement of learners.

Using analogies from the world of sports, Martin (1993) described how all corporations can benefit from team think. As a starting point, he recommended that corporations define clearly their mission statement, philosophy, and yearly and long-term goals. These should be concise and understandable. He cited examples such as Shell Oil Company's mission statement, "To meet the energy needs of mankind" (p. 10); statements of philosophy such as "People come first" and "To treat our clients' interests as if they were our own" (p. 14–15). Goals also need to be stated simply. Progress toward the goal should be measurable. Employees can contribute to reaching goals only if they know and understand the goals. Drucker (1993) stated that, "The knowledge-based organization, therefore, requires that everyone take responsibility for that organization's objectives, contributions, and indeed, for its behavior as well" (p. 108). Drucker went on to say:

> There is a great deal of talk today about "entitlement" and "empowerment." These terms express the demise of the command and control-based organization. But they are just as much terms of power and rank as the old terms were. We should, instead, be talking about responsibility and contribution. For power without responsibility is not power at all; it is irresponsibility. (p. 109)

For every employee to perform responsibly, clear statements of mission, philosophy, and goals are not enough. There must be leadership that manifests concern for each employee and a reward structure that recognizes achievements. Salary alone is not enough. Special recognition programs, stock options, and a manifest interest in employee welfare by the leadership is necessary. Martin (1993) even recommended that termination should be done with care, consideration, compassion, and clarity. This, of course, sends a valuable message to employees who are not terminated.

Teams as a Learning Group

Whether in school or corporate settings, the central purpose of teams is to learn how to do something better. This brings into play all of the factors discussed in earlier chapters, as well as principles that are included in subsequent chapters. Consistent with the learning principle, "The most important thing influencing learning is what the learner already knows," I bring into play both the richness and diversity of knowledge, skills, and attitudes of the various team members—and also the problems associated with each person's idiosyncratic view of the world. To capitalize on the diversity represented in the team, I need to begin by reviewing the mission, philosophy, and goals relative to the work to be done and to reach some consensus on the tasks at hand. Leadership in this early process could be by a more experienced or more senior team member. However, every team member can and should play a leadership role in some capacity.

In my classes, I have frequently used teams with four to six members, and then, after the goals were agreed on, each team subdivided into subteams of two or three persons to tackle specific aspects of the whole team's program. When class schedules allow for two or more projects to be undertaken, I insist that persons who played a smaller leadership role in the first project accept a larger leadership role in the second or third project. Often students are themselves surprised how well they can play leadership roles in team settings. My role in the program is similar to that of a head coach for an athletic team. I help to define goals and procedures for the teams and subteams, and then work with teams individually as they progress in their project.

In the corporate setting, most of my coaching work has been to help team members understand the nature of knowledge and nature of learning and to assist them in organizing their knowledge using concept maps and Vee diagrams. Almost without exception, the latter tools are new to all team members, so there is commonly a half-day coaching session needed to help them understand and learn how to use these tools.

Using Concept Maps and Vee Diagrams

With a relatively small investment of time, school students and corporate employees can acquire sufficient skill in concept mapping and Vee diagramming to use these tools to advance their learning. Although it would seem to make sense to begin by using the Vee because this tool can incorporate concept maps as part of the left side and right side of the Vee, our early experiences in a junior high school setting indicated that students (and teachers) can be overwhelmed with the Vee if it is presented before concept mapping skills are acquired (Novak, Gowin, & Johansen, 1983). With relatively few exceptions, we have found this to be true with high school, university, and corporate learners as well. Some of the reasons for this were discussed in chapter 6. On the other hand, we have found that it only takes most people an hour or two to gain enough skill in concept mapping to build a reasonably good first cut concept map for a given knowledge domain. Therefore, we have found it highly useful to use concept maps for team problem solving even when none of the team members have had prior experience with this tool.

Some of our most successful work has been in corporate settings because effective team problem solving has become so overwhelmingly important in the highly competitive corporate environment. In most cases, we have been very successful in capturing the essential knowledge structure for any problem area in as little as a half-day session. Sessions running 2 or 3 days have permitted refinement of preliminary concept maps and discussion of alternative strategies that were suggested by the concept maps. Participants find an all-day concept mapping session a real brain drain, but they typically come away highly motivated. There is a natural excitement and stimulation to seeing the big picture of a problem area laid out in front of you. For example, a participant in one of our corporate sessions observed:

> Peter: I was really enthusiastic, especially the day we worked through the mapping and started seeing some of the concepts come out because those were questions that I've had. I've been with the company for 4 years, and I have worked on these compounds for 1 year, and so I started seeing concepts coming out that I had been questioning people about that had been working in the field for a while. You know, it's like "okay now, how do you know that you need to call this the hydrophobe? . . . which activator?" Some of these concepts started coming out, and I think this would have a real value for onboarding new hires. We could have real value for onboarding people into the team that haven't worked on these compounds before or even the idea of taking the compounds and applying them in a new area for new products. (Personal communication, July, 1995)

Commenting on the value of concept maps for communications with other team members on other projects, this participant said:

> Peter: Concept maps would be very useful for each team that I interact with because I interact with teams on totally different projects, like 3 or 4 different projects. Each team is at different stages of development, but it would be nice to be able to say, for instance, now what are we going to do to get this product to market? What are the things we have to fill in in our maps to have the knowledge, and to gain the confidence of, to present to managers that this is our recommendation, this is our technical recommendation, this is what we want to go with. Or for instance, having something that's further upstream when we're still under the development stage, talking with someone about, hey, now this is what we think this interaction is, or we don't quite understand this interaction? Do you have any feedback? Do you have any data that can help us make this connection here? (Ibid, 1995)

Commenting on the value of the experience, this participant said:

Peter: I thought that is was actually very informative because I've only worked in the area for a year, and it was very good to work with a group of people, technologists who had worked in the area for say 10-15, 20 years and to *start seeing the concepts that they have intuitively in their minds start to come out onto the map and to the paper.* (Ibid, 1995)

I cited in the previous chapter the value concept maps played to help a new research team member understand the knowledge the Rhizobotany group was using to guide their research. In corporate work, I have found that the knowledge structure necessary to understand and resolve problems is often an order of magnitude more complex than what is needed in academic research programs. Is it any wonder that corporations often waste so much time and resources in trying to create and bring to market superior products or services? Ten years from now, I doubt if there will be any major corporations that will not find value in using concept maps, and the psychological and epistemological ideas that give them more meaning. There is nothing more disempowering to an employee than feelings of stupidity, and especially for new employees or new members joining project teams, this is all too often the feeling they experience.

Once team members are comfortable with making and using concept maps, it is not difficult to help them understand and use the Vee heuristic. Part of the value in employing the Vee is that it helps to keep in front of participants those global ideas that are too easily ignored. The corporate mission statement can easily be modified, if necessary, to provide a good world view for any project. The statements on corporate philosophy or fundamental beliefs may also contribute to the world view and/or to the philosophy, theory, and major principles guiding project work in the company. Consideration of Value Claims early in project planning can help to clarify what the major value(s) are that the work seeks to achieve. For example, the Ford Team Mustang may have written: "The new Mustang will be fuel efficient, high performance, and fun to drive." Considering the Knowledge Claims in advance could help to define tasks of chunk teams, for example, "The fuel injection system will have these performance characteristics. . . ."

As with concept maps, the Vee representing the knowledge creation work to be done by a team can be drawn on a single page. Posted in team members' work areas, it helps them to keep the big picture of the job to be done in clear view. It also can serve to provide imagery and language to help workers communicate with one another, addressing questions such as, "Are those measurements you propose to make really supported by the theory and principles x, y, and z, and will they be valid?" Or, another example, "Are the value claims we believe we can make, based on our data, consistent with our assessment of customer wants?" As a project progresses, there will be a need to prepare Vees for each subteam, and perhaps, for each of several studies undertaken by subteams. Even with these multiple Vees, there remains a basic simplicity and connectedness because all of the subproject

Vees will contain many of the same elements, such as the operative World View guiding the work.

The problems of communication among team members can be overwhelming. Most project teams in corporations involve 10 to 30 or more members, drawn from a variety of backgrounds and corporate cultures. Table 7.3 illustrates this diversity for eight company projects (from Nonaka & Takeuchi, 1995, p. 77).

We can see from Table 7.3 that constructive interaction among team members with such diverse backgrounds would not be easy, and indeed, we observed this to be the case at Kodak in the example cited in chapter 6. By contrast, I have observed the enormous facilitating effects the use of concept maps and Vee diagrams can have in both academic and corporate settings.

TABLE 7.3

Functional Backgrounds of Product Development Team Members*

| Company | Functional Background | | | | | | | |
| | Sales | | | | Quality | | | |
(Product)	R&D	Production	Marketing	Planning	Service	Control	Other	Total
Fuji Xerox (FX-3500)	5	4	1	4	1	1	1	17
Honda (City)	18	6	4	—	1	1	—	30
NEC (PC 8000)	5	—	2	2	2	—	—	11
Epson (EP101)	10	10	8	—	—	—	—	28
Canon (AE-1)	12	10	—	—	—	2	4	28
Canon (Mini-Copier)	8	3	2	1	—	—	1	15
Mazda (New RX-7)	13	6	7	1	1	1	—	29
Matsushita Electric (Automatic Home Bakery)	8	8	1	1	1	1	—	20

*Reprinted by permission of Oxford University Press.

The communication problem is common in most organizations. This problem is being addressed by groups such as The Institute for Research on Learning (IRL), where the idea of a community of practice has been developed. Peters (1994) asserted:

> Becoming a member of a community of practice is literally a requirement of modern-day job success. Non-members, IRL researchers insist, can't succeed in an age of knowledge. IRL has examined everything from airline operations centers to insurance companies. In the latter, for example, new insurance claims processors become effective to the extent that they are accepted into (and wish to join) a local community of practice. IRL's Etienne Wenger claims that a knowledge-age organization is nothing but "an ensemble of interconnected communities of practice." Nice. (p. 174)

Waitley (1995) went so far as to assert there is "no creation without communication" (p. 164). The bottom line is that, in any team project setting, better methods for improving communications among members are needed. There is little hard data to support this claim, but there is an abundance of soft data from many different sources that do support the claim. In time, I believe we shall see good empirical evidence that concept maps and Vee diagrams can facilitate team communications and team effectiveness in creating new knowledge and new useful products. These tools, when wisely applied, will markedly alter the context for teaching and learning needed for knowledge creation.

8

The Context for
Education/Management

THE IMPORTANCE OF CONTEXT

Education is an event that always occurs in a specific context. The context includes emotional, organizational, physical, and cultural characteristics, and each of these include other factors. One of the reasons education is too often ineffective or even destructive results from a limiting context. Some of the complexity of the context for education is shown in Fig. 8.1.

As with all other concepts in my theory of education, each of the concepts shown in Fig. 8.1 interrelate with all the others, some in more significant ways than others. For example, the audio-tutorial lessons we developed for elementary school science lessons, described in the previous chapters, created a special context (an equipped carrel unit) in a traditional classroom in a traditional elementary school in a representative New York State school system. Our primary motivation for developing these lessons was to exercise careful control over the knowledge presented, but important secondary goals were to utilize a wide range of hands-on materials, apparatus, and visual aids to allow some learner control over the pace of instruction and to use examples that were emotionally neutral or positive for students, and also culturally sensitive. Certainly we fell short of the ideal, but the significant, enduring, positive effects on students' achievement indicated that we had a measure of success exceeding that of typical elementary school science learning. An anecdotal comment made by one of our cooperating teachers was, "About the only time George really seems to pay attention in class is the 15 to 20 minutes a week he spends in the science carrel." Our evaluation interviews indicated that George was indeed engaged in learning in the carrel because his performance exceeded that of most of his peers. Kahle and her colleagues (Kahle, 1976) found that the most striking

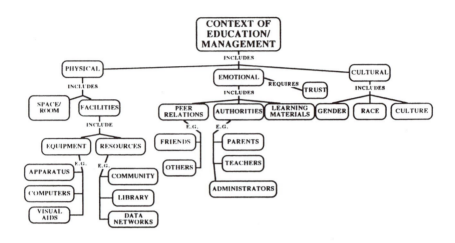

FIG. 8.1. The variety of factors involved in creating the context for education.

difference between Black high school students using audio-tutorial biology lessons compared with their classmates receiving conventional instruction was their substantially higher class attendance rates.

With the explosion of new technology now accruing and increasing access to electronically mediated learning in contexts where the learners can increasingly exercise his or her preferences, we may see before the turn of the century radical changes in the way education is delivered and selected. One of my goals for this book is to guide the process by which education can be improved for the more traditional as well as electronically mediated contexts.

THE EMOTIONAL CONTEXT

The Importance of Feelings

When do people begin to be cognizant of how they feel, and how others around them are feeling? According to Dunn (1987) and Lewis (1995), children begin to manifest recognition of how they feel in their first year of life. By age 20 months, they evidence clearly not only concern for themselves but also concern for the feelings of others. For example, an older sibling may give a crying baby her or his pacifier or a favorite toy. The meanings human beings construct for events include feelings. Penfield (1952) found that when electrodes placed in the brain were used to stimulate specific regions of the brain, the subject not only recalled the details of some event but also the feelings that were experienced during the event. Human beings integrate their thinking, feeling, and acting in some form for every experience they have.

Can people learn to enhance their positive feelings about themselves and become more sensitive and more concerned with the feelings of others? The answer from many sources is a resounding yes! However, caring, sympathy, concern, responsibility, and commitment are not simply the unfolding of our genetic endowment as we grow older; they are traits that need to be learned and practices—with learning and practice continuing throughout our lifespan.

Harris (1969), in his popular book, *I'm OK—You're OK,* drew on the earlier work of Berne (1964) to describe *transactional analysis* (TA), a technique used by many psychiatrists and others to help people understand their own feelings and the feelings of others. The theory behind TA is that we all experience feelings of "You're okay, I'm not okay" as we move through infancy and early childhood. The basic unit of TA is when one person says or does something to another person. Berne defined three emotional states he labeled as Parent, Child, and Adult. The Parent state is that huge store of recordings we have from our growing-up experiences with parents and other authority persons. The recordings: "Don't touch that; you might break it"; "Wear your coat and cap when you go out today—it's cold"; "Don't associate with John or Mary because they are nasty people"; and so forth. The admonitions may or may not have validity, but they are recorded as truth and we are supposed to feel bad or inadequate if we violate them. The child, on the other hand, is the records we make of our feelings when we are subjected to Parent transactions. They lead to feelings of "You're okay; I'm not okay." By 10 months, children begin to have sufficient control that they can act on their environment and achieve a certain amount of control over their environment. The child begins to record ways he or she can consciously control his or her environment, including using smiles or kisses to get adult approval. The child begins to develop his or her Adult. The Adult is the rational person who can achieve rational control over events and people. The feelings of the Adult move toward "I'm okay, You're okay".

Too often, teachers or managers issue instructions with little or no rationale, or a rationale that is patently fraudulent. They are acting as Parent, and elicit in students or subordinates feelings of Child. This is obviously not the way to empower people to achieve their best performance. And yet, an hour's observation in almost any classroom or work setting will probably reveal multiple instances of Parent transactions eliciting Child feelings and actions. Of course, we all offer and experience Parent, Child, or Adult transactions from day to day in our lives, but most of us manage to maintain an Adult emotional posture most of the time. When we deviate widely from this, as under periods of great stress, we may become candidates for the psychiatrist's care.

It is a constant challenge for the teacher/manager to interact with others in ways that will do nothing to diminish their I'm okay image and everything possible to enhance their image. The most robust criterion is at once simple and profound: How can I organize the transaction so that it may become an optimal meaningful learning experience? As Maslow (1984) pointed out, emotional needs of individuals need careful consideration. This will be a theme stressed in this chapter, as it has been in other chapters.

The Art of Loving

At first blush, you might think I am referring to the sexual act of making love. Although I believe the latter is important, and there are whole sections in most bookstores dealing with sex, I wish to discuss the kind of loving Fromm (1956) stressed in his book, *The Art of Loving*. In his chapter on "The Theory of Love," Fromm stated:

> Envy, jealousy, ambition, any kind of greed are passions; love is an action, the practice of human power, which can be practiced only in freedom and never as a result of a compulsion.

> Love is an activity, not a passive affect; it is a "standing in," not a "falling for." In the most general way, the active character of love can be described by stating that love is primarily *giving*, not receiving. (p. 18)

By giving, Fromm was not referring only or even primarily to material things. When one seeks to help someone else enhance his or her I'm okay image, that is giving. The truly loving (giving) person is attractive to others not by the materials things they offer, but by the understanding, compassion, and search for meaning they offer. It is not surprising that many of us have at least on some occasions experienced the love of an effective teacher or an effective manager. Occasionally, unfortunately, this apparent love may degrade into no more than sexual exploitation.

Fromm (1956) discussed another important concept of love: fairness.

> *Fairness* means not to use fraud and trickery in the exchange of commodities and services, and in the exchange of feelings. "I give to you as much as you give to me," in material goods as well as in love, is the prevalent ethical maxim in capitalist society. It may even be said that the development of fairness ethics is the particular contribution of capitalist society.

> The reasons for this fact lie in the very nature of capitalist society. In precapitalist societies, the exchange of goods was determined either by force, by tradition, or by personal bonds of love or friendship. In capitalism, the all-determining factor is the exchange on the market. Whether we deal with the commodity market, the labor market, or the market of services, each person exchanges whatever he has to sell for that which he wants to acquire under the conditions of the market, without the use of force or fraud. (pp. 108–109)

However, Fromm went on to express his skepticism that fairness and other concepts of love can operate in a capitalistic society: "The *principle* underlying capitalistic society and the *principle* of love are incompatible" (p. 100).

People capable of love, under the present system, are necessarily the exceptions; love is by necessity a marginal phenomenon in present-day Western society. Not so much because many occupations would not permit of a loving attitude, but because the spirit of a production-centered, commodity-greedy society is such that only the non-conformist can defend himself successfully against it. Those who are seriously concerned with love as the only rational answer to the problem of human existence must, then, arrive at the conclusion that important and radical changes in our social structure are necessary, if love is to become a social and not a highly individualistic, marginal phenomenon. The direction of such changes can, within the scope of this book, only be hinted at. Our society is run by a managerial bureaucracy, by professional politicians; people are motivated by mass suggestion, their aim is producing more and consuming more, as purposes in themselves. All activities are subordinated to economic goals, means have become ends; man is an automaton—well fed, well clad, but without any ultimate concern for that which is his peculiarly human quality and function. If man is to be able to love, he must be put in his supreme place. The economic machine must serve him, rather than he serve it. He must be enabled to share experience, to share work, rather than, at best, share in profits. Society must be organized in such a way that man's social, loving nature is not separated from his social existence, but becomes one with it. If it is true, as I have tried to show, that love is the only sane and satisfactory answer to the problem of human existence, then any society which excludes, relatively, the development of love, must, in the long run, perish of its own contradiction with the basic necessities of human nature. Indeed, to speak of love is not "preaching," for the simple reason that it means to speak of the ultimate and real need in every human being. That this need has been obscured does not mean that it does not exist. To analyze the nature of love is to discover its general absence today and to criticize the social conditions which are responsible for this absence. To have faith in the possibility of love as a social and not only exceptional-individual phenomenon, is a rational faith based on the insight into the very nature of man. (pp. 111–112)

Much as I admire what Fromm has written on the Art of Loving, and I know of no recent books or articles as cogent and powerful as his work, I believe he may be wrong about the incompatibility of capitalism and loving (as he saw it). With the emerging globalizations of businesses and the constantly increasing competitive pressure, there is a growing number of economist and other writers who see business success over the long term as requiring those elements that Fromm sees as necessary for loving. Fromm may have been right for capitalism up to the 1990s, but now we have entered what Drucker (1993) called the Post-Capitalist Society. In this society, knowledge and knowledge creation become the principal resources for increasing profitability. But how do you create knowledge and enhance the utilization of knowledge at all levels of a corporation? Certainly not by top-down dictates from the management. As Drucker observed:

The knowledge-based organization therefore requires that everyone take responsibility for that organization's objectives, contribution, and, indeed, for its behavior as well.

This implies that all members of the organization must think through their objective and their contributions, and then take responsibility for both. It implies that there are no "subordinates"; there are only "associates." Furthermore, in the knowledge-based organization all members have to be able to control their own work by feedback from their results to their objectives. All members must ask themselves: "What is the one *major* contribution to this organization and its mission which I can make at this particular time?" It requires, in other words, that all members act as responsible decision makers. All members have to see themselves as "executives." (p. 108)

The community that is needed in post-capitalist society—and needed especially by the knowledge worker—has to be based on *commitment and compassion.* . . . (p. 174)

And how does Drucker believe we get commitment and compassion from the corporate workers?

"Loyalty" from now on cannot be obtained by the paycheck; it will have to be earned by proving to knowledge employees that the organization which presently employs them can offer them exceptional opportunities to be effective. Not so long ago, we talked about "labor," increasingly, now, we are talking of "human resources." This implies that it is the individual knowledge employee who decides in large measure what he or she will contribute, and how great the yield from his or her knowledge can or should be. (p. 66)

In knowledge and service work, partnership with the responsible worker is the *only* way to improve productivity. Nothing else workers at all. (p. 92)

Drucker is not the only economist calling for a new view of capitalism. Virtually every leading economist is telling us that we have entered a truly new era. For example, Nonaka and Takeuchi (1995) show the necessity for commitment and responsibility at all levels of the organization:

For any organizational knowledge creation on a global scale to succeed, the following three conditions must be met. First, top management of the participating organizations should show strong commitment to the project. This visible support provides the first step in persuading project members to commit themselves to the project. Second, assigning capable middle managers to the project as "global knowledge engineers" is critical. . . . Third, participants in the project should develop a sufficient level of trust among themselves. Building trust requires the use of mutually understandable, explicit language and often prolonged socialization or two-way, face-to-face dialogue that provides reassurance about points of doubt and leads to willingness to respect the other party's sincerity. (p. 222)

Waterman (1995), in his book, *What America Does Right,* made a similar observation:

What makes top performing companies different, I would urge, is their organizational arrangements. Specifically:

- They are better organized to meet the needs of their *people,* so that they attract better people than their competitors do and their people are more greatly motivated to do a superior job, whatever it is they do.
- They are better organized to meet the needs of *customers* so that they are either more innovative in anticipating customer needs, more reliable in meeting customer expectations, better able to deliver their product or service more cheaply, or some combination of the above. (p. 17)

Furthermore, to succeed, corporations need to acquire a new view of customers and their needs. It is necessary to recognize that we need to dialogue with customers to come to understand their needs:

Most customer's needs are tacit, which means that they cannot tell exactly or explicitly what they need or want. Asked "What do you need or want?" most customers tend to answer the question from their limited explicit knowledge of the available products or services they acquired in the past. This tendency points to the critical limitation of the one-way questionnaire format employed in traditional market research. (Drucker, 1993, p. 234)

I would go further. I believe the successful corporations of the future will become education corporations. They will seek to negotiate meanings with customers to understand better their needs, and to help educate consumers on the best way for them to meet their needs. If the company is truly an educating company, it will seek to make its products the best for the consumer's needs.

Peer Relations

For many students, a major motivation for going to school is to be with their friends. In fact, a major incentive for expelled or drop-out students to return to school is to be with their friends. However, when schooling fails for a substantial percentage of students, their friends may not be found in schools but in shopping centers, in street gangs, or, in worst cases, in prisons. The challenge to educators is to encourage peer relationships that build mutual trust and a sense of caring and being cared for. Some of the growing popularity of cooperative learning (Johnson, Johnson, & Holubec, 1988; Slavin, 1982) approaches in classrooms is recognition that students can assist each other in a learning task structured as a team effort. There may be competition between groups, which can add motivation to excel, but the criteria for high performance in the groups must be structured so that no group is unwarrantedly disadvantaged. A variety of strategies for achieving this have been promulgated by the writers cited and by many others.

One strategy I have found effective in building trust and encouraging positive peer relationships is concept mapping. When done individually and shared with a group, concept maps can show that all learners see a view of the larger conceptual picture and no one has the perfect map of the domain. The individuals who are more ego secure, or more in need of recognition, will usually offer their maps early in a discussion, but as recognition builds that each person has something to contribute, all members of a class or cooperative learning group will express ideas. It is a bit like the proverbial story of the blind men and the elephant—each saw a piece of the whole and collectively the group can construct a better picture of the knowledge domain. After constructing individual concept maps, members of a cooperative learning team can work together to construct a team map, and a healthy competition may occur as individuals vote on which team map (with names omitted) wins the prize. A similar process is effective with Vee diagrams.

When sensitivity is used in structuring cooperative learning groups, the results can reduce bias favoring male or female gender, race or cultural differences, and personality differences.

Personality factors are complex and their influences on learning are equally complex. There have been numerous studies in education dealing with such factors as intrinsic versus extrinsic motivation tendencies, internal versus external locus of control, that is, beliefs about who controls my destiny, me or other forces, and dogmatic versus open-minded characteristics. The fundamental issue is, however, how an individual seeks to achieve an ego status of "I'm okay." Education and employment practices that encourage peer relations that enhance the "I'm okay" feelings of all should be the goal of the contexts we construct.

Peer relations in the workplace are perhaps as important as in schools. In one of our studies, we found that dissatisfaction with peer relations between two staff members was the result of failure to understand clearly neither their own job characteristics or their associates' job characteristics (Fraser, 1993). When we prepared concept maps describing each staff member's jobs (see Fig. 8.2) and these were shared, Gwen could see why Catherine was performing as she did and vice-versa. In a matter of minutes, they resolved conflicts that had festered for some 2 years, and 6 months later, both staff members reported continuing satisfaction with their peer relationships.

In the corporate setting, constructing concept maps to better understand a problem, search for new problem solutions, and to seek better ways to organize and represent knowledge can lead to improved peer relations as a consequence of the empowerment conferred to all team members. The latter application was discussed in chapter 6.

Evaluation practices can enhance or damage peer relations in either work settings or school settings. Higgins (1995) pointed out in his book, *Innovate or Evaporate,* that corporations that promote innovation need a variety of approaches to recognize and reward creativity. Money alone is not the solution.

As we shall see in chapter 9, we need to place less emphasis on evaluation practices that place individuals in direct competition with their peers and more emphasis on practices that can be mutually ego enhancing to groups of students or employees. Moreover, we need to emphasize evaluation of the feeling aspect of an

Fig. 8.2a

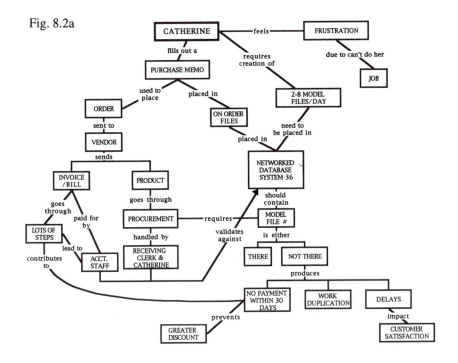

Fig. 8.2b

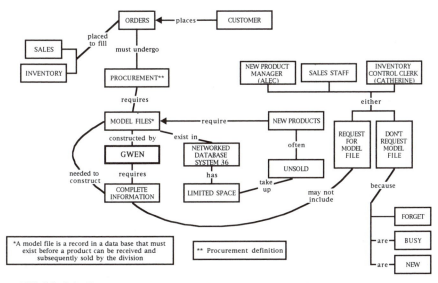

FIG. 8.2a & b. Concept maps showing the job characteristics and feelings as seen by two staff members in a computer sales office. When Gwen and Catherine shared their maps with each other, conflicts were quickly resolved.

161

educational experience much more than we currently do in most settings. Questions relating how a learner feels toward their peers and how they believe their peers feel toward them can be informative and productive.

Learning Materials

Learning materials carry the potential for strong positive (ego-enhancing) or strong negative (ego-destructive) effects. For example, learners who have had negative experiences with mathematics may respond negatively to a learning task where mathematics is involved even when they are in a comfortable physical or cultural context and have considerable knowledge about the subject. What does an educator do when the level of understanding of a domain we desire requires understanding mathematical ideas? The solution may not be easy, but usually we can find another pathway.

A key problem in learning mathematics is that most instructional materials are *conceptually opaque,* that is, they do not present the concepts and concept relationships needed to understand the meaning of the mathematical ideas involved. This is almost a universal problem, beginning in early grades and continuing in many college math courses. What is usually presented are procedures for obtaining answers to problems.

To illustrate concepts in mathematics, let us begin with Fig. 8.3, that shows the key concepts needed to understand the concept *number.* It also illustrates some of the sources of confusion in math problem solving. For example, many people do not understand clearly that numbers used to designate units, such as pounds, inches, or hours, have a separate meaning from numbers used to perform operations, such as add, multiply and divide. While 2 + 2 may equal 4 as an operation, 2 hours plus 2 minutes equals 122 minutes, not 4 hours or 4 minutes.

Professor Henderson, a colleague and distinguished senior mathematician, who helped me prepare Fig. 8.3, said he only recognized the sharp distinction I have described late in his career. It is obviously not obvious that the concept *number* has two distinct meanings, one to represent units and another used in operations such as addition or division. The failure to understand clearly the very elementary concepts in Fig. 8.3 is one of the reasons mathematics is so confusing to so many people. The problems multiply as we move into more advanced mathematics and applications of mathematics in sciences and other fields. The long-term result is math anxiety experienced by so many people, but most research studies on math anxiety fail to consider the conceptual opaqueness of almost all instruction in mathematics or fields using mathematics. I believe if we made strong efforts to make mathematics as conceptually transparent as suggested in Fig. 8.3, it could become one of the easiest and most emotionally rewarding subjects people could study. At this writing, only a very small minority of the mathematics education community agrees with me, but these numbers (people units) are increasing.

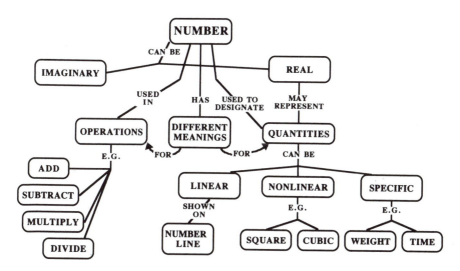

FIG. 8.3. Key concepts involved in understanding the mathematical concept of number.

There remains today a mystique that the only learning that is of value is learning that derives from discovery by the learner of the concepts, principles, or relationships we seek to teach. Thus, the context for learning becomes one of extensive manipulation of materials, experimentation and practice of the Scientific method. As noted in chapter 5, most so-called discovery learning can be just as rote, just as meaningless as poor reception learning. It is true that the extensive didactic methods of much schooling in the 19th century, and even today, results in little usable knowledge. For example, Thorndike (1922) reported that math students who worked textbook problems such as squaring $(x + y)$ could not square $(B_1 + B_2)$. The solution is not necessarily dependent on students working with graph paper or models; it does require that teacher and learner seek to identify and comprehend meaningfully the concepts and principles involved. This is as true for learning in the workplace as it is for learning in classrooms.

What I have described as the problem of conceptual opaqueness is evident at this time in almost every field of study. In my early school years, I had a substantial dislike for history for it was presented as little more than memorizing dates, names, and places. In later years when I recognized that history was a tapestry of human experiences, the toil and suffering of the poor and oppressed and the aggrandizement of the rich and powerful and similar relationships, I found history exciting, easy, and satisfying to study, and even dates, names, and places were easy to remember when they were fitted into the tapestry of human experiences over time.

There have been a few notable efforts to organize content in a way that made learning the content fun and exciting. Bonner's (1962) *The Ideas of Biology,* Cannon's (1932) *Wisdom of the Body,* Commoner's (1971) *The Closing Circle,*

Dethier's (1962) *To Know a Fly,* and Muller's (1958) *The Loom of History,* are a few of the books that brought excitement into my education. Commoner's book, for example, presents five metaphors, which, if understood, explain why it is important to work to sustain and improve our environment: One of these, "There is no such thing as a free lunch," applies not only to ecology but to many domains of knowledge. Metaphors can be very powerful for building communications. In *Metaphors We Live By,* Lakoff and Johnson (1980) showed how so much of our thinking and acting can be explained by common metaphors. Metaphors can be powerful tools for organizations as well as for individuals. Nonaka and Takeuchi (1995) described the Tall Boy metaphor used by Honda to mobilize a team to create a new car ideal for cities.

In 1963, the National Science Teachers' Association's (NSTA) Committee on Curriculum held a conference to identify the big ideas of science that could serve as the organizing ideas for curriculum design from grades kindergarten through college. Seven conceptual schemes were identified (Novak, 1964) and promulgated by NSTA. The work attracted considerable attention and some strong criticism, but the idea of using foundational major concepts as one set of superordinate concepts to be developed and elaborated on over the years never took hold. For one thing, behavioral psychology and associated emphasis on behavioral objectives dominated school learning ideas. The powerful ideas of Ausubel's (1962, 1963) cognitive learning theory had just been put forward and were then not generally known in the United States (or now, for that matter!). The powerful tool of concept mapping had not yet been developed; it was difficult to show how powerful superordinate ideas could be used to facilitate meaningful learning of the myriads of concepts and principles of science. Science learning for most students remains today largely the memorization of facts and problem-solving procedures, most of which are forgotten 6 months after they are studied.

Despite the many years of effort of the Social Science Education Consortium (SSEC), headquartered in Boulder, Colorado, to promulgate basic concepts of social sciences that could serve as the foundations for school studies in this field, most social science classes remain largely the memorization of isolated facts. The SSEC remains today one of the few organizations committed to teacher education and curriculum development that emphasizes understanding of basic social science concepts.

Probably every reader of this book has experienced courses where understanding basic concepts played little or no role. You may recall how emotionally unrewarding these experiences were, except for the extrinsic reward of teacher approbation and high grades—if you played along with this meaningless game. For those learners who do not, disapproval by parents, teachers, and peers, or even ridicule, can have dire emotional consequences creating many learning disabled (read school disabled) people, school dropouts, and, in worst cases, criminals.

THE PHYSICAL CONTEXT

The Sameness of School Facilities

Working with a team of colleagues, we completed a nationwide study in 1971 of exemplary school science facilities and programs (Novak, 1972). Nominations for exemplary facilities were sought from various school leaders, architects, and equipment companies. Some 600 schools were nominated and after screening by phone calls or visits by local colleagues, 140 schools were selected as showing the most promise. Each of these were visited by one or more members of our study team, and some schools were visited two or three times.

The most striking finding was that even most of the schools nominated as exemplary were, in most respects, highly traditional and similar in both facilities and programs. The typical pattern was schools with an auditorium, gymnasiums, many rooms for 25 to 30 students, a library/learning center, and administrative quarters. The room facilities usually included fixed laboratory benches, either at the room perimeter or in a rear section of a room, and two-student tables or arm-tabled chairs. Less than a dozen facilities and programs departed radically from this arrangement with open-space arrangements for multiple groups, carpeted floors, furniture that could be arranged in many configurations, student project space, and supply and materials centers.

It was this latter kind of facility we recommended for new or remodeled schools with two important provisos: (1) extensive staff education was needed for new curriculum development, building skills in using these flexible facilities, acquiring skills in managing more interactive student and staff relations; and (2) support staff, equipment centers, and a different curriculum were needed. Most schools that attempted to build new, more open and flexible facilities failed to provide the staff education and support needed to make successful use of the facilities. Many reverted to traditional patterns, walling-up open spaces and bolting down furniture. The study illustrated an important thesis of this book: You cannot improve education by modifying only one element of the five elements of education. In some cases, students and staff felt that the new facilities were worse than the old!

Little has changed in most school facilities since 1971. A recent report by Arzi (in press) calls for a need for more flexibility in facilities, the same kind of problem described in my 1972 report. The major addition has been computer laboratories, usually by taking over standard classroom space. Little has changed in the instructional programs, although we are hearing less and less about behavioral objectives and more about the need for students to construct their own knowledge. However, for most students, schooling is still memorizing information in preparation for frequent objective quizzes and multiple-choice tests. It is an exceptional classroom in an exceptional school where these are not the common educative events.

The Ideal Learning Environment for Education

From the standpoint of the physical context for education, the ideal depends on what we hope to teach and the strategies we select to use. For the teaching of a foreign language, the ideal context might be a tutorial approach in a marketplace setting in the culture where the language is spoken. Here learners could see, smell, feel, and hear all that is associated with the language. Obviously this is not possible for most learners, especially those in traditional classrooms where the dull memorization of English word synonyms and rules of grammar predominate. The creative teacher, even in a traditional school, can find ways to use visual aids, food samples, plays, audio and/or video tapes and other resources to help approximate the real thing.

If one is teaching science, some aspects of physics, for example, might be brought to life in a playground with slides, teeter-totters, swings, and pulleys. In the classroom, we can use models of these things, visual aids, and computer simulations. Much good mathematics could also be taught in this setting.

The issue at the core of our concern is how to help learners experience the regularities coded by the concept labels and concept relationships we seek to teach. Recall again the relationships between the psychological constructions we seek to help learners make and the epistemological origins of these constructions. Remember, the universe is made up only of events and objects (or *happenings* and *things* may be better descriptors for young children). The language we use to code regularities and relationships in those events and objects takes on greater meaning the closer the educative experience duplicates or models the world we seek to understand. Some of the most advanced applications of computers for education is in pilot training. All airline pilots obtain at least some of their education flying aircraft using computer simulations. It is not only very expensive to fly large jet planes to practice flying skills and the application of knowledge in special situations, but it is clearly impossible to practice emergency routines that may occur just prior to or during crash conditions. In a personal interview with an airline pilot of one of the major airlines, this captain commented on the very high quality of the training programs for her airline (personal communication, December, 1997).

At this writing, we stand on the brink of what I believe to be a revolutionary advance in our ability to use electronic resources to provide a good simulation of almost any learning environment. Computer arcades in shopping malls already illustrate the wide range of sights, sounds, and feelings we may experience with electronic devices, and there may already be some devices that emit smells as well. The exponentially growing capabilities of computer-driven simulations would suggest that we are only years away from creating extraordinary learning environments electronically. Long before this book is as old as my first *Theory of Education* (1977a), I predict we shall see this extraordinary capability manifested, not in shopping malls but in all businesses, homes, and maybe eventually in most schools.

The open question is, "Can schools as we know them (at all levels) continue to exist when such an extraordinary learning opportunity can be brought into the home?" It can be argued that humans are social beings and learning at home with electronic devices is asocial. But we do not need to be in social settings 16 hours each day. Moreover, pairs, teams, and network groups can interact together with many constructive social exchanges. Many of the negative social exchanges that now occur in schools could be reduced or avoided. Given the potential educative power of well-designed electronic educational packages, 3 or 4 hours of on-line time would be all that would be needed to achieve much higher levels of achievement than learners experience in schools today.

The central issue then becomes, "How do we create these well-designed electronic learning resources? The short answer is: "We build them on the basis of a solid theory of education." I believe the theory put forth in this book is more than adequate for the task, and the theory will improve as it is applied, tested, and revised. What evidence do I have to assert this?—Not much, but then there has not been a great deal of effort to design and evaluate such theory-based educational experiences, or the theories that have been applied in the past have had major shortcomings, for example, theories based on behavioral psychology or Piaget's developmental psychology.

Let us examine again what was achieved and evaluated in our 12-year longitudinal study of science concept learning. We provided 191 first- and second-grade children some 15 hours of carefully designed, theory-based audiotutorial lessons dealing with basic concepts of science, including concepts of matter, energy, living things, and human anatomy and physiology. Although audio-tutorial lessons have some advantages over electronically delivered learning experiences, such as working with real things in real demonstrations, they also have severe limitations compared with electronically mediated lessons. The latter can provide virtually unlimited access to visual (still and motion) images, learner-selected sequences of text and images, interactive experiences where successive materials offered depend on prior materials selected and/or evaluation information, and easy updating with addition or deletion of materials. But even with their limitations, the audio-tutorial lessons provided to many of the students enough development in understanding basic science concepts that the mean achievement for students receiving this instruction was much greater than that of uninstructed students for the balance of their schooling (refer again to that discussion in chapter 7). Remember that this instruction was given only in grades 1 and 2 (6- to 8-year-old children). One can only speculate on what achievement would be possible if such quality instruction were given from grades 1 through 12.

There is an ominous side to the possibilities suggested. Children in the most affluent homes may be the only recipients of this kind of learning opportunity in their homes. A new kind of school with new kinds of home, school, workplace, and community relationships needs to be created. These changes are not likely to occur as a smooth transition with equality and justice for all. Is it too early to begin to plan for this transition?

THE CULTURAL CONTEXT

Heredity and Environment

Is nature (heredity) more important than nurture (environment) in forming who we are and what we can do? The finest seeds will not produce healthy plants without proper nutrients and light. The child with the best possible genetic endowment will be severely limited in development in a poor environment. The issue is, "How can we capitalize on the genetic endowment of every individual by creating the most favorable environment?" As with most important issues, there are no easy solutions.

There is the need to consider the physical environment as well as the emotional environment. Obviously, the child of an alcoholic or drug-abusing mother will be damaged in developing his or her potential due to the deleterious effect of drugs on fetal development. Less obvious, but in some cases more significantly, the child may suffer from strong negative and little positive emotional support from both parents who are drug addicted. Nutrition and health care may be additionally limiting factors in childhood when drug costs and drug impairment compete with food purchases and preparation. For these problems, we must look to long-term societal changes that are at the root of the problem, albeit heredity has been shown to be a factor in drug addiction and mental health. Radical improvement in education can contribute to better retention of drug users and their children in educational programs, but at best this is a long-term solution to the problems. Quick-fix attempts at outlawing drugs (already on the books), imprisoning drug dealers, and interdicting drug supplies are, at best, only moderately successful with no evidence that these by themselves can solve the problem. Programs for nutrition supplements (such as federally funded Women, Infants, and Children Programs) can be helpful, but they, too, are not the long-term solution to the problem. In the end, our best hope for radical reduction in these problems is radical improvement of educational programs, including new kinds of programs based on a viable theory of education.

There are those who believe that some races are, on average, better endowed genetically than others—Hitler, Jensen (1969), and Herrnstein and Murray (see *The Bell Curve,* 1994). For Hitler, there was a political agenda that required and fed this belief, and for Jensen and Herrnstein and Murray, there is the press of the academic publication game that drives some people to take controversial positions to gain recognition (or notoriety?). There certainly are genetic differences among the races, in skin color, for example, but to assert that mental tests demonstrate hereditary differences between the races is to illustrate naiveté both as regards psychometric issues of testing and issues associated with differential performance on tests of any kind. I deal with some of these issues in chapter 9. Many scholars, including Keddie (1973), *The Myth of Cultural Deprivation,* Kamin (1974), *The Science and Politics of IQ,* and Gould (1981), *The Mismeasure of Man,* have shown that the arguments made to assert genetic differences in mental capabilities between races are naive at best. Sternberg (1996b) provided one of the best recent summaries of the myths and truths about intelligence issues I have seen. The April 1995 issue of *Educational Leadership* presented papers by Molnar (1995) and others critical of the Herrnstein and Murray book.

The nature–nurture debate has gone on for decades, and it is not likely to be resolved in the near future. Those who argue that heredity accounts for most of the variance in human abilities and performance tend to look at data in ways that support their position, whereas persons who argue that nurturing, better homes, and better schools can profoundly influence aptitudes and performance look at different data in different ways. Bronfenbrenner and Ceci (1994), in their bioecological model saw heredity as playing a significant role, but they also saw a synergistic effect where an enhanced environment early in development leads to progressively greater enhancement in abilities and performance as the child matures. One of the problems for society is that this early, preschool environment is not easily augmented. Bronfenbrenner, who is credited with a major role in creating the Head Start Program in the United States, has long argued that more concern and attention must be paid to ways to improve family life, especially for preschool children. This remains a daunting social challenge.

> It is always tempting to value most what we ourselves possess—and, in the process, to scapegoat other groups. It is happening in ethnic wars around the world. And one might argue it happens when Herrnstein and Murray (1994) cheerfully note that most readers of their book are members of the cognitive elite (p. 47) and other elite groups. We need to remember that, over time and space, those at the higher rather than the lower end of the various intellectual spectra have been those most likely to be persecuted or scapegoated. However it is defined, intelligence is only one attribute of human beings and one attribute leading to certain kinds of success, but tests of intelligence can, at best, provide measures of certain cognitive skills (Keating, 1984); they are not measures of human worth. (Sternberg, 1996b, p. 15)

With regard to gender, there are again obvious genetic differences, in hormonal levels and associated secondary sex characteristics such as breasts and facial hair, but no obvious differences in intellectual capacity. Scholars such as Gilligan (1982), Belenky, Clinchy, Goldberger, and Tarule (1986), and Keller (1985) have shown that in personality and social characteristics, there appear to be patterns of differences between males and females that are innate. But the influence of environment is also evident and may account for much of the gender differences observed in Western cultures because some of these patterns are not observed in other cultures. Best (1983) showed that even by Grade 1 (6 years old), boys manifest different patterns of action toward girls, other boys, and their teacher than are manifested by girls. However, these patterns of differences mirror the patterns of the adults of our culture, and they can be modified by appropriate educational intervention.

Gender Issues

In her book, Best (1983) described the actions and attitudes toward the teacher and school tasks as strikingly different patterns for boys and girls. While in kindergarten, both girls and boys sought affection from their teacher. By the end of grade 1, this pattern began to shift for boys who now sought affection and approbation from their peers. By grade 2, membership and status in peer groups was far more important for boys than girls. Best reported that in one classroom where the teacher was ill from March until June and a succession of substitute teachers occurred, 9 of the 12 girls showed lower achievement in June than in January, and the other three showed no change.

> What was astonishing, however, and not only to me but to all those with whom I discussed it, was the finding that the academic achievement of the boys had not suffered any adverse affects whatsoever from the teacher's long-term absence. Eight of the twelve boys had scores in the same range in June as they had had in January. And four had even higher scores. None had suffered learning setbacks. All those who lost ground in the teacher's absence were girls. (p. 13)

Best explained the result as a consequence of the independence of the boys on need for teacher approval for achievement, with greater reliance on peer approval as supporting achievement.

There is also a hidden message here that Best did not discuss but is implicit in the gender differences observed. Boys more than girls socialize more toward becoming autonomous learners—the consequence being over time, boys more often than girls take charge of their own meaning making. Sometimes the boys overtly reject the teacher's agenda, especially when it requires work that they see as meaningless, or as what they classify as women's work, such as household chores. The long-term net result is that boys more than girls seek to excel in those things seen as man's work—and these tend to be the jobs and professions that are most rewarded by society.

There is a downside to the male tendency to identify more with peers than with their teachers. Best reported that boys rejected by their peer group experience reduction in school achievement rather than substantial increases. The pressure on boys to be part of the gang is severe, for better and worse.

In an effort to study a curriculum that included discussion of gender issues, Best (1983) worked with the fourth-grade students, discussing issues of sex-role stereotypes, supplying them with vocabulary to discuss sex, and attitudes toward gender. Her initial reaction was that her efforts over the school year were not successful in changing attitudes or behaviors. However, when the students returned to school after the summer holiday, Best observed:

> There seemed to have been an incubating effect in process during the summer hiatus. Seeds had apparently been planted the year before that were now beginning to bud. Only now, in fifth grade, did the boys and girls I was working with begin to talk to

one another. But when they did, it proved to be a critical event. They seemed now to be ready to leave the stereotypes behind them and work toward new ways to relate to one another. (p. 141)

We see in Best's work a study of how the school context can reinforce the gender stereotypes of the society. We also see that modifying the curriculum to include frank and sustained discussion of issues of sexism and stereotyping can have a strong positive effect, Best reported that the language used in fifth grade repeatedly expressed the recognition by boys and girls that common stereotypes were invalid at best and often the reverse of reality. Once again, the power of high quality, meaningful learning experiences shows payoff not only in the knowledge acquired by the students but also in the attitudes and values expressed by the learners. While Benbow and Stanley (1982) puzzled over observed gender differences in mathematical reasoning where the gap between males and females appears to increase with schooling, we found some evidence to support the thesis that females socialize into playing the school game (i.e., learning by rote) more than males, and this leads in time to significant gender differences favoring males in mathematical and science reasoning tasks (Ridley & Novak, 1983). In most cases, gender differences in cognitive abilities tend to be exaggerated (Hyde, 1991). There are ways that schools can help to reduce gender bias and gender stereotypes. The American Association of University Women's report (1995) *Growing Smart: What's Working for Girls in Schools,* has many suggestions for schools to recognize and deal with gender problems.

In our society, traits associated with masculinity are often seen as desirable and traits associated with femininity are less desirable. As Gilligan (1982) observed:

The repeated findings of these studies is that the qualities deemed necessary for adulthood—the capacity for autonomous thinking, clear decision-making, and responsible action—are those associated with masculinity and considered undesirable as attributes of the feminine self. The stereotypes suggest a splitting of love and work that relegates expressive capacities to women while placing instrumental abilities in the masculine domain. Yet looked at from a different perspective, these stereotypes reflect a conception of adulthood that is itself out of balance, favoring the separateness of the individual self over the connection to others, and leaning more toward an autonomous life of work than toward the interdependence of love and care. (p. 17)

The impact of culture on the thoughts, feelings and attitudes of people is also profoundly severe in the business world. Tannen (1994), in her book, *Talking from 9 to 5,* described well the different patterns in the way males and females express their thoughts and feelings. Some years ago, Gilligan (1982) described how women speak "in a different voice."

"I have a very strong sense of being responsible to the world, that I can't just live for my enjoyment, but just the fact of being in the world gives me an obligation to do what I can to make the world a better place to live in, no matter how small a scale that may be on." Thus while Kohlberg's (male) subject worries about people interfering with each other's rights, this women worries about "the possibility of omission of your not helping others when you could help them." (p. 21)

Tannen (1994) took this gender difference further and showed how, in the business world, men do not express the world they see the same as women.

Amy was a manager with a problem: She had just read a final report written by Donald, and she felt it was woefully inadequate. She faced the unsavory task of telling him to do it over. When she met with Donald, she made sure to soften the blow by beginning with praise, telling him everything about his report that was good. Then she went on to explain what was lacking and what needed to be done to make it acceptable. She was pleased with the diplomatic way she had managed to deliver the bad news. Thanks to her thoughtfulness in starting with praise, Donald was able to listen to the criticism and seemed to understand what was needed. But when the revised report appeared on her desk, Amy was shocked. Donald had made only minor, superficial changes, and none of the necessary ones. The next meeting with him did not go well. He was incensed that she was now telling him his report was not acceptable and accused her of having misled him. "You told me before it was fine," he protested.

Amy thought she had been diplomatic; Donald thought she had been dishonest. The praise she intended to soften the message "This is unacceptable" sounded to him like the message itself: "This is fine." So what she regarded as the main point—the needed changes — came across to him as optional suggestions, because he had already registered her praise as the main point. She felt he hadn't listened to her. He thought she had changed her mind and was making him pay the price.

Work days are filled with conversations about getting the job done. Most of these conversations succeed, but too many end in impasses like this. It could be that Amy is a capricious boss whose wishes are whims, and it could be that Donald is a temperamental employee who can't hear criticism no matter how it is phrased. But I don't think either was the case in this instance. I believe this was one of innumerable misunderstandings caused by differences in conversational style. Amy delivered the criticism in a way that seemed to her self-evidently considerate, a way she would have preferred to receive criticism herself: taking into account the other person's feelings, making sure he knew that her ultimate negative assessment of his report didn't mean she had no appreciation of his abilities. She offered the praise as a sweetener to help the nasty-tasting news go down. But Donald didn't expect criticism to be delivered in that way, so he mistook the praise as her overall assessment rather than a preamble to it. (pp. 21–22)

Whether the differences between the voice of men and women are, in part, genetic or entirely a consequence of the socialization differences for males and females, the consequences are that real differences do exist in how males and females converse and how they interact with others. Given that management has been dominated for most of history by males, women who seek to succeed in management face what is called a glass ceiling. Tannen (1994) described it this way:

Here is a brief explanation of how conversational-style differences play a role in installing a glass ceiling. When decisions are made about promotion to management positions, the qualities sought are a high level of competence, decisiveness, and ability to lead. If it is men, or mostly men, who are making the decisions about promotions — as it usually is — they are likely to misinterpret women's ways of talking as showing indecisiveness, inability to assume authority, and even incompetence. All the conversational-style differences discussed thus far can work against women who use them in an office setting. For example, a woman who feels it is crucial to preserve the appearance of consensus when making decisions because she feels anything else would appear bossy and arrogant begins by asking those around her for their opinions. This can be interpreted by her bosses as evidence that she doesn't know what she thinks should be done, that she is trying to get others to make decisions for her.

Again and again, I heard from women who knew they were doing a superior job and knew that their immediate co-workers knew it, but the higher-ups did not. Either these women did not seem to be doing what was necessary to get recognition outside their immediate circle, or their superiors were not doing what was necessary to discern their achievements and communicate these upward. The kinds of things they were doing, like quietly coming up with the ideas that influenced their groups and helping those around them to do their best, were not easily observed in the way that giving an impressive presentation is evident to all.

Even so small a linguistic strategy as the choice of pronouns can have the effect of making one's contributions more or less salient. It is not uncommon for many men to say "I" in situations where many women would say "we." One man told me, "I'm hiring a new manager; I'm going to put him in charge of my marketing division," as if he owned the corporation he worked for and was going to pay the manager's salary himself. Another talked about the work produced by all the members of his group in the same way: "This is what I've come up with on the Lakehill deal." In stark contrast, I heard a woman talking about what "we" had done, but on questioning, discovered that it was really she alone who had done the work. By talking in a way that seemed to her appropriate to avoid sounding arrogant, she was inadvertently camouflaging her achievements and lessening the chances they would be recognized. (pp. 136–137)

Tronto (1993) observed that the perception of women as caregivers places them at a disadvantage in our competitive, male-dominated society. Women are not supposed to be the aggressors, but rather the supporters of males in competitive situations.

A more recent report by Swiss (1996) found that in a survey of 325 women, 65% indicated that attitudes of senior management influenced gender inequity to a great extent and 68% indicated that their compensation had been limited by their gender. These and other findings indicate that American businesses still have a long way to go to eliminate gender inequities.

In the sciences, similar gender differences favoring men have been reported. Sonnert and Holton (1996) commented on a conversation with a female scientist who observed:

"Men . . . stood in the hallways and found the great men and went over to them and shook their hand or asked them to have a drink with them or something, and women couldn't do that in my day . . . They took themselves very seriously and they said any kind of that came into their head. I call it 'professor talk' . . . And I found that a waste of my time." Sonnert and Holton remarked, "'Professor talk' may indeed be a waste of time in terms of exchanging research information or gaining scientific insights. But it may be anything but wasteful in terms of its hidden agenda. What other respondents called a 'bull session' or 'chatty self promotion' may have the function of a bonding ritual. And the social bonds thus forged may have beneficial effects on a scientist's research and career. (p. 68)

The struggle of women in the sciences has a long history (Rossiter, 1982).

Whatever one may conclude about the pros and cons as regards differences in male and female styles of interaction, the undeniable fact is that gender does play a powerful role in setting the context for teaching and learning in any organizational setting.

Race

As noted earlier, there have been repeated attempts to associate intellectual potential (and other traits) with genetic racial differences. Usually the motivation has been to establish the superiority of the dominant race, also the majority race, over the minority race. There is political motivation behind this, as Kamin (1974), Gould (1981), and others have noted, but the sustaining force for these kinds of prejudices is a problem of ego needs, especially of males, to feel "I'm okay," and perhaps also "You're not okay." Rooted in childhood, and too often in early experiences in school, these emotional needs tend to persist into adulthood and beyond. In some cases, they become overwhelming, leading to drug abuse and a variety of antisocial or pathological actions. Because they are often emotionally deeply rooted, racial biases or prejudices are not easily modified. Objective data or rational discourse is often not sufficient to reduce or eliminate racial biases or prejudices.

Perhaps even more than gender, race plays a role in shaping the interaction between individuals, and the effect is typically deleterious to the minority members in any national or local context. The literature on this issue is voluminous, and any effort to cull key points from this literature would probably prove deficient. I shall not deal with it extensively, not because race is not important, but rather because I believe that many of the problems and issues that have race as a root cause can best be dealt with by applying the ideas and tools presented in this book.

We must recognize that the problems that now plague many minorities and underprivileged are almost certain to get worse as world economies move increasingly to globalization. We have seen low-pay, low-skill jobs move from Japan to Taiwan to Korea and more recently to China and Vietnam. Under pressures from global competition, the better-paying jobs will require significantly better-educated workers. The problems we face in many of the United States' larger cities where racial minorities predominate are likely to get worse if despair in these communities increases.

Unfortunately, many of the remedial programs designed for minority students tend to place even greater emphasis on rote mode learning practices and testing for rote recall than is typical for schools in general. Moreover, these remedial programs tend to be even more boring than conventional programs. These school programs lead to progressively greater disempowerment of students—and greater despair as regards employment opportunities. Some very conscientious students in these programs hone their skills in rote learning and manage to succeed in schools, only to find they are poorly prepared for college work, especially for better colleges and universities.

There is also the reality that in general, conventional school testing disadvantages Blacks and other minorities and advantages White and some Asian students. The growing public pressures for increasing accountability lead to increasing the kind of testing that is already disadvantaging Blacks and others. The resources required to evaluate student performance in nondiscriminatory ways are probably at least an order of magnitude greater than what is typically available.

As the power and role of technology in education increases, the students from advantaged homes are likely to have much greater access to these resources than students from disadvantaged homes. My expectation is that at least for the near term, the increasing value for meaningful learning that will be conferred by new technologies will exacerbate the problem of the discrepancies between racial minorities and privileged White students.

THE ORGANIZATIONAL CONTEXT

Democratic Versus Authoritarian

School organization varies from country to country, state to state, and city to city. The degree of autonomy for individual schools varies considerably, although in general, schools must follow state or national mandates regarding curriculum, certification of personnel, salary and retirement compensation, tenure, and graduation requirements. In most schools, there are also relatively rigid structures. Although individual teachers have some autonomy in selecting learning materials, instructional strategies, and evaluation, for the most part they must follow dictates imposed on them. Even in so-called alternative schools that pride themselves on their freedom and inventiveness, what is commonly observed is more cosmetic than substantive. Ted Sizer, former Dean of Education at Harvard University, and a leading proponent of school reform, describes most school reform as similar to fine-tuning a Model T Ford. What is really needed are truly substantive reforms, and these are very difficult to achieve (see O'Neil, 1995a).

Some states and some school districts in the United States have tried to employ for-profit corporations to run privatized schools. However, the reports to date on contract or for profit schools are not overwhelmingly favorable (see, e.g., Farrell,

Johnson, Jones & Sapp, 1994). The problem, as I see it, is that most school reform does not deal with truly fundamental issues, namely, how do we modify our teaching and administrative structure to help teachers help learners take charge of their own meaning making? To achieve this, there needs to be a new vision for education and leadership that helps to create and share the vision with parents, students, teachers, and administrators. This cannot be done by an authoritative top-down administration, but for most schools, this remains the overwhelming characteristic of school reform.

A controversial problem in many schools is the placement of students into different tracks. Parents whose children qualify for high or honors tracks usually defend the practice, and often they are the most vocal at school board meetings. The evidence regarding tracking is that while students in honors or high tracks may benefit, students in lower tracks may suffer, both socially and academically (Gamoran, Nystrand, Berends, & LePore, 1995). The net effect over time is a widening gap in achievement and opportunity between students in high versus low tracks. Apart from the inequalities in achievement that result from tracking, there are also the social consequences, including segregation of peer groups. It is evident that it is not a desirable condition in a democracy and for future economic development where low-track students will need to become skilled technicians in an increasingly sophisticated job market.

Currently, the new fetish for school reform is so-called site-based management (SBM). In theory, SBM encourages parents, teachers, administrators, and sometimes students, to plan, collaboratively, programs that will meet student needs. In practice, what occurs is that constraints of union contract, state legislative requirements, funding restrictions, and ordinary resistance to change subvert most efforts at truly positive reform.

The overriding problem in all school reform issues comes in dealing with teacher unions. Some 85% of public school teachers are unionized, and rules and procedures negotiated by unions determine, to a large part, how schools will operate. Randy Moore (1996) cited examples such as the following:

> In Michigan, a group of young teachers wanted some extra training in math. Since their school system couldn't afford to pay the teachers for the training, the teachers agreed to do the training without pay. Veteran teachers protested, pointing out that the union contract forbids unpaid work. The training never took place. (p. 260)

Moore went on to identify 12 satirical steps for "How Unions Can Ensure Excellence in Education." His steps included: Protect mediocre and incompetent teachers by rewarding longevity, not performance; Abolish quality-based incentives, and oppose quality by opposing all measures of quality; and Build your program on gimmicks, not substance. At Cornell University, Bacharack studied factors that influence decision making in schools, and he concluded, "Three principal factors are determinant, union contracts, union contracts, and union contracts" (Bacharach, personal communication, 1987). For better or worse, the reality that exists now regarding the context for school education is overwhelmingly determined by union contracts (Shedd & Bacharach, 1991). There are some 16,000 independent school districts in the United States, but for most of them, the operating policies are determined in union contract negotiations.

For many reasons, systemic change has been slow and is likely to continue to be slow. As one teacher put it:

> My conclusion is this: If *systematic* changes are made in schools, site-based management might succeed. So far, that has not happened. At Wilson Magnet, a school with a reputation for making SBM work, the teachers can't even get enough people to run in-site elections to fill out our numbers. By now, most of us have figured out the drawbacks: trying circumstances and long hours for minuscule results. (Geraci, 1995, p. 52, italics added)

The overriding problem is that schooling in America, and I would include tertiary education, is a huge bureaucracy, run autocratically mostly from the top down. State legislative actions, partly under pressures from strong teachers' unions, are more designed to preserve the autocracy than to modify it in significant ways. Some millions of parents have simply given up on public and private schools and are doing home schooling. Financially difficult as this is in most cases, without the benefit of tax revenues, endowments, or other sources of income, parents who choose to do home schooling seek to take back from the bureaucracy, to the extent that laws allow, the responsibility for the education of their own children. It is for them, in regards to schooling, similar to the early American frontier days, when each family had to be almost completely independent. Important differences now, of course, are the huge reservoir of knowledge available in libraries, museums, nature centers, and exhibits, and electronically through the Internet. Problems and issues regarding school organization are discussed further in chapter 10.

Corporations suffer from the same top-down autocratic management as do schools. In fact, in many ways, they have been the model followed by schools. The problem is that such organizations are poor for empowering people in the organization to learn, and to facilitate learning by the organization. Senge (1990) described such organizations as learning disabled—and, the disability is widespread, if not universal. Senge pointed out that one third of the firms in the Fortune 500 in 1970 had vanished by 1983! These were large companies, many of whom were at one time leaders in their industry. They failed, according to Senge, because the organization did not know how to learn:

> But, what if high mortality rate is only a symptom of deeper problems that afflict *all* companies, not just the ones that die? What if even the most successful companies are poor learners—they survive, but never live up to their potential? What if, in light of what organizations *could* be, "excellence" is actually "mediocrity"?

It is no accident that most organizations learn poorly. The way they are designed and managed, the way people's jobs are defined, and most importantly, the way we have all been taught to think and interact (not only in organizations, but more broadly) create fundamental learning disabilities. These disabilities operate despite the best efforts of bright, committed people. Often the harder they try to solve problems, the worse the results. What learning does occur takes place despite these learning disabilities—for they pervade all organizations to some degree.

Learning disabilities are tragic in children, especially when they go undetected.(Consider Andrew's case.) They are no less tragic in organizations, where they also go largely undetected. (p. 18)

Senge is not alone in his analysis. Nonaka and Takeuchi (1995) also saw corporations as poor learners and poor creators of new knowledge. They argued that corporations need a new management organization they described as middle-up-down where new ideas flow freely up and down the organizational structure. Peters (1992) also called for the need to "demolish the corporate superstructure" (p. xxxii) if real, sustained change is to be effected. Higgins (1995) advised bluntly in his book, *Innovate or Evaporate,* that corporations need to become much better at developing constructive innovations; in short, much better at learning.

Organizations can learn. As Nicolini and Meznar (1995) stated, two things are required: "1) the modification of organizational cognitive structures (which constitute a form of cognition in action), and 2) the process of representation, formalization, and normalization of such knowledge" (p. 743). The ideas and tools described in this book are a way to achieve this.

Schools, too, are poor as learning organizations. In a conversation with Senge regarding schools, O'Neil (1995b) related:

The Fifth Discipline *explains the characteristics of "learning organizations." Schools are considered to be institutions of learning, but are most of them learning organizations?*

Definitely not. A learning organization is an organization in which people at all levels are, collectively, continually enhancing their capacity to create things they really want to create. And most of the educators I talk with don't feel like they're doing this. Most teachers feel oppressed trying to conform to all kinds of rules, goals and objectives, many of which they don't believe in. Teachers don't work together; there's very little sense of collective learning going on in most schools.

By the way, I also disagree with your assumption that schools are institutions of learning for students.

Why is that?

We say school is about learning, but by and large, schooling has traditionally been about people memorizing a lot of stuff that they don't really care too much about, and the whole approach is quite fragmented. Really deep learning is a process that inevitably is driven by the learner, not by someone else. And it always involves moving back and forth between a domain of thinking and a domain of action. So having a student sit passively taking in information is hardly a very good model for learning; it's just what we're used to. (p. 20)

Katzenbach (1995) and his colleagues at McKinsey and Company combined their experiences consulting with companies to identify characteristics of truly effective change leaders. Some of the outstanding characteristics they found for real change leaders (RCLs) were:

RCL's establish individual—and team—accountability measures by doing two simple things:

1. Establishing measures, assessments, and goals that put real meat behind the change effort, and link it to performance priorities that people can understand.

2. Avoiding "the activity trap," in which lots of measured actions are viewed as surrogates for results. (pp. 40–41)

In both schools and corporations, assessment of performance and learning in truly valid ways is not easy. These problems are addressed in the next chapter.

And, just as schools are caught up with archaic organizational bureaucracies, so are most corporations. But there is one important difference—in today's global economy, the corporation that does poorly in reorganizing, in learning as an organization, will soon disappear! Therein lies some hope for new leadership in the world for better ways to organize and operate to make organizations far better learning environments. From changes in corporations and their new insights may arise new promise for schooling in America—and in the whole world.

9

Evaluation and Rewards

THE IMPORTANCE OF EVALUATION

From the time we are born, we are weighed, measured, and evaluated in various ways until we die. In fact, even before birth, our heartbeat, fetal position, and other characteristics may be evaluated. Those who are highly weight conscious may stand on the scales several times per day—or fear the day they must be weighed. Being evaluated may not involve much thinking for the moment, but most of the evaluations we face will involve thinking, feeling, and acting to varying degrees. And when we die, many religions hold that we face the eternal judgment, a judgment based on the life we have led.

In the world of work, we also face evaluations of various kinds, some of which lead to advancement in position, usually with higher earnings and/or higher status and privileges. Some rewards may be special recognition or increased opportunity for self-expression and creative pursuits. Although this chapter will focus on evaluation issues common in school settings, many of these also apply in work settings. Conversely, rewards and recognitions apply in school settings, albeit they are usually not monetary. Key ideas regarding evaluation and rewards are shown in Fig. 9.1.

Too often evaluation is equated with testing; that is, the kind of paper-and-pencil tests we take in school or to qualify for a driver's license. The latter may require performance evaluation also as we try to parallel park and do the other tasks required, at least to some criterion level of skills with perhaps 70% or better success. Performance evaluation occurs in schools also, especially in schools of dance, music, art, and design, but also in science laboratories, language classes, and increasingly in all kinds of classes.

Using the Vee heuristic as a framework to understand the role of evaluation, we see that the fundamental problem in measurement is to obtain valid and reliable
180

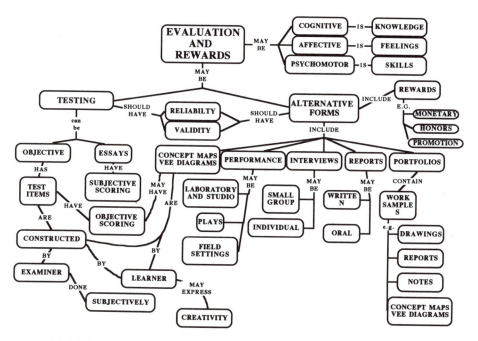

FIG. 9.1. Key ideas regarding evaluation/rewards.

measures of key variables involved in the event we are observing. In education, we can never observe and measure all relevant variables (e.g., the subject's mood at the moment of test taking) but we must strive to measure what we believe are the most important, relevant variables. Here is where a theory of education can be helpful in deciding on what to record. Specific concepts and principles relevant to the event (shown on the left side of a Vee diagram for the event) will assist us in determining key variables and appropriate measures of these variables. Refer to Fig. 9.2 and note that measurement is a way to make records of events. These may be transformed using statistics or other tools; however, the claims derived can be no better than the quality of the records we make. This is one reason why evaluation is so important.

MEASUREMENT

One of the reasons the natural sciences have advanced more rapidly than the social sciences is that the measurement of significant variables in the social sciences is much more difficult than in the natural sciences. Furthermore, the social sciences have been theory-poor and hence we have not been clear on what the key variables are that influence human thinking, feeling, and acting, to say nothing about how to measure these variables appropriately. A theory of education, including a theory of

THE KNOWLEDGE VEE

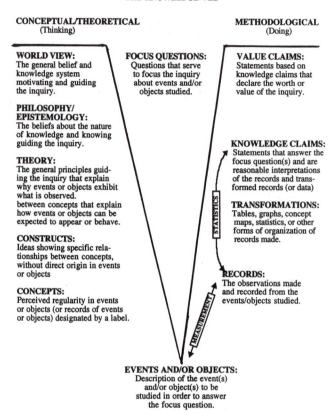

CONCEPTUAL/THEORETICAL
(Thinking)

METHODOLOGICAL
(Doing)

WORLD VIEW: The general belief and knowledge system motivating and guiding the inquiry.

FOCUS QUESTIONS: Questions that serve to focus the inquiry about events and/or objects studied.

VALUE CLAIMS: Statements based on knowledge claims that declare the worth or value of the inquiry.

PHILOSOPHY/ EPISTEMOLOGY: The beliefs about the nature of knowledge and knowing guiding the inquiry.

THEORY: The general principles guiding the inquiry that explain why events or objects exhibit what is observed. between concepts that explain how events or objects can be expected to appear or behave.

CONSTRUCTS: Ideas showing specific relationships between concepts, without direct origin in events or objects

CONCEPTS: Perceived regularity in events or objects (or records of events or objects) designated by a label.

KNOWLEDGE CLAIMS: Statements that answer the focus question(s) and are reasonable interpretations of the records and transformed records (or data)

TRANSFORMATIONS: Tables, graphs, concept maps, statistics, or other forms of organization of records made.

STATISTICS

RECORDS: The observations made and recorded from the events/objects studied.

MEASUREMENT

EVENTS AND/OR OBJECTS: Description of the event(s) and/or object(s) to be studied in order to answer the focus question.

FIG. 9.2. The Vee heuristic can serve to illustrate ideas presented in this module.

learning, can do much to bring clarity and specification to the assessment of human characteristics and thus contribute to the advance of measurement in education, business, and in the social sciences in general.

According to *A Theory of Education* (Novak, 1977a), the most important factor influencing humans is the extent to which meaningful learning has occurred and well differentiated, hierarchical cognitive structure has developed. Most of this learning is domain specific, that is, it relates to knowledge in specific subject matter areas. There is also some learning that transcends knowledge domains and concerns what we know about learning strategies, problem-solving strategies and similar metacognitive knowledge, and this has been only poorly measured in the past.

Based on my theory, our central concern in evaluation of cognitive learning should be with the ability of the test instrument to assess the conceptual and propositional frameworks held by the subject, or the extent to which knowledge is learned substantively and nonarbitrarily, which is the case in meaningful learning. Test items that require no more than recall or recognition of specific information may be adequate for evaluation of rote learning but they fail to assess the extent to which functional conceptual frameworks have been established or modified by the learner. It is the latter that influence and give power for future learning, problem solving, and creativity.

Records are often transformed to produce graphs tables or charts, often with the use of statistical tools. These transformations also need to be guided by theory.

TESTING

The Objective Test

Every student in education programs learns that there are objective tests and subjective tests. Multiple-choice or true–false tests are examples of objective tests, and short-answer or essay exams are examples of subjective tests, the latter being subjective because the evaluator must make a subjective judgment on the accuracy and appropriateness of the response. What is seldom discussed is the highly subjective process by which objective test items are constructed. The test maker chooses the specific subject matter to be covered, the exact wording of the question, and the exact wording of the choices in multiple-choice exams. Although there are strategies for evaluating the extent to which various domains of subject matter are sampled by a given objective test, and item analysis techniques for identifying test items that may have a faulty structure, the bottom line is that the test maker subjectively decides what will be accepted as correct answers. Only the scoring is objective; that is, the testee chooses the right answer as judged by the test writer or the answer is marked wrong.

Let us consider for a moment what this means. In general, it means that the meaning of the content tested must be expressed in the exact words of the test maker. If the testee constructs his or her meanings in a somewhat different, but equally valid, form, the answer chosen may be wrong. Look at this example from a national achievement test:

Is each of the following foods rich in protein?

(a) lettuce   yes   no

(b) fruit   yes   no

The correct answer is "no" for each of these items because the bulk of these two foods is water and, compared with meats or eggs, the amount of protein per serving is low (poor). However, a student may know that lettuce and fruits are made of cells and that except for the cell walls and the water and sugars in the cells, much of the remaining substance in these foods is protein. This would be good reasoning, but it could lead to the wrong answer. This is the kind of reasoning that Hoffman (1962) argued goes unrewarded. The kind of thinking that is rewarded is rote memorization of the four food groups and that a high level of protein is found in the meat and eggs group whereas the fruit and vegetable group is high in fiber and vitamins. Too often, objective tests, even those that are comparatively well designed, tend to encourage verbatim, nonsubstantive, and arbitrary memorization of information. The typical teacher-made test too often penalizes the meaningful learner who has constructed their idiosyncratic but valid meanings for a domain of knowledge. Unfortunately, national standardized tests and textbook tests are not much better, and Holden (1992) reported that "95% of the items in school math tests rely on 'lower level thinking skills' such as memorization, and fail to measure 'higher order' functions that are involved in creative problem solving" (p. 541). In reviewing proposed new test items recently for a national exam, I raised the same concerns to the test makers.

Two of the concepts of measurement that enter into testing are reliability and validity. Reliability is the extent to which a test assesses a given domain of knowledge consistently. A test is reliable when individuals with the same fund of knowledge obtain the same scores, or if a given individual obtains the same score when the exam is repeated with no change of knowledge occurring between tests. Obviously, the conditions needed for these situations are almost impossible to establish, so more commonly, reliability is estimated by methods such as computing the correlation between frequency of correct answers on even-numbered items with the answers on odd-numbered items. Unfortunately, if subjects were guessing on answers for all items, we could get a high correlation between right or wrong answers on odd, compared with even, items, but the reliability coefficient obtained would have little value on assessing the reliability of the test.

Validity is the extent to which test items assess the competencies they are intended to assess. There are no easy ways to establish the validity of a test. A common practice is to solicit expert judgment on individual items or the test as a whole. Although this practice has merit, it is very difficult to judge the validity of a given test item or test without knowing what specific instruction was given, the prior knowledge of testees before instruction, and the conditions or context in which the test was or will be given. Another method of assessing test validity is to determine the correlations of scores on the test with scores on some other test that is assumed to be a valid test of the same or similar abilities. Thus we may see claims that a given achievement test is valid because it has significant correlation with IQ test scores. There are at least two problems with this kind of correlational validity. First, even relatively low correlations (commonly $r = 0.2$ to $r = 0.4$) will be statistically significant with large sample groups. But we need to recognize that the amount of variation in test scores that one test predicts for another test is only equal to the correlation coefficient squared, or 4% to 16% in our example. What accounts for the remaining 84% to 96% of variation in test scores? God only knows. A second problem is that a high correlation coefficient (say $r = 0.8$ to 0.9) only means that the two tests tend to be measuring the same competencies, but both could be poorly measuring the true competencies we seek to assess! We are back to a judgment call on the validity of both tests. Typical multiple choice tests often show validity problems (cf. Glanz, 1996).

Another problem that is too often ignored by educators is that the distribution of scores on any test is a function of the competence of the testees and the item difficulties. Item difficulty is the percent of testees who pass a given item, now more frequently referred to as *item ease*. A test item with a high percentage of testees answering correctly has a high ease value (and a high item difficulty value). Based on experience with a set of test items administered to similar sample groups over time, it is possible to establish item ease values that will show stability for a pool of test items. We can then select test items that will produce almost any score distribution we desire. Figure 9.3 shows the score distribution using a test with many items with high ease index, and Fig. 9.4 shows the expected score distribution for the sample group of testees for many items with a low ease index. In practice, tests are usually designed to produce a normal curve, using test items with items having a range of ease indices from relatively low to relatively high.

Selection of items with various ease values can affect the validity of a test. For example, if we construct a test with test items of relatively low-ease values, the test can be a good (valid) measure of the excellent and good testees but a poor measure of the competencies of the average or below-average testees (see Fig. 9.4). We are

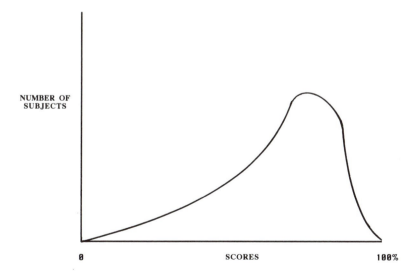

FIG. 9.3. Score distribution obtained when many test items are easy, that is, have high ease values or item difficulty values.

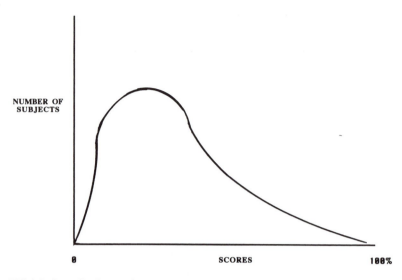

FIG. 9.4. Score distribution obtained when many test items are hard, that is, have low ease values or item difficulty values.

not good at assessing their competencies relative to others in their group. Their scores are bunched up at the low end of the distribution. On the other hand, such a test might have higher validity for selecting the top 10% of a group who should participate in gifted programs. The reverse selection of items might be effective for selecting students to receive remedial help.

Given the wide recognition of problems with conventional testing, one would expect that there would be a concerted effort to write better tests. The problem is that test items that require higher levels of understanding and thinking are usually missed by most students, with the result that these items have zero discriminability. That is, they fail to separate those students who know more from those students who know less. Test made up with such items would give essentially a chance score distribution and lack both validity and reliability. In 1956, Bloom proposed a taxonomy of educational objectives, wherein test items that measure only rote recall of specifics were rated as 1.0 level items and items that required synthesis or evaluation were rated as 5.0 or 6.0 items, respectively. Most studies of the taxonomy levels of most tests show that overwhelmingly, the test's items rank only 1 or 2 on Bloom's taxonomy. For example, a million dollar study supported by the National Science Foundation found that close to 95% of test items used in school math tests relied on lower-level thinking skills and failed to measure higher order functions that are involved in creative problem solving (Holden, 1992). There exists what I like to refer to as the *psychometric trap*—tests items that require higher levels of thinking will produce results that show little or no discriminability among students, and hence must be rejected. Thus we perpetuate the testing problems decried by so many thoughtful and critical observers.

There are other ways to make objective tests more effective. Much research has been done on common misconceptions (or faulty conceptions) of students, especially in sciences and mathematics (Helms & Novak, 1983; Novak, 1987a; Novak & Abrams, 1993). These studies have identified concepts and concept relationships that interfere with or do not permit valid interpretations of certain events. It is possible to design multiple-choice test items that give alternative answers that are wrong, but appear valid to testees with specific misconceptions. The result can be a test that can produces below-chance scores (below 20% on five-choice, multiple-choice items) for testees and still have high validity and reliability. For example, Sadler (1995) found that when test items in astronomy were developed using as alternative answers statements of common misconceptions held by students, even items with low difficulties can be very discriminating. Furthermore, he found that when student performance on a given item is plotted against student ability, students of low ability may actually perform better than students of nearly average ability. This pattern was repeated on the majority of the 47 test items given to a large sample of school students. What the data indicates is that, as students gain some pertinent information, they may actually strengthen their misconceptions and perform more poorly (see Fig. 9.5). The data also call for careful sequencing of concepts taught to minimize that latter problem and enhance overall achievement. Objective test data can be useful in curriculum design when the kind of sophisticated item analysis is done as is illustrated in Sadler's work.

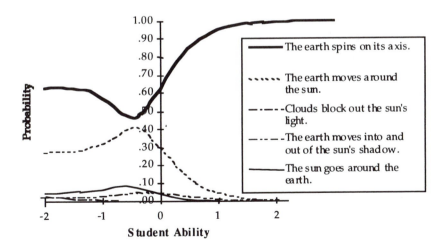

FIG. 9.5. Average ability students may perform more poorly than low ability students on test items that are designed to include common misconceptions that arise from partial knowledge of what causes day and night. From Sadler, 1995. Reprinted with permission.

Likert Scales

A common type of testing where there may not be right or wrong answers but rather expressions of feelings or attitudes was devised by Likert (1932). In this form of testing, testees are given statements to which they may reply on a scale, usually 1 through 5 or "strongly agree" to "strongly disagree." For example, one of the Likert scales we devised dealing with preferences for learning approaches contain these items:

I try to relate new material, as I am reading it, to what I already know on that topic. (SA = meaningful learner)	SD	D	U	A	SA
I prefer to follow well tried out approaches to problems rather than trying anything too adventurous. (SA = rote learner)	SD	D	U	A	SA
While I am studying, I often think of real life situations to which the material I am learning would be useful. (SA = meaningful learner)	SD	D	U	A	SA
I find I tend to remember things best if I concentrate on the order in which the teacher or book presented them. (SA = rote learner)	SD	D	U	A	SA

It is not easy to determine why a given individual chooses to agree or disagree with a statement, but validation of Likert scales can be achieved by doing interviews on a sample of the target population to ascertain whether or not the testees' belief structure is being accurately assessed by the test items. Our experience, in a variety of studies using Likert scales, is that they are at best limited in their validity for assessing individuals' beliefs about their learning preferences, views on the nature of science, tendency to believe they control their destinies, and similar attitude or preference measures. Nevertheless, compiling the direction of preferences of an individual on 10 or more Likert items can have predictive validity on, for example, how that person will approach learning in a given domain. Bretz (1994) found that students with Likert-scale preferences for rote-learning approaches described their learning strategies as essentially rote in interviews, and the reverse was true for students who showed meaningful learning preferences in a college chemistry course designed to help students understand and approach the science of chemistry.

Meaningful learners generally performed better in the course than rote learners, especially on those test items that required novel applications of knowledge.

Likert scales were first developed to assess feelings and they continue to be useful in this way. For example, Alaiyemola, Jegede, and Okebukola (1990) used such tests of student anxiety to study the effect of concept mapping on the reduction of anxiety. They found that students using concept mapping showed significantly lower anxiety toward science study compared with nonmapping students after a 6-week treatment of learning selected science topics. Although these findings may not generalize to study of other science topics, the findings do point to the positive affective results from use of a strategy that can facilitate meaningful learning. We see affirmation here of the theory put forth in this book.

Up to this point, I have focused on tests for cognitive learning and tests that involve feelings or affective learning. There are also tests for our actions or psychomotor learning, but these are usually quite different in character. Figure 9.6 illustrates the range of concepts and principles involved in measurement, and I shall turn next to other forms of evaluation, some of which are commonly called

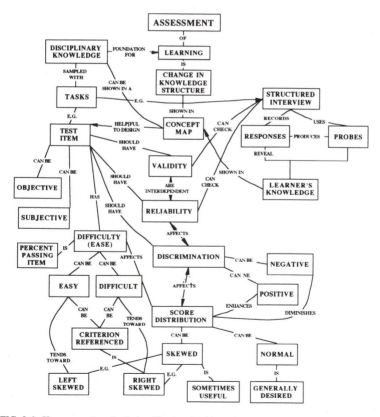

FIG. 9.6. Key concepts and relationships involved in understanding measurement.

alternative assessment that are discused later (see, e.g., example, Herman, Asch-bacher & Winters, 1992).

OTHER FORMS OF EVALUATION

Performance Evaluation

Perhaps the most common performance evaluation faced by people in developed countries is the test for a driver's license. Usually a written test is first required and the knowledge needed to pass this exam, together with test-taking skills, have only limited relevance to the driving test. Skillful, experienced drivers sometimes fail the written portion of the exam. This suggests, in part, a need to improve the kind of written exams given to qualify for a driver's license. Because thinking, feeling, and acting must be constructively integrated to be a skillful driver, or to perform any psychomotor task skillfully, it should be possible to design written tests that better match the cognitive and attitudinal attributes associated with skillful driving.

Music, art, architecture, photography, dance, and all sports are domains where performance evaluation predominates and usually identify the distinguished from the undistinguished performer. But it is important to recognize the crucial support-ing role that cognition and affect or feelings play in skillful performance. The successful performers must get their thoughts and feelings organized, as Herrigel (1973) so nicely described in *Zen and the Art of Archery.*

One of our graduate students, Nadborn (see Novak & Gowin, 1984), found that when his junior varsity basketball team developed concept maps to better under-stand and communicate, their game performance went from a previous 3 win and 8 loss record to 8 wins and 3 losses. Smith (1992) found that when students in nursing were asked to prepare concept maps and review a Vee diagram for each week's instruction in nursing skills, they performed 7 out of 10 skills significantly better than students not using these learning tools. Baranga (1990) found that fifth-grade students who prepared concept maps prior to writing stories and poems performed at levels much beyond the typical student performance at that age.

The use of metacognitive tools for enhancing performance is still a rare event, and I believe this is a highly promising area for research and educational develop-ment. Currently we are working with research teams with each member employing concept maps and Vee diagrams to conceptualize their research. Preliminary data suggest substantial enhancement of research productivity. Given the importance of knowledge creation in both academic and corporate settings (Drucker, 1993), research that shows substantive enhancement in new knowledge production by individuals instructed in the use of metacognitive tools could be even more exciting than the results that have been found in enhancement of school learning.

One of the fields in which performance testing has been utilized commonly is in the health sciences. Some of our work with nursing students was discussed previously. On the surface, it would appear self evident that performance tests would have high validity because they require subjects to perform the kind of tasks that subsequent application of their learning will necessitate. However, testing is always to some extent a contrived experience, and when one takes into account the problems of scoring or ranking performance, this type of evaluation can also be problematic. Swanson, Norman, and Linn (1995) presented a concise synopsysis of lessons that have been learned from work in the health professions. Their lessons are shown in Table 9.1.

It is evident from the issues cited in Table 9.1 that performance testing is not without its problems. Whether in the school or the workplace, more care and attention is needed when performance testing is used for assessment, especially

Table 9.1

Lessons Learned In the Health Professions
Regarding Performance Testing

Lesson 1:	The fact that examinees are tested in realistic performance situations does not make test design and domain sampling simple and straightforward. Sampling must consider both context (situation/task) and construct (knowledge/skill) dimensions, and complex interactions are present between these dimensions.
Lesson 2:	No matter how realistic a performance-based assessment is, it is still a simulation, and examinees do not behave in the same way they would in real life.
Lesson 3:	Although high-fidelity performance-based assessment methods often yield rich and interesting examinee behavior, scoring that rich and interesting behavior can be problematic. It is difficult to develop scoring keys that appropriately reward alternate answers that are equivalent in quality, both because of poor consensus on scoring keys and because of scoring artifacts resulting from variation in response style.
Lesson 4:	Regardless of the assessment method used, performance in one context (typically, a patient case) does not predict performance in other contexts very well. In-depth assessment in a few areas results in scores that are not sufficiently reproducible for use in high-stakes testing.
Lesson 5:	Correlational studies of the relationship between performance-based test scores and other assessment methods targeting different skills typically produce variable and uninterpretable results. Validation work should emphasize study of threats to the validity of score interpretation, not general relationships with other measures.
Lesson 6:	Because performance-based assessment methods are often complex to administer, multiple test forms and test administrations are required to test large numbers of examinees. Because these tests typically consist of a relatively small number of independent tasks, this poses formidable equating and security problems.
Lesson 7:	All high-stakes assessments, regardless of the method used, have an impact on teaching and learning. The nature of this impact is not necessarily predictable, and careful studies of (intended and unintended) benefits and side-effects are obviously desirable but rarely done.
Lesson 8:	Neither traditional testing nor performance-based assessment methods are a panacea. Selection of assessment methods should depend on the skills to be assessed, and generally, use of a blend of methods is desirable.

when the assessment is the basis for determining promotion or rewards of any consequence.

Concept Maps

I have shown in earlier chapters examples of concept maps that we have used in our research and teaching projects. Concept maps were developed by our research group to meet a need for an evaluation tool that can show easily and precisely changes in students' conceptual understanding. I now routinely use concept maps as an evaluation tool in my own courses. Figure 9.7 shows an example of a concept map prepared by a student in my course, Theory and Methods of Education.

What is evident in Fig. 9.7 is that an enormous amount of knowledge is represented. My approach is to provide students with a list of 20 to 30 concepts and ask them to map these, adding at least 10 or 20 more concepts of their choosing. This, of course, is a fairly demanding task, and I often give these as take-home exams. The construction of the map requires considerable creativity in organizing the structure of the map, selecting important, relevant concepts to add to the map and searching out salient cross-links, indicating relationships between concepts in different sections of the map. Needless to say, the map becomes an important learning experience for my students as well as a unique evaluation experience. Of course, one must give students weeks of practice and constructive feedback in building smaller concept maps, and maps of the size shown would be inappropriate for elementary school students. Those teachers in secondary schools and tertiary schools who use comprehensive concept mapping assignments for end-of-year evaluations report positive results both in terms of comprehensiveness in evaluating learning and in terms of students' affective responses.

One of the problems of traditional testing is that true–false or multiple-choice exams can never sample more than a small portion of the relevant knowledge considered in the instruction. Try to guess at how many multiple-choice questions would be required to evaluate students' ability to understand and relate all the concepts and propositions shown in Fig. 9.7. Furthermore, there would be no opportunity for students to show how they organized their knowledge nor the creativity demonstrated in selection of additional concepts included in the map organization. In my view, concept maps are the most powerful evaluation tool available to educators, but they can be used only when they are also first used to facilitate learning. Perhaps by 2050 we shall see widespread and worldwide application of this tool in busines and also in education.

There are the issues of reliability and validity that need to be addressed with use of concept maps. The validity issue is relatively transparent because it is obvious that the fundamental characteristics of constructivist learning is exemplified in a well constructed concept map. For any competent evaluator, it is relatively easy to see if propositions indicated on the map are valid and to determine if the superordinate/subordinate nature of concepts in the structure makes sense.

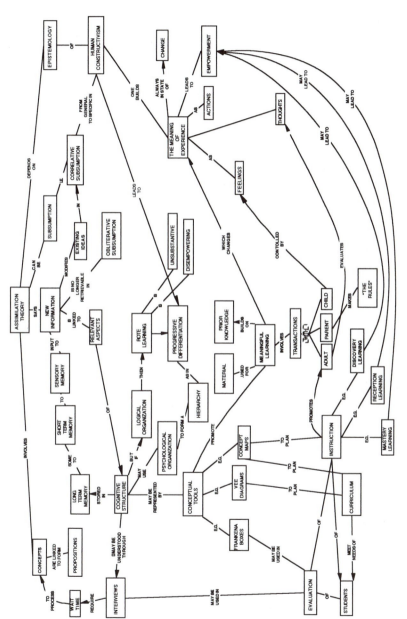

FIG. 9.7. A concept map constructed by a student for a mid-term examination in my course, Theory and Methods of Education. Thirty concept labels were given, and students were asked to supply additional concepts to complete their map.

It is now generally agreed among researchers that changes in learners' conceptual frameworks may be most thoroughly evaluated by use of clinical interviews. The problem is that use of interviews for evaluation requires skilled interviewers and relatively costly interviewer time. There remains the problem of the interpretation of the knowledge expressed in interviews; in fact, this problem led our research group to devise the concept mapping tool. We have also developed a variety of scoring algorithms to give numerical scores to concept maps, permitting statistical tests and comparison with other tests (Novak & Gowin, 1984). Scoring a concept map, when scoring criteria have been established, requires only 3 to 10 minutes, depending on the complexity of the map (Ruiz–Primo & Shavelson, 1996). If interviews remain the gold standard for evaluation of cognitive structures, how does the concept map compare? Edwards and Fraser (1983) showed that concept maps constructed by students were as revealing of their knowledge structures as clinical interviews of students. Over the past 2 decades, in dozens of studies by our research group and other researchers, concept maps have been shown to be highly reliable assessment instruments.

An obvious advantage in using concept maps for evaluation is the ease with which new tests can be devised. By simply adding or subtracting one third or so of the concepts from the list of concepts to be mapped by students, a new test has been devised. As already noted, it is comparatively easy to cover large domains of knowledge with opportunity for creative expression. Although there is some subjectivity in scoring the maps, the great freedom given to individuals to demonstrate their idiosyncratic meanings for the subject matter removes an important source of bias and subjectivity that is present when the test writer chooses the specific content and form in which answers must be selected. One of the powerful attributes of using concept maps for instruction and evaluation is the extent to which they encourage meaningful learning and discourage rote learning. In one of our studies, Gurley–Dilger (1982) asked her school psychologist to interview members of her class regarding their thoughts and feelings on her use of concept maps with instruction in high school biology. The following are some quotations from the psychologist's interview:

"Given a choice, well I probably wouldn't do it. I don't like doing ' em, but . . . the map shows out the more important things."

"I always use my maps. If you just read the book it's different 'cause you might not see the main point of the chapter and how it all fits together. Concept maps are easier to understand. It puts it a different way than the book says it. It gives you the concepts in your own way. They're worth the time—it's easier to learn, for me."

"I can't use concept maps. I'd rather read the chapter over and over. Concept maps are more work. It's different than memorizing—it's all related."

"Concept maps are hard to study from. When you're doing it though, you're sorta studying it. If ya make 'em good they can help you. They make ya read the book. I'd rather not do them." (Gurley–Dilger, 1982, p. 155)

We see that in general, students recognized the value of concept maps both as a learning tool and a tool evaluating their learning. Also evident is that it is hard work to construct your own meanings and a minority of her students preferred just to memorize information. After years of school practices that emphasize the latter, it is not surprising to see that students find taking responsibility for constructing their own meanings to be challenging—but most also see this as rewarding. Unfortunately, we have found some of the greatest resistance to use of concept maps among medical students for whom meaningful learning is essential if they are to perform competently. Their previous successes with rote-learning approaches make them very insecure in moving to meaningful learning strategies.

Vee Diagrams for Evaluation

As with concept maps, Vee diagrams are both a tool to facilitate learning and a tool for evaluation. Their use is especially appropriate when the focus of interest is on an event, such as a demonstration, performance, laboratory or field event, or any creative event. For example, in some of my courses I ask students to construct a Vee diagram for their class project. The usual events I ask them to create are interviews with subjects on any topic they choose with any kind of sample group they choose. Figure 9.8 is an example of a Vee diagram created by one of my students. The Vee diagram presents the ideas that guided the inquiry on left side, and a summary of the results on the right side. The student planned to be a dairy farmer, hence the choice of the topic.

Vee diagrams help learners recognize the complexity and also the basic simplicity of the knowledge construction process. If done thoughtfully and with reflection, they help learners see that every element interacts with and influences every other element and all are necessary for understanding how and why we construct the knowledge claims and value claims for the focus question(s). Vees can be very successfully employed in group settings. They allow for creative expression, partly by the selection of salient elements on the left side, in construction of the focus question(s), description of the event(s) observed, and description of the elements on the right side. Although the basic form of the Vee is given, and hence students often report that Vees are easier to construct than concept maps, the Vee is more comprehensive. In fact, one can incorporate a concept map in the Vee to represent concepts, constructs, principles, and theory on the left side of the Vee.

The very comprehensiveness of the Vee may explain in part why Vee diagrams are currently less popular than concept maps, both as a learning tool and as an evaluation tool. As noted in chapter 6, the pervasive positivism in schools and even

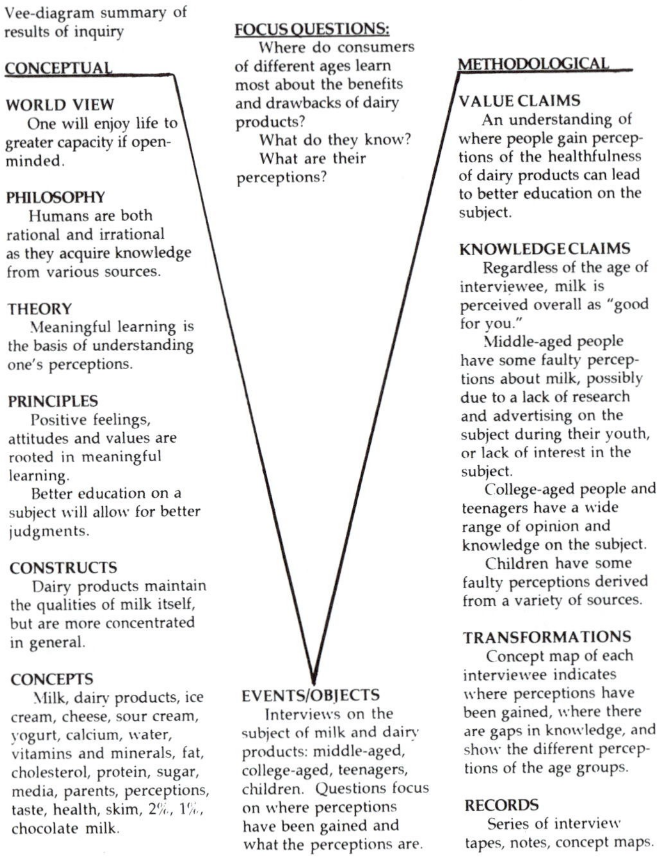

Vee-diagram summary of
results of inquiry

CONCEPTUAL

WORLD VIEW
One will enjoy life to
greater capacity if open-
minded.

PHILOSOPHY
Humans are both
rational and irrational
as they acquire knowledge
from various sources.

THEORY
Meaningful learning is
the basis of understanding
one's perceptions.

PRINCIPLES
Positive feelings,
attitudes and values are
rooted in meaningful
learning.
Better education on a
subject will allow for better
judgments.

CONSTRUCTS
Dairy products maintain
the qualities of milk itself,
but are more concentrated
in general.

CONCEPTS
Milk, dairy products, ice
cream, cheese, sour cream,
yogurt, calcium, water,
vitamins and minerals, fat,
cholesterol, protein, sugar,
media, parents, perceptions,
taste, health, skim, 2%, 1%,
chocolate milk.

FOCUS QUESTIONS:
Where do consumers
of different ages learn
most about the benefits
and drawbacks of dairy
products?
What do they know?
What are their
perceptions?

EVENTS/OBJECTS
Interviews on the
subject of milk and dairy
products: middle-aged,
college-aged, teenagers,
children. Questions focus
on where perceptions
have been gained and
what the perceptions are.

METHODOLOGICAL

VALUE CLAIMS
An understanding of
where people gain percep-
tions of the healthfulness
of dairy products can lead
to better education on the
subject.

KNOWLEDGE CLAIMS
Regardless of the age of
interviewee, milk is
perceived overall as "good
for you."
Middle-aged people
have some faulty percep-
tions about milk, possibly
due to a lack of research
and advertising on the
subject during their youth,
or lack of interest in the
subject.
College-aged people and
teenagers have a wide
range of opinion and
knowledge on the subject.
Children have some
faulty perceptions derived
from a variety of sources.

TRANSFORMATIONS
Concept map of each
interviewee indicates
where perceptions have
been gained, where there
are gaps in knowledge, and
show the different perceptions of the age groups.

RECORDS
Series of interview
tapes, notes, concept maps.

FIG. 9.8. A Vee diagram constructed by one of my students in the course, Learning To Learn.
This Vee shows the ideas used to plan and evaluate subjects on their knowledge of dairy
products.

in research laboratories tends to make use of the Vee as a learning and evaluation
tool less attractive to many. Using the Vee heuristic with enthusiasm requires a
commitment to constructivism, not only of the trivial kind that recognizes learners
must construct their own knowledge, but also the radical kind (to use von Glasersfeld's, 1984, terms) that recognizes the tentative and evolving nature of knowledge.

Referring again to the work of Gurley–Dilger (1982), the following are some
quotations from interviews with her students by her school psychologist:

"I don't like them. I'd rather have lab questions. They're easy. I guess you understand
what you're doing better with a Vee."

"You learn the stuff you need to talk about on the left side. The Vee helps me remember 'cause I write it all out. I don't mind Vees. They're easy and don't take a lot of time."

"I get more out of lab using a Vee. Not these lab questions. Vees are easy once you get used to it. Questions you could just skim, Vees make you tie everything together and work on it." (p. 160)

We see again that students regard construction of their own meanings to be challenging—but also rewarding. In the several dozen studies carried out by our research group at Cornell University and increasingly by colleagues at other universities and school systems, similar results are being reported not only in science learning but also in the study of literature (Baranga, 1990; Moreira, 1977), mathematics (Fuata'i, 1985; Kahn, 1994), and other fields.

Reports

In all of my courses, I require each student to prepare oral and/or written reports using data from an inquiry designed by the student. Typically, reports count 40 to 50% of the grade with concept maps and other work assignments comprising the remaining 50 to 60 %. In smaller classes (30 or fewer), I usually require oral reports partly because I believe students need more opportunity to prepare and make presentations to a group. Their oral reports on their project work is typical of the kind of reports they may need to make in almost any white collar employment and increasingly in blue collar employment as well. Oral reports consume class time, so one must consider the value of time used this way, compared with other class activities. Written reports require considerable time for students to prepare and for the evaluator to read. For educators working with large groups (50 or more), both oral and written reports may be impractical unless special time allowances are made or competent assistance in evaluation is available.

It is necessary to provide learners with clear and sufficient guidance as to how to prepare their reports and how to deliver them. Samples of reports done by previous groups can be helpful as well, and I usually make available both exemplary reports and reports that might have been improved, including remarks that indicate why the reports were evaluated as they were. I also use video tape to illustrate good oral presentations (with permission of the presenters). As with any evaluation, ambiguity regarding the standards for excellence have negative attitudinal consequences and diminish performance. If we want learners to demonstrate clearly their successes in constructing meanings and presenting these new meanings, they need guidance and assistance, as well as practice to do this well.

One can raise validity issues regarding reports. There is the obvious concern with the bias of the evaluator, but there are also issues regarding the comparative skills of individuals to deliver written and/or oral reports. We face decisions that we must recognize as value decisions that must be confronted in education. How can we raise the level of written and oral expression of learners unless we require written and oral expression in our evaluation programs? There are ways to recognize individual differences in these abilities and to ameliorate the potentially disempowering effects of unrealistic standards for learners who come from cultures where written and oral expression in English is inordinately demanding. To evade or ignore these issues is to shortchange the futures of our students and also to contribute to a decline in the competence and competitiveness of the American work force. The long-term result is a lowering in the standard of living enjoyed by Americans, a trend already in progress and contributing to a growing sense of frustration and lowered aspirations of American youth. (See, e.g., Marshall & Tucker, 1992; Senge, 1990).

Portfolio Evaluation

In brief, portfolios are collections of learners' work used to demonstrate their competencies. They may include artwork, compositions, music (written or recorded), videos of performance, concept maps, Vee diagrams, and a host of other products of the learner's efforts. The validity issue disappears when portfolios allow for a full range of evidence of the learner's thinking, feeling, and acting. In practice, portfolios may be required that present a more restricted sample of work, and hence selective bias is introduced.

The reliability of the assessment issue hinges on the extent to which the learner has the resources to consistently produce the work samples requested and the competence of the evaluator to judge the work samples. One must carefully consider these issues when portfolios are employed as a substantial element in the evaluation process. Race, culture, socioeconomic status, and gender differences could introduce highly significant biases, both in opportunity to produce portfolio materials and in their evaluation. Nevertheless, because they are real work samples of the learner and can bear a close relationship to the kinds of competencies required in real world settings, portfolios need to be included as at least part of any comprehensive evaluation programs.

Martin, Miller, and Delago (1995) reported on a study done in California involving some 500 science teachers and reviewed 4,000 portfolios. Teachers attended two statewide portfolio training and development sessions, as well as regional implementation meetings, and they also participated in scoring portfolios. Students were asked to submit three portfolio entries dealing with real world applications of science concepts. In general, there was good consensus between two independent raters for each portfolio. They found that female students obtained higher scores than males, in contrast to score averages on a multiple choice type test, where male students scored slightly higher. Ethnicity did not show differences between performance on portfolios and other measures of performance, although there were not sufficient numbers of portfolios submitted by African-Americans to make statistical comparisons. Portfolio scores correlated $r = 0.3$ with multiple choice test scores in chemistry, and $r = 0.4$ with biology test scores. Thus, some 84 to 91% of variance in portfolio scores was not accounted for in multiple choice test scores. Clearly, portfolio performance gave students a good alternative way to express their understanding of science.

Unfortunately, using portfolios as an evaluation tool as well as a method of instruction requires more work on the part of the teacher. Students often need more guidance, schedules need to allow for library work or work off of the school premises, and grading cannot be done by simply comparing answers with those on a scoring key. Unless use of portfolios is adopted as part of a school's policy and standard curriculum, it is not likely to be adopted and continued over time.

A variant on typical portfolio evaluation is the use of computers to generate electronic documents that combine information, pictures, video clips, and so forth into a composite electronic portfolio. Krajcik, Spitulnik, and Zembal (in press) reported good success in using this technique with high school science students and preservice teachers. Of course, this form of instruction/evaluation requires that students have access to relatively good computers, Internet connections, and instructors competent to guide them. The potential for such instruction and evaluation will increase exponentially with advances in computers and information highways. However, we are looking at instructional practices that will require more resources and teachers motivated and competent to lead this kind of work. It will probably be a few decades before these capabilities become commonplace in public schools.

AUTHENTIC ASSESSMENT

There has been substantial criticism in recent years of traditional testing practices together with documentation on the low predictive validity of tests as indicators of real world performance or competence. This has lead to a call for more authentic assessment. Wiggins (1989) identified a number of characteristics of authentic tests, as shown in Table 9.2. Reviewing these characteristics, one would have to conclude that authentic testing is certainly the way to go! The problem is that it is extraordinarily difficult to implement the kind of evaluation program that would achieve many of these characteristics. Portfolios and performance tests would have some of these characteristics, but as we have seen earlier, these are not easy to implement, nor are they trouble-free. Puckett and Black (1994), who cite Wiggins' work, provided a good handbook of practices, but they also had no easy answers to achieve authentic assessment.

Although concept maps and Vee diagrams are no panacea for authentic assessment, they satisfy many of the criteria for such evaluation, and if they are also used as instructional tools, they can be highly effective at any level of schooling. They can also be effective in business settings when used in conjunction with various forms of data collection regarding consumer knowledge and interests, or as self-

TABLE 9.2

Characteristics of Authentic Tests[*]

A.	**Structure and Logistics**
1.	Are more appropriately public; involve an audience, a panel, and so on.
2.	Do not rely on unrealistic and arbitrary time constraints.
3.	Offer known, not secret, questions or tasks.
4.	Are more like portfolios or a *season* of games (not one-shot).
5.	Require some collaboration with others.
6.	Recur—and are *worth* practicing for, rehearsing, and retaking.
7.	Make assessment and feedback to students so central that school schedules and policies are modified to support them.
B.	**Intellectual Design Features**
1.	Are "essential"—not needlessly intrusive, arbitrary, or contrived to "shake out" a grade.
2.	Are "enabling"—constructed to point the student toward more sophisticated use of the skills or knowledge.
3.	Are contextualized, complex intellectual challenges, not "atomized" tasks, corresponding to isolated "outcomes."
4.	Involve the student's own research or use of knowledge, for which "content" is a means.
5.	Assess student habits and repertoires, not mere recall or plug-in skills.
6.	Are *representative* challenges—designed to emphasize *depth* more than breadth.
7.	Are engaging and educational.
8.	Involve somewhat ambiguous ("ill-structured") tasks or problems.
C.	**Grading and Scoring Standards**
1.	Involve criteria that assess essentials, not easily counted (but relatively unimportant) errors.
2.	Are not graded on a "curve," but in reference to performance standards (criterion-referenced, not norm-referenced).
3.	Involve demystified criteria of success that appear to *students* as inherent in successful activity.
4.	Make self-assessment a part of the assessment.
5.	Use a multifaceted scoring system instead of one aggregate grade.
6.	Exhibit harmony with shared schoolwide aims—a *standard*.
D.	**Fairness and Equity**
1.	Ferret out and identify (perhaps hidden) strengths.
2.	Strike a *constantly* examined balance between honoring achievement and native skill or fortunate prior training.
3.	Minimize needless, unfair, and demoralizing comparisons.
4.	Allow appropriate room for student learning styles, aptitudes, and interests.
5.	Can be—should be—attempted by *all* students, with the test "scaffolded up," not "dumbed down," as necessary.
6.	Reverse typical test-design procedures: they make "accountability" serve student learning (Attention is primarily paid to "face" and "ecological" validity of tests).

check tools for individuals or teams working on any form of project. I expect we shall see the use of these tools increase slowly, but by the mid-21st Century, I would not be surprised to see them used widely.

Assessment problems are pervasive, profound, and in many ways, intractable. As a fifth element involved in educating, assessment cannot be treated casually, for faulty assessment practices can negate some of our best efforts at organizing and delivering knowledge to learners. It can also have devastating effects on individuals' egos, and in some cases, irreparable harm can be done. My counsel is that one can never take too seriously how best to evaluate achievement and accomplishment.

10

Improving Education in Schools and Corporations

A BASIS FOR OPTIMISM

Are Improvements in Education Possible?

In 1977, I observed in *A Theory of Education* that change in education was much like Brownian motion, as Toffler (1970) described it: constantly churning but going nowhere. I asserted then, and I would assert even more forcefully now, that this characterization is likely to persist unless educators in every educational setting, businesses as well as schools, seek to base change on a comprehensive theory of education. As noted in chapter 1, in spite of enormous increases in per-pupil expenditures on school education (even in inflation-corrected dollars), there is little evidence that schooling is improving in terms of the usual criteria of success, namely various achievement test measures. Moreover, we have noted repeatedly the limitations of standardized achievement testing and argued repeatedly that more powerful, more demanding standards of achievement are needed. One of the reasons I believe we have been making so little progress in improving education is that when our evaluation methods measure little more than trivial achievements, it is difficult to discern changes in programs that produce truly substantive changes in human understanding. We can and we must move toward the wider use of better evaluation measures.

It may have been argued that military expenditures restricted our opportunities to invest in education, but the Cold War is over now and military expenditures have declined enormously, especially in constant dollars, or as a percentage of our gross domestic product (GDP). Health care costs have soared far beyond inflation and now represent a new financial crisis; how much of these costs are a product of poor health education and preventative care and/or inadequate education of health care professionals? Welfare and crime costs, too, are at least partly a result of failed educational programs. With a prison incarceration rate in the United States of .615 per thousand, we lead other industrialized nations with six to eight times as many prisoners. The numbers for youth homicide, youth suicide, and births to unmarried White females cited by Stallings (1995) are going up exponentially (Fig. 10.1). It is difficult to estimate the societal costs of these statistics. These and Social Security and health care payments are the big-ticket items in our budget and the budgets of all developed countries. Without radical improvements in education of all kinds, none of these costs will be contained, let alone reduced. Add to the equation that since 1980 we moved from the largest creditor nation to the largest debtor nation and the fiscal crises looming on the horizon are nothing short of frightening to the informed person.

Another fact of life that permeates our lives now, but was just beginning in 1977, is the globalization of the economy. For centuries, countries have traded products and their banks have exchanged currencies. But these trades were comparatively a mere trickle in the world flow of money, goods, and services compared with that

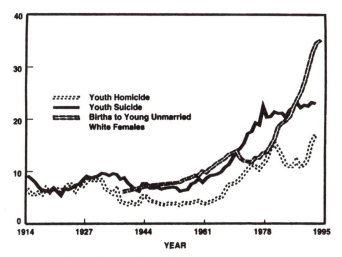

Note. Suicide and homicide deaths calculated as rates per 100,000 members of the age group 15–24 years old. Births to young unmarried White females calculated as rates per 1,000 members of the age group 15–19 years old. Numbers of left ordinate represent rates per specified number.

FIG. 10.1. Rates of White male youth homicides and suicides, 1914–1991, and births to unmarried White females, 1940–1992. From Stallings, 1995. Copyright © 1995 by the American Educational Research Association. Reproduced by permission of the publisher.

which is occurring now and what we can expect to occur in the next 2 or more decades. Just recently, the United States Congress has ratified overwhelmingly the General Agreement on Trade and Tariffs (GATT) that surely will lead to acceleration of the globalization of the economies of all developed countries and somewhat uncertain futures for the weakest economies. We are rapidly moving to a time when any product, good, or service can be produced almost anywhere and sold everywhere—if the price is right. The import of this for business can only be conjectured at this time. As Marshall and Tucker (1992) pointed out, we have entered a new economic era:

> One of America's most important advantages in the 19th and early 20th centuries was its extraordinary store of raw materials and cheap energy sources. But the steady advance of technology after the Second World War has greatly diminished our natural advantage in raw materials . . . The extent to which ideas, skills and knowledge are being substituted for natural resources is suggested by the fact that 50 to 100 pounds of fiber glass cable (made from sand) transmits as many telephone conversations as one ton of copper wire.
>
> . . . Thus human resources—ideas, skills and knowledge (have) replaced natural resources as a major source of production and wealth. (pp. 34–35)

We have not seen the last shock wave to run through the economies of the world. Nanofabrication, the new emerging technology that permits building products atom by atom from relatively inexpensive raw materials, is just in its infancy. Nobody can predict how economies will adjust to these emerging technologies, but the message is clear: The old economic rules no longer apply and the number one source of wealth in the future will be new knowledge. As Drucker (1993) asserted:

> The basic economic resource—the means of production, to use the economist's term—is no longer capital, nor natural resources (the economist's "land"), nor "labor." *It is and will be knowledge.* The central wealth-creating activities will be neither the allocation of capital to productive uses, nor "labor"—the two poles of nineteenth- and twentieth-century economic theory, whether classical, Marxist, Keynesian, or neoclassical. Value is now created by "productivity" and "innovation," both applications of knowledge to work. . . . (p. 8)

Educated in the sciences, I had grown to believe that the enormous advances in the sciences and in associated technologies derived from the explanatory and predictive power that the theories constructed by scientists permitted. Yes, some of these theories have been modified or discarded over time, but they were useful to advance the sciences when they were created. True, people do not behave as do atoms or molecules, but there are regularities in the ways people and organizations are structured and the ways in which they function. I believed it should be possible to construct a theory of education that would have explanatory and predictive power in 1977, and I am convinced now that audacious attempt has been vindicated. When *A Theory of Education* (Novak, 1977a) was first published, a close friend and respected scholar, Ned Bingham, wrote to me saying that "the theory explained why what I had learned . . . in 40 years as an educator, worked." The late scholar, Ralph Tyler, was kind enough to write a gracious foreword to the book.

Despite these good words, and translations of the book into Spanish and Portuguese, and just recently into Basc, *A Theory of Education* has not had a major impact on education in the United States or in most countries. Spain may be an exception in recent years. The theory has had a major impact on my research program and programs of some of my colleagues in this country and abroad.

There is the saying that nothing succeeds like an idea whose time has come. In retrospect, it seems clear to me now that educators were not ready for, nor did they desperately need, a theory of education. Older educational practices, rooted largely in the now discredited behavioral psychology (see Brown, 1994) seemed to be good enough to carry on the business of education, not only in schools but also in the professions and in corporations. But as another saying goes, we are in a new ball game! The accelerating globalization of the world economies is putting new demands on education of all people. As Marshall and Tucker (1992) observed:

> The new forms of work organization will not work unless management understands that it is just as important for front-line workers to learn constantly and to put that learning to work as it is for management. By learning enough to take over many functions previously reserved for management, they not only contribute directly to great productivity improvements, but they also reduce the compartmentalization of the organization, which once again increases the organization's learning capacity. In all these ways, the learning organization makes possible gains in quality and productivity that are not achievable in any other way. And, ultimately, it makes it possible for modern societies to substitute ideas, skills, and knowledge for physical resources. (p. 102)

It is not enough for individuals in an organization to learn. The organization as a whole must also be a learning organism. Commenting on the fact that one third of the Fortune 500 companies in 1970 had vanished by 1983, Senge (1990) observed:

> What if high corporate mortality rate is only a symptom of deeper problems that afflict *all* companies, not just the ones that die? What if even the most successful companies are poor learners—they survive but never live up to their potential? What if, in the light of what *could* be, "excellence" is actually "mediocrity"?
>
> It is no accident that most organizations learn poorly. The way they are designed and managed, and the way we have all been taught to think and interact (not only in organizations but more broadly) create fundamental learning disabilities. (pp. 17–18)

The ideas and tools presented in this book are as relevant to individual learners as to organizations that seek to learn. They are now being applied to some organizations in the United States and abroad.

To return to the question in the title of this section, I believe that the examples presented in this book suggest a resounding "yes!" to the question, "Are improvements in education possible?" I have tried to show how theoretical ideas can guide and accelerate the process of improvement of education in every kind of setting. Furthermore, I believe the economic pressures will force substantive changes in schools in the next few decades. Schools cannot do this alone, and corporations cannot become highly effective knowledge creating and knowledge utilizing organizations without better schools. A new partnership in creating, sharing, and using new educational ideas is needed. An overview of the ideas presented in this chapter is shown in Fig. 10.2.

IMPROVING ORGANIZATIONS

School Organization

In most countries, school policies are established by the national government. In the United States, responsibility for education is delegated to the states, with the exception of special programs such as school lunch programs. States provide financial support together with support from local communities and also set policies on licensure for teachers, administrators, and other school personnel. In general, licensure policies deal with college course credit hours rather than broad intellectual competencies and skills. Thus certain courses are required for various specializations. This rigidity in licensure policies is perhaps the major deterrent to creative programs for educators, but the rigidity of schools of education and other agencies preparing educators can be equally stagnating. There are efforts to break away from these conventions, such as the Coalition of Essential Schools, headquartered at Brown University. Some states have relaxed restrictions to allow for experimental programs in Essential Schools, and some colleges are collaborating to modify preparation programs for staff in these schools. For the vast majority of schools in the United States, innovations and variation in preparation of the staff and in instructional programs are modest at best.

School Reform

When the National Commission on Excellence in Education published, in 1983, its report, *A Nation At Risk: The Imperative for Educational Reform,* many schools, organizations, and state bureaucracies cited the report as justification for radical changes in schools. So, more than a decade later, what has happened? At best, the results have been modest, and in some school districts, the situation has gotten worse. Sarason (1993) in his book, *The Predictable Failure of Educational Reform,* observed that the long-standing educational structures, coupled with the needs of various groups to defend their power, stifled reform efforts. Sarason offered ideas on how educators can make significant reforms that produce substantial, long-last-

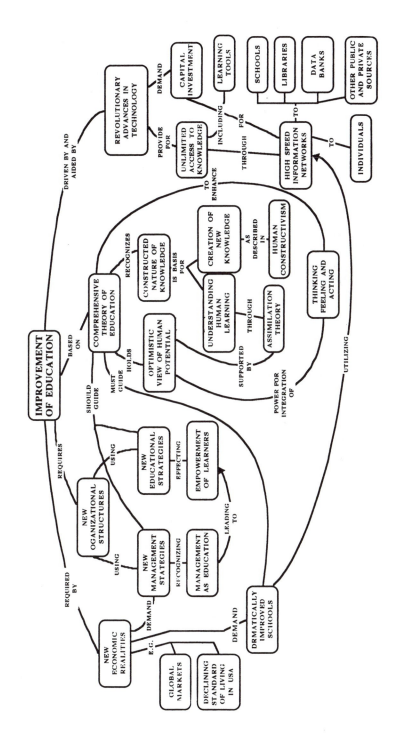

FIG. 10.2. An overview of ideas presented in chapter 10.

ing results, but still, such changes are slow in coming. The September 1993 issue of *Educational Leadership* published a series of articles dealing with system change, and I cite some articles in this issue.

What happened in most states after publication of *A Nation at Risk* (National Commission on Excellence in Education, 1983) was that legislation was passed that required higher standards for teacher certification and prescribed standards for student achievement in basics, and testing to assess if the standards were being met. Of course, such legislation did little to change the system. College courses for teachers, patterns of instruction well established in the classroom, curriculums, and textbooks—all these remained substantially the same. There was little new learning taking place either on the part of teachers or administrators. In short, little was happening to change the organization.

In the area of science and mathematics, the National Science Foundation (NSF) launched a program in 1990 to encourage systemic reform. This program recognized that many of the previous NSF programs to improve textbooks and teacher education dealt only with parts of the education enterprise. Other factors operating in schools tended to dilute these efforts at best and in some cases, totally undermine them. Systemic reform has as its goal to deal with most of the factors that affect the quality of school science and math instruction (Lawler, 1994). Based on competitive proposals, the NSF selected 25 state programs and a number of urban systems to receive support for innovative programs involving teacher enhancement, equipment purchases, new evaluation procedures, and use of TQM strategies such a benchmarking and feedback from customers; that is, parents, students, and employers. Unfortunately, the 100 million dollars allocated annually to this program is a mere drop in the bucket of funding that would be needed to reform schooling in America, although the intent was to provide model programs. If these funds were used for only two or three school districts, there might be a chance that, over time, some revolutionary change might be effected, but given the politics of Washington, this would be impossible to fund and sustain. Moreover, the approach even in best cases is similar to TQM and reengineering efforts in corporations, modifying largely the processes by which science and mathematics is taught and evaluated but not modifying substantially how the schools empower teachers and students to create and use new knowledge. The pessimistic view I took regarding curriculum reforms in science and mathematics in the 1950s and 1960s (Novak, 1969) was based on my belief that those programs failed to recognize and apply new knowledge on teaching and learning processes, and I do not believe the systemic reform efforts will do much better. Too little of what is done incorporates the kind of ideas and activities suggested in our books, *Teaching Science for Understanding* (Mintzes, Wandersee, & Novak, in press), and *Aprendizaje Significativo: Tecnicas y aplicaciones* (Gonzales & Novak, 1996).

Part of the problem has been the lack of leadership with the vision and talent to bring about truly valid educational improvement. Brandt (1993) cited the example of the superintendent for Edmonton, Alberta, Canada, who used his status and 20 years of experience to turn power over to individual schools and gave them control over 87% of the school budget. Individual school principals would work with teachers, parents, and community groups to modify instruction and programs. Such leadership is rare, however, and most school superintendents' tenure is only 3 to 5 years. Even with changes that confer more power for local control, schools can do little to change teacher preparation, quality of textbooks, and collective bargaining practices, and a host of other factors that influence day-to-day classroom instruction. Feynman's (1985) scathing critique of the way in which textbooks for schools in California are selected would be equally valid in many states today.

Beginning in 1979, a group of school leaders formed a group that became known as The Coalition of Essential Schools. This group sought to effect changes in their individual schools and exchange ideas on things that work and things that were unsuccessful. There are now some 800 schools loosely attached to the Coalition, but only 50 or so are really doing things significantly different from the mainstream (O'Neil, 1995a). With leadership from Ted Sizer, former Dean of Education at Harvard, and funding from a variety of foundations, the Coalition continues to encourage improvement in schools. Even with substantial foundation contributions, the Coalition has had relatively modest successes, and some notable failures. In a *Wall Street Journal* article, Stecklow (1994) noted that evaluation data on the success of the schools is mostly anecdotal. Admittedly, it is not easy to do valid evaluation studies for schools that try to do truly innovative things, and a proposal to fund such a study was turned down by Exxon Foundation, one of the Coalition supporters. As noted in chapter 9, good evaluation programs can do much to advance good school programs, and poor evaluation programs do the reverse.

In an interview with Peter Senge, O'Neil (1995b) reported:

> Nothing will change, no matter how fascinated you are by a new idea, unless you create some kind of a learning process. A learning process is a process that occurs over time whereby people's beliefs, ways of seeing the world, and ultimately their skills and capabilities change. It always occurs over time, and it's always connected to your domain of taking action, whether it's about relationships or about your professional work. Learning occurs "at home," so to speak, in the sense that it must be integrated into our lives, and it always takes time and effort. (p. 23)

The kind of systems thinking Senge (1990) recommended is difficult to implement when so few components of the system can be controlled and changed through the learning of the people involved in the system.

Privatization. Given the slow progress of school improvement, there has been growing support for privatizing schools, that is, using public funds to contract with for-profit organizations to educate children. There have been private schools for many years, but these are schools where the parents pay the tuition and fees. On the whole, private schools have enjoyed inordinate success by criteria such as admission to better universities and later job success of graduates. The problem is that a high proportion of students in private schools come from homes where economic and social resources are much better than average. Could private schools operated by for-profit corporations achieve similar results for all children?

One form of privatization has been formation of charter schools. Bierlein and Mulholland (1994) described charter schools in this way:

> In its purest form, a charter school is an autonomous educational entity operating under a contract negotiated between the *organizers* who manage the school (teachers, parents, or others from the public or private sector), and the *sponsors* who oversee the provisions of the charter (local school boards, state education boards, or some other public authority).

> Charter provisions address such issues as the school's instructional plan, specific educational outcomes and their measurement, and management and financial issues. A charter school may be formed from a school's existing personnel and facilities or from a portion thereof (for example, a school-within-a-school); or it may be a completely new entity with its own facilities.

> Once approved, a charter school is an independent legal entity with the ability to hire and fire, sue and be sued, award contracts for outside services, and control its own finances. Funding is based on student enrollment, as it would be for a school district. With a focus on educational outcomes, charter schools are freed from many (or all) district and state regulations often perceived as inhibiting innovation—for example, excessive teacher certification requirements, collective bargaining agreements, Carnegie units, and other curriculum requirements. (pp. 34–35)

In theory, charter schools have the opportunity to innovate in ways that would not be possible in regular public schools. In practice, many of the constraints that operate to impede truly innovative programs in public schools also operate in charter schools and similar private schools. As Molnar (1994) observed in his article, "Education for Profit: A Yellow Brick Road to Nowhere":

> Privatization seems attractive because it provides a comforting illusion of change without the sacrifices that would be necessary to bring about real improvement. It helps perpetuate the myth that the fundamental problems of urban schools are caused by bureaucracies, incompetence, and the self-interested greed of unions instead of crushing poverty, racism, and a lack of jobs. (p. 71)

Home Schooling. An alternative some parents choose is to educate their children at home. Sometimes parents choose this option for religious reasons, but increasingly, parents seek to offer more education quality and opportunity than they believe can be provided by public, private, or parochial schools. They often do so at considerable personal and financial sacrifice because they continue to pay for public education but may receive no tax relief nor other support for their home school. In some cases, a home–public school partnership is established, where children use school facilities and participate in sports and other extracurricular activities. An advantage to public schools is that they typically receive state aid for local home schooled children, but do not have the full burden for educating these children.

Home schooling is becoming an increasingly popular option with some one million children now receiving their education through such schools. With growing opportunities for learning via the Internet and other media sources, we are likely to see the popularity of home schooling continue to increase. If tax dollars are provided to parents for home schooling, either in direct funding or as tax credits, the growth in home schooling could accelerate greatly.

There is a certain security, if not outright complacency, in maintaining the status quo in schools. Most parents believe their local schools are doing an adequate or very good job in educating their children. By the standards of their own past experience in schools, their beliefs may be justified. By the standards required for graduates to compete in the new global economic scene, the standards are far short of the mark. For the one fifth of our students who drop out of school, schools have clearly failed them, and yet these people will need employment. Even for those who graduate from high school or college, the reports on their intellectual competencies are grim. For example, a recent article in the local newspaper reports that 46% of 1994 high school graduates who entered public colleges read below the eighth-grade level and 60% of students entering Florida colleges are below this level (Moloney, 1996). In science and math, eighth-grade students ranked 17th and 28th, respectively, when compared with students in 40 other developed countries (Hegarty, 1996).

Why? Why are schools performing so poorly? There are, of course, many difficult and complex societal issues involved, as we noted previously. Changing demographics with some urban schools almost 100% non-White, nonnative-born who speak various languages; drug abuse with both parents and students; physical safety in schools threatened with knives and guns—just to name a few! There are no easy solutions to any of these problems. And yet, I see the overriding failure in schools contributing to the problems listed is the failure to empower learners to take charge of their own meaning making. Why? For one thing, most school administrators with whom I have worked do not understand what is required for the latter condition to occur in their schools. They are either uneducated or badly educated in understanding how humans learn and how to organize school experience to empower learners. In 3 decades of teaching at Cornell University, I have had only one student in school administration enroll and complete my course in Theory and Methods of Education. The leadership in school administrations remains largely blind to the revolutionary changes that have taken place in understanding how humans learn and the nature and structure of knowledge. In reviewing recent textbooks on school administration, only two of six books have any information on student learning, and this was only 1½ pages in one book and one half page in another. Administrators who are concerned with empowering learners are rare indeed, and those who do care feel themselves trapped by the system.

I see little hope for public schools in the United States working their way out of the organizational and political problems they are in within the next 10 years. I am much more optimistic that we can see changes along the lines suggested in this book in some foreign countries and in corporate America. Spain, for example, has as a national education commitment and determination to move forward on helping learners learn how to learn and to make school learning meaningful! The Spanish Ministry of Education and Science (MEC) published in 1989 the White Book for the Reform of Education, putting forth an agenda for improvement of education that placed a central emphasis on the need to encourage meaningful learning. Unfortunately, promising and in some ways visionary as this White Book is, the transformation of teaching and learning in Spanish schools and colleges is no more easily done than are major educational overhauls in any country.

Corporate America, especially the for-profit organizations, have pressures public schools do not face to a significant degree at this time: They must compete to survive! They cannot tap the public purse by increasing taxes to pay for their failures. Although I fear the near-term consequences of using taxpayer funds to support private schools, it seems to me inevitable that this will occur before the turn of the century. To date, no state has legislation to provide taxpayer support to home schools. For one thing, it would be difficult for states to assure that funds to home schools were not being misused. However, if parents who home school do get some assistance from state funds in the future, their growth might be explosive. I expect to see increasing pressures for taxpayer support for schools other that public schools in the future. Public schools in many areas may have to die before they can be born again with the central commitment not sorting successful from unsuccessful learners, but rather empowering all learners. The organizational structures of most states, localities, and schools in the United States are simply not prepared for, nor organized to seek, empowerment of learners as a overriding commitment.

For-Profit Organizations

As already noted in the quote from Senge, for-profit corporations are also learning disabled. For decades I found my overtures to introduce A Theory of Education (Novak, 1977a) ideas to American business silently rejected. Often very junior corporate executives hearing of our work at a conference or seminar would respond with great enthusiasm and ask if I would be willing to visit with their colleagues. The calls never came. I am sure that when the junior executives spoke about our efforts to understand learners and knowledge, the senior officers saw little or no relevance to issues that were important to them. As Senge said, American business corporations have been learning disabled. All of this has changed since the early 1990s, not dramatically, but in significant ways. Some corporate executives, again especially in foreign countries, are interested in theory-based methods and tools for improving learning in corporations and in facilitating knowledge creation (see earlier note on one major corporation employing these tools and ideas, pp. 145-146).

One evidence of the changing Zeitgeist is illustrated with our book, *Learning How To Learn* (Novak & Gowin, 1984). When it was published in 1984, none of the many Japanese publishers translating books by Cambridge University Press were interested in translation rights. In 1990, a prominent publisher in Japan approached the Press for translation rights to the book and published this in 1992. During the 1980s when the United States was moving from the largest creditor nation to the largest debtor nation, Japan was doing the reverse. As Prestowitz (1988) observed, we were trading places. Part of the problem was and is with research productivity. To quote Prestowitz,

> The United States gets very little bang from its R & D bucks. It not only spends less on commercial research and development as a percentage of gross domestic produce [1.6 percent of our GNP versus 2.9 percent for Japan], but it gets less out of what it spends.
>
> We must strive for a more rational organization of our R & D programs. . . . (p. 106)

Yes, we must improve our capability for creation of new knowledge. What Prestowitz did not say, but Drucker (1993) and others are saying, is, "In the knowledge society (we are now in), people have to *learn how to learn*. Indeed, in the knowledge society, subjects matter less than the students' capacity to continue learning and their motivation to do so" (p. 201, italics added).

I believe the Japanese see this, and I am told by the author of the translation that the Japanese version of *Learning How To Learn* is being well received (Yumino, 1994). Will Japan pick up the learning how to learn ball and run with it while American schools and corporations languish? I hope not.

Corporate Learning.   Almost every book or article published in recent years on ways to improve business success has as a key claim that corporations must become better at learning, not only learning by upper management, but by everyone in the organization. Senge (1990) proposed that organizational learning required five component technologies:

1. Systems thinking—ways of thinking that help people see the whole pattern of factors involved in any given problem domain. For example, to develop a truly revolutionary automobile, all the component factors—powertrain, body, suspension, customer's wants, and so forth, must be considered together with the interactions of these components with one another.
2. Personal mastery—"the discipline of continually clarifying and deepening our personal vision, of focusing our energies, of developing patience, and of seeing reality objectively" (Senge, 1990, p. 7). Part of the process of gaining

personal mastery is employing systems thinking, and becoming more effective in the following component technologies.

3. Building better mental models—we all come to a new task with some kind of model of how the thing or process works. Often our mental models inhibit new learning. For example, most teaching interns come to their practice teaching experience with the mental model that teaching is lecturing, for this is the model they have seen in most of their school and university classes. It takes time and practice for them to see that guiding teams, cooperative planning with students, and critiquing computer activities are what make excellent teaching. In the corporate setting, dealing with stomach acid and heartburn can be modeled as providing compounds to neutralize the acid as with Tums or Rolaids, or we can conceive a new, more effective model where stomach acid secretion is diminished, as with Zantac, Tagament, or Axid. Our conceptual frameworks underlie our mental models, and the challenge is how to enrich, modify, and/or substitute new conceptual frameworks to achieve new problem solutions.

4. Building shared vision—partly because each individual holds his/her own mental models, and often these are not clearly evident to the person or the group, it can be very difficult to create a shared vision in schools or corporations. One of the reasons positive change in schools is so difficult is that there is so little shared vision as to what constitutes good education and an exemplary school. We saw in chapter 8 (see Fig. 8.2) the problems we identified at one major corporation and the concept maps that showed little evidence of a shared vision. Senge (1990) observed:

> When there is a genuine vision (as opposed to the all-too-familiar "vision statement"), people excel and learn, not because they are told to, but because they want to. But many leaders have personal visions that never get translated into shared visions that galvanize an organization. All too often, a company's shared vision has revolved around the charisma of a leader, or around a crisis that galvanizes everyone temporarily. But, given a choice, most people opt for pursuing a lofty goal, not only in times of crisis, but at all times. What has been lacking is a discipline for translating individual vision into shared vision—not a "cookbook," but a set of principles and guiding practices. (p. 9)

5. Team learning—All of us work in teams, even the prairie pioneer farmer worked with his family and neighbors as teams. Senge (1990) asserted, "Team learning is vital because teams, not individuals, are the fundamental learning unit in modern organizations" (p. 10). We all know that teamwork is essential in most sports. Martin (1993) used the sports model as the basis for his book, *Team Think: Using the Sports Connection to Develop, Motivate, and Manage a Winning Business Team.* Martin emphasized that business teams need a leader or coach, and he argued that "To be an effective manager,

you must become a leader" (p. 34); and he contrasted the old style manager with the team leader thus:

- A manager administers, a leader innovates.
- A manager maintains, a leader develops.
- A manager plans, a leader sets a direction.

Senge (1990) emphasized the importance of dialogue and genuine thinking together as essential to effective learning by the team. I would be more specific and say that the team must effectively negotiate old and new meanings held by team members and work to modify and improve the conceptual frameworks of all team members. In sports, the goal of the team is generally clear, for example, to score the most touchdowns, field goals, and conversions possible. Peters (1992) suggested that corporations need more participation in management by all members of the organization. In school learning or business, teams need leaders to help define the goals and lead (guide) the team. This requires skill and understanding of all of Senge's five component technologies. Senge (1990) observed:

Despite its importance, team learning remains poorly understood. Until we can describe the phenomenon better, it will remain mysterious. Until we have some theory of what happens when teams learn (as opposed to individuals in teams learning), we will be unable to distinguish group intelligence from "groupthink," when individuals succumb to group pressures for conformity. Until there are reliable methods for building teams that can learn together, its occurrence will remain a product of happenstance. This is why mastering team learning will be a critical step in building learning organizations. (p. 238)

My contention is that team learning needs to be seen as basically an educational problem. The tools and ideas presented in this book have been effective in team learning, as well as in aiding individuals to gain mastery in both school and corporate settings.

Hamel and Prahalad (1994) distinguished between vision and foresight. Industry foresight helps managers answer three critical questions. Hamel and Prahalad cautioned that vision, vanity, and foresight are not the same:

Visions that are as grandiose as they are poorly conceived deserve to be criticized, as do companies that seem to prefer rhetoric to action. All too often, "the vision" is no more than window dressing for a CEO's ego-driven acquisition binge. Chrysler's purchase of an Italian maker of exotic sports cars and its acquisition of a jet aircraft manufacturer were driven more by the ego and whim of the company's erstwhile chairman, Lee Iococca, than by a solid, well-founded point of view about what it would take to succeed in the automotive business ten years hence. They were a side trip. Any vision that is simply an extension of the CEO's ego is dangerous. On the other hand, it is equally simplistic and dangerous to reject the very notion of foresight simply because some corporate leaders can't distinguish between vanity and vision. (p. 75)

Katzenbach (1995) and his associates found that the real change leaders in successful companies they studied had an effective working vision that served the following functions:

- *Give meaning* to the changes expected of people;

- *Evoke clear and positive mental images* of what "it should be like around here";

- *Create pride, energy, and a sense of accomplishment* along the way; and

- *Link change activities and business-performance* results. (p. 66)

If we see management as essentially the task of educating or teaching, we can apply much of what has been presented in the earlier chapters as the tools and ideas needed to build, share, and execute a more powerful vision for schools and corporations.

THE PROMISE OF NEW TECHNOLOGIES

The Internet

The Internet originated as a governmental network called ARPANET, which was created in 1969 by the Defense Department so that defense contractors and researchers could continue communications after a nuclear attack. Computer resources were distributed in various locations so that destruction of some would still permit communications with others. Proven to be popular with scientists and computer specialists, the network evolved into what is now called the Internet. It is a loose collection of commercial and noncommercial computer networks tied together by telecommunications lines. When federal funding for ARPANET was discontinued in 1989, the Internet was born, with support from various user groups.

Initially, the Internet served primarily to provide electronic mail service to research organizations, computer companies, scientists, and graduate students. More recently it has served to carry information from Web services set up by organizations or individuals. The availability of free software needed to browse Web sites has made access to the Internet popular with anyone who owns a computer with sufficient power to use the Web services. The World Wide Web, or www, is now accessed by millions of people all over the world.

As personal computers continue to become more powerful and/or less expensive use of the Internet will continue to expand. The major limitation for home use now is the speed with which information can be transmitted using telephone lines and currently available modems. There are also limitations on the availability of Internet access in many countries, especially in remote locations. Transfer of large quantities of information over Information Highways, except for locations with direct fiber optic cable connections, is currently slow and not appropriate for good two-way video transfer. Undoubtedly, there will be great strides and maybe new break-throughs in solving the problem of transferring huge amounts of information between computers in the next decade. However, even with current capabilities, there are extraordinary opportunities for gaining new knowledge via the Internet. Most schools and businesses today are far from utilizing the resources that already exist.

Two-Way Video Conferencing

Current computer technology and Internet capabilities already allow for two-way video conferencing. Cornell University's CU See Me Program allows dialogue and video exchange between students or experts located in classrooms or offices almost anywhere in the United States, as well as in foreign countries. Although video quality is marginal at this time, it should become good-to-excellent in the next 10 years. For schools, this can mean access to many new knowledge resources, as well as collaboration on research projects between students located in different schools. For children in home–school programs, the new resources could give each child unprecedented opportunities for learning and collaboration.

In the corporate world, opportunities for two-way video conferencing can also afford new ways for teams to collaborate, including collaboration between mem-bers at almost any location on the globe. As the globalization of business continues to increase, video conferencing and other knowledge exchange forms will undoubt-edly increase exponentially.

Currently computer linked white boards allow conference teams to interact with electronic pens that record marks on both the originating and on remote white boards. These records are also stored in computer files and can be retrieved, modified, and printed out. Thus, conferencing can proceed in real time, or individu-als and groups can work on documents whenever their schedules permit. Smart Technologies, Inc., is developing white boards and computer software that allows easy use of concept maps for knowledge representation, and this technology is advancing rapidly. Undoubtedly, other companies will eventually offer products with similar capabilities.

Concept-Map Based Electronic Knowledge Storage and Retrieval

A major project is now underway with the Navy and NASA to capture the knowledge held by experts, many of whom will retire in the near future. Interviews and concept maps will be used to capture and store this knowledge. Concept maps will also provide the basis for easy access to this knowledge. One of the major difficulties faced in using and retrieving information stored electronically is that traditional search strategies can provide thousands or even millions of references if one or several pertinent keywords are used to generate the search. Most of these references have little or no relevance to the searcher's needs, but adding more explicit keyword combinations can eliminate desired information as well as irrelevant information.

The advantage of using computer search engines based on information stored in concept maps is that knowledge is highly organized in a concept map, and each proposition in the map is set in a context, thus aiding the searcher by providing relatively easy selection of the most pertinent information. Maps can be stacked hierarchically, where selecting and clicking on a concept on a global map can bring up on the screen a subordinate or more explicit concept map with greater detail. Any number of map hierarchies can be programmed into concept maps for a given domain of knowledge. Furthermore, a searcher can easily scroll across and up and down a concept map to see other related concepts and propositions, some of which might never have been known or considered if only keywords were used to guide the search. Thus, information stored as concept maps is contextualized, not random bits, and locating knowledge is a much more orderly process. Such search processes have already been built into AI programs to train physicians with astonishingly good success (Canas & Ford, 1992; Canas, Ford, & deBessonet, 1993; Ford, Stahl, et al., 1991).

During a sabbatical leave in 1987 and 1988 at the University of West Florida, I worked with Bruce Dunn to experiment with using concept maps and questions relating to concept maps as stimulus material for subjects who were connected to an apparatus to measure the electrical activity of their brains. Dunn had the apparatus and experience for study of electroencephalographic (EEG) measures of brain activity. We wanted to ascertain whether subjects performing simple concept map-related tasks differed in their EEG patterns from subjects performing more cognitively complex tasks. Simple tasks included replacing a concept that had been deleted from the concept map prepared by that subject, whereas complex tasks included finding a new crosslink between different segments of their map. The apparatus setup is shown in Fig. 10.3. Briefly, the results showed very high statistically significant differences in EEG patterns for these two kinds of tasks, suggesting, in part, the validity of concept maps as knowledge representation tools and the greater cognitive activity needed for more complex tasks (Dunn, Novak, Hill, MacQueen, & Wagner, 1989). There are now more sophisticated instruments and techniques for studying brain activity during cognitive tasks, and this is an area of accelerating research activity. I expect that in the first half of the 21st century, we shall begin to acquire explicit knowledge about how the brain acquires, stores, and processes knowledge and the biological structures that mediate these activities. This knowledge will undoubtedly have great significance for education just as current work in genetic engineering is having profound effects on agriculture, medicine, and numerous manufacturing processes.

The most fortunate part of my sabbatical at UWF was getting acquainted with Dunn's close friend, Kenneth Ford. We began to collaborate late in my sabbatical and, subsequently, worked together in developing strategies for using concept maps in the field of artificial intelligence in which Ford was a recognized international leader. Ford and his associates published a number of their AI studies and project descriptions, some of which I just cited. But I believe the most exciting work lies ahead as Ford assumes his role as Director in the newly created Knowledge Systems section of NASA. With increasing pressure from the U.S. Congress for agencies such as NASA and the Department of Navy to work collaboratively with industry in developing and using new knowledge, I expect an extraordinary growth in the development of computer tools and strategies for using concept maps to create, acquire, store, and utilize knowledge. I predict that this government agencies-and-industry partnership will revolutionize the way we think about knowledge, teaching, and learning. In due course, these developments are bound to have a revolutionary impact on education, perhaps first in excellent home schooling programs and some public schools, then in contract schools, and finally in public schools in general. Driven by global competitiveness and the increasing necessity for a highly educated work force combined with use of new technologies, I expect to see many new forms of collaboration between governmental agencies, corporations, and the schools. The path may not always be smooth and ascending, but I think revolutionary changes in education are inevitable.

FIG. 10.3. The laboratory arrangement used to monitor students' EEG patterns during their performance with their concept maps.

New Forms of Curriculum Development

Across the years, curriculum development has meant production of new textbooks, study guides, and course syllabi. For example, the numerous federally funded alphabet programs to improve science and mathematics education in the United States in the late 1950s and 1960s were mostly focused on the production of such materials. PSSC, BSCS, ESS, and MMST were all federally funded curriculum projects of this kind. None of these, however, were based on a theory of education, and the theories of learning, when considered, were either Piagetian developmental theory or behavioral psychology (Novak, 1969). Except for the BSCS (Biological Sciences Curriculum Studies), most of the curriculum development groups have become history, along with the materials they developed. The several billions of federal dollars that were invested in developing these materials and training teachers to use them now show little or no impact on the quality of science and mathematics teaching in the United States, or in other countries where the materials were adapted. Similar results occurred in the social sciences, where politically sensitive materials that were developed were widely criticized.

Educators and publishers continue to develop and offer to schools new books and syllabi, perhaps including CD-ROM visual materials to extend the print materials. No doubt this kind of work will continue well into the 21st century. But there are new opportunities for developing curriculum materials made possible by the technology revolution that is taking place. Because learning is necessarily idiosyncratic and meaning making must be done by the individual learner, the best curriculum development is that which the learner constructs.

A first step toward this kind of curriculum development is illustrated in the work of Krajcik and his associates at the University of Michigan (Krajcik, Spitulnik, & Zembal, in press). With both high school students and preservice teachers, they have developed strategies to aid learners in developing artifacts (Fig. 10.4) on computers that combine text Internet resources, visuals (including videos), and other resources that illustrate some major concept in science. The development of the computer-based montage or artifact of materials is guided by a teacher, but the end result is created by the learner. Furthermore, future students can review artifacts created by previous students, modify, and build on these and develop new materials. The possibilities for developing new learning materials are limitless and can be done in any discipline. Teacher guidance is needed, both to help steer learners over obstacles, including their own prior misconceptions and problems with using technological resources. In addition, teachers, or a new breed of curriculum planners, need to identify key concepts that are crucial foundations for under-standing any discipline, and these need to be included, in some useful sequence, in planning assignment of student artifact constructions. This is not a trivial problem, but here again, use of the system will help to determine what the most powerful sequences of experiences in artifact construction may be. This, I predict, may become the curriculum development activities of the mid-21st century, if not earlier.

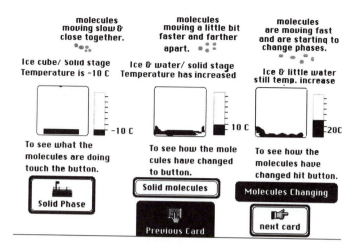

FIG. 10.4. One screen of a computer generated artifact showing two students' ideas regarding phase changes for water. Note common misconception on comparative space between molecules in solids and liquids. Reproduced with permission from Krajcik, Spitulnik, & Zembal, in press.

There will be no obsolescence of textbooks or syllabi, for the curriculum will be created from current as well as historical resources.

THE CUSTOMER AS TEACHER AND LEARNER

What will be the new wave of change that flows through the corporate world? In the 1980s it was TQM with the idea that using various strategies for systematic evaluation of customer needs, product quality, and manufacturing efficiencies could lead to enhance productivity. To some extent, these strategies, first introduced by Deming in the United States, but implemented widely by Japanese corporations, showed promise. American companies, especially the automobile industry, sought to implement many of these strategies, and management consultant firms rushed to spread the gospel. TQM is essentially a management approach providing guidelines on how to manage people and resources. In the 1990s, a new gospel has emerged: The rush today is to become, in the words of Nonaka and Takeuchi (1995), the knowledge-creating company. Both application of TQM and emphasis on knowledge-creation strategies have contributed to business competitiveness. In fact, the latter movement is now very much in progress and, hopefully, this book will contribute to increased effectiveness in knowledge creation by corporations.

So what does the future hold? Who will be the new leaders, and what will be the new strategies? Minkin (1995) identified 100 global trends he saw based on his experience and consulting practices. Among his predictions are that small entrepreneurs will become more numerous, with younger people and more women swelling the ranks of small business managers. J. Moore (1996) in his book, *The Death of Competition,* observed:

> Not that competition is vanishing. In fact, it is intensifying. But competition, as most of us have routinely thought of it, is dead—and any business manager who doesn't recognize this is threatened. Let me explain. The traditional way to think about competition is in terms of offers and markets. Your product or service goes up against that of your competitor, and one wins. You improve your product by listening to customers, and by investing in the processes that create it.

> The problem with this point of view is that it ignores the context—the environment—within which the business lies, and it ignores the need for co-evolution with others in that environment, a process that involves cooperation as well as conflict. Even excellent businesses can be destroyed by the conditions around them. They are like species in Hawaii. Through no fault of their own, they find themselves facing extinction because the ecosystem they call home is itself imploding. A good restaurant in a failing neighborhood is likely to die. A first-rate supplier to a collapsing retail chain—a Bradlees, Caldor, or Kmart—had better watch out. (p. 3)

Hamel and Prahalad (1994) in their book, *Competing for the Future,* argue that:

> Competition for the future is competition for *opportunity share* rather than market share. It is competition to maximize the share of future opportunities a company could potentially access within a broad *opportunity arena,* be that home information systems, genetically engineered drugs, financial services, advanced materials, or something else. (p. 31)

One of the methods they see as necessary to increase opportunities is to move decisively into markets, preempting the competition. For example:

> In a reversal of such [previous] misfortunes, P&G managed to preempt its Japanese rival, Kao, in the race to take super-absorbent diapers to world markets. In 1985, Kao surprised P&G by launching a technologically advance, superabsorbent diaper in Japan. The new diaper quickly overtook Pampers as the market leader. But with little distribution or brand power outside Asia, Kao could do little to capitalize on its innovation in global markets. Thus, P&G was able to launch its own version of a superabsorbent diaper around the world with virtually no opposition from Kao. In the end, it was P&G, more than Kao, that profited from the new diaper technology. While global distribution power alone can't substitute for a lack of competencies in other areas, it is an absolutely critical multiplier of the returns to innovation. (pp. 246–247)

Another trend Minkin (1995) identified is changes in when and how we learn. He saw education and entertainment as merging, with the development of new technologies:

> The decline of learning in the United States and its ripple effect on the economy and society leads many of us to believe that education can no longer be entrusted to the educational or governmental bureaucracies but instead requires a major shift in focus.

The answer to when will we learn? is when "edutainment," the combining of education and entertainment, through interactive multimedia, saturates the classroom and corporate training rooms. Interactive education will be a huge business as global competition, new technology and other forces continue to provide occupational growth in areas requiring more training and education. (pp. 126–127)

Regarding the need to learn from our customers, J. Moore (1996) observed that we can learn most from early adopters. Sometimes they are the most educated, most advantaged individuals, but not always. For an example, from a relatively primitive setting:

> The ideal customers are those who will tolerate a primitive version of the final offer, knowing that, even in the rudimentary form, the value is sufficient to improve their lives or businesses.

> Somalians nicely fit the bill. They will patiently wait days to get a phone call because the alternative is not talking to certain people at all. Moreover, they will provide useful feedback about the service and how to improve it, and they will often contribute to its improvement by creating support systems of their own. Finally, even though they are early adopter customers, they are representative enough of other sorts of customers that any information gleaned from then can be applied more broadly. (pp. 120–121)

In his autobiographical book, *The Road Ahead,* Gates (1996) also saw technology as playing a major role in new educational opportunities. With regard to business, he spoke of the need to learn from customers. New communications technologies such as Teledesic's plan to place several hundred inexpensive satellites in low orbit will permit communications with people anywhere, even in remote areas. Gates observed:

> If it succeeds, Teledesic could transform millions of lives by bringing state-of-the-art communication and the Internet's educational, commercial, and entertainment content to an audience that might not be able to connect up otherwise. It's easy for those of us in developed countries to forget that two-thirds of the world's people have never even made a phone call. Where telephone service is available, it's provided over analog, copper-wire networks that are often antiquated and unlikely to be upgraded to a digital, broadband capability any time soon outside the most developed markets. While many places in the world are connected by fiber, so far it is used primarily for the trunk lines between countries and for telephone company switches. Fiber to homes and offices is expensive to install even in high-density areas, and it is unclear when it will ever be feasible to justify running fiber extensively in low-density areas. (p. 272)

Whether it will be Teledesic or some other organization that creates the potential to link all people of the world is too soon to say. That it will happen is a certainty, and we are probably only about a decade away from this. It is impossible to forecast the extraordinary educational potentials that can derive from this.

As corporations move toward seeing customers as both teachers and learners, they need to take cognizance of several principles from the theory of education presented in this book that should guide their programs. This we know about education:

1. There must be motivation to learn. No learning will take place unless the learner chooses to learn.
2. We must understand and engage the learner's existing relevant knowledge, both valid and invalid ideas.
3. We must organize the conceptual knowledge we want to teach.
4. Learning takes place in a context and we must consider what will be a facilitative context for educating.
5. Learning can be aided by a teacher who is knowledgeable and sensitive to the learner's ideas and feelings.
6. Evaluation is necessary to assess progress and further motivate the learner.

These six principles are fundamental for any substantive learning to occur. We shall review briefly the meaning of each of these principles as they pertain to marketing research and advertising programs. Each of the six principles influences action on all of the other principles, so there is an interconnectedness that needs to be recognized.

1. Motivation derives from some unsatisfied need or desire on the part of the learner. There are both thinking or cognitive aspects and feelings or affective aspects to customer's needs and desires. Market research must probe carefully how the target population for a given product or service thinks and feels about that product or service.

Although there are many ways to assess consumers' thoughts and feelings, the most powerful is the personal interview. The design of the interview is critical and is best done through an iterative sequence of identifying concepts and feelings that are pertinent to the product or service, concept mapping this knowledge, designing questions based on these concept maps that probe the customer's thoughts and feelings, concept mapping the thoughts and feelings of individual customers and customers taken collectively, then redesigning the interview based on the insights from the concept maps. Usually three to five iterations of this process will produce excellent interview protocols.

Zaltman and Higie (1993) at Harvard University and my students and I at Cornell University have found that a sample of 6 to 10 representative customers given carefully designed, executed and evaluated interviews can give a complete and reliable picture of individual's thoughts and feelings on any topic, product, or service for a given target population. Thus we can assess the underlying motivational factors of customers toward any product or service. The concept maps prepared from interviews can also be used to design more effective questionnaires that can be distributed to large numbers of customers and provide an additional data source. For more on these techniques, see Novak and Gowin (1984).

2. Well-designed interviews properly conducted will provide knowledge of the ideas and feelings held by customers. We must recognize that these are the conceptual glasses through which the customer sees his or her world. New information will be interpreted by the customer based on these ideas. Therefore, we need to build advertising copy and illustrations that will make sense to the customer based on the knowledge and feelings they have. However, we must be careful not to strengthen misconceptions and work toward replacing these with more valid ideas. There is a large body of literature that deals with this problem.

3. For any product or service, it is possible to create a concept map representing the knowledge of experts and customers that is pertinent to understanding the properties, merits, and value of the product or service. This knowledge should be competently concept mapped and used as a basis for steps 1 and 2. These concept maps also help to communicate ideas between R&D teams and marketing personnel. They serve as a foundation for creative work by R&D and marketing staff.

4. *Context,* or the setting in which learning will take place, needs to be carefully considered. Copy and visuals appropriate for a package or store display may need to be quite different from those in home mailings or television. If consumer interviews are well designed and well executed, they will provide information on various contexts in which consumers learn about products or services.

5. Gender, culture, race, age, education, economic status, and other customer attributes must be recognized and treated with sensitivity. A person offended by product or service presentations as regards any of the this will not be a customer, at least not for long. The source for information pertinent here is once again carefully designed and executed personal interviews and the concept maps developed from these interviews.

6. Information that provides the customer with a means to evaluate the value of a product or service needs to be provided. The customer needs a way to assess if they are getting what they want and what they are paying for. Similarly, the company needs a way to assess if they are providing what the customer wants and their comparative degree of satisfaction with the product or service.

There is, of course, much detail that could be added to the hows, whys, and wherefores for each of these ideas. Nevertheless, the items presented are complete in terms of what we know about the basic components involved in teaching and learning with our customers. They are the essential ingredients for any corporation that wants to become an educating corporation.

THE ROAD AHEAD

Gates (1996) described well where we are and where we are likely to go in the near future as regards developments in technology and its application in business and education. What he did not discuss is what new knowledge and tools regarding the teaching and learning processes may bring, nor how the potential radical changes that will take place in how corporations create and use knowledge will change the world we live in. The latter is what I have attempted to present in this book. Gates did see education as important:

> Education is not the entire answer to the challenges presented by the Information Age, but it is part of the answer, just as education is part of the answer to a range of society's problems. H.G. Wells, who was as imaginative and forward-looking as any futurist, summed it up back in 1920. "Human history," Wells said, "becomes more and more a race between education and catastrophe." Education is society's great leveler, and any improvement in education goes a long way toward equalizing opportunity. Part of the beauty of the electronic world is that the extra cost of letting additional people use educational material is basically zero. (p. 293)

As we approach the time when any person can get any information at any time, anywhere—for little or no cost—we enter a whole new realm of possibilities for education. Yes, the invention of the printing press in 1460 made access possible to the great books for at least all of the more affluent. We now are on the brink of a period when almost everything known can be accessed—free—by almost anyone. The problem is, how do we use this potential to improve the lives of human beings the world over? As I have noted repeatedly, information does not automatically translate into knowledge, and what is required is the empowerment of people to access and use this information to construct new meanings! This is the principal challenge we face. I believe we now know many things to achieve a much higher level of meaning making by all people. At the present time, on a scale of 1 to 10, I believe most schools and corporations are only operating at a level of 2 or 3, in terms of capitalizing on what we know about knowledge, learning, ego enhancement, and personal empowerment. There is much to be done in applying this knowledge more broadly, perhaps to achieve a 6 or 8 in effectiveness. There is also much to be done in creating new knowledge about learning and knowledge creation. My hope is that this book may contribute to this enterprise.

Appendix I:
How To Build a Concept Map

1. Identify a focus question that addresses the problem, issues, or knowledge domain you wish to map. Guided by this question, identify 10 to 20 concepts that are pertinent to the question and list these. Some people find it helpful to write the concept labels on separate cards or Post-its™ so that they can be moved around. If you work with computer software for mapping, produce a list of concepts on your computer. Concept labels should be a single word, or at most two or three words.

2. Rank order the concepts by placing the broadest and most inclusive idea at the top of the map. It is sometimes difficult to identify the broadest, most inclusive concept. It is helpful to reflect on your focus question to help decide the ranking of the concepts. Sometimes this process leads to modification of the focus question or writing a new focus question.

3. Work down the list and add more concepts as needed.

4. Begin to build your map by placing the most inclusive, most general concept(s) at the top. Usually there will be only one, two, or three most general concepts at the top of the map.

5. Next select the two, three, or four subconcepts to place under each general concept. Avoid placing more than three or four concepts under any other concept. If there seem to be six or eight concepts that belong under a major concept or subconcept, it is usually possible to identify some appropriate concept of intermediate inclusiveness, thus creating another level of hierarchy in your map.

6. Connect the concepts by lines. Label the lines with one or a few linking words. The linking words should define the relationship between the two concepts so that it reads as a valid statement or proposition. The connection creates meaning. When you hierarchically link together a large number of related ideas, you can see the structure of meaning for a given subject domain.

7. Rework the structure of your map, which may include adding, subtracting, or changing superordinate concepts. You may need to do this reworking several times, and in fact this process can go on indefinitely as you gain new knowledge or new insights. This is where Post-its™ are helpful, or better still, computer software for creating maps.

8. Look for crosslinks between concepts in different sections of the map and label these lines. Crosslinks can often help to see new, creative relationships in the knowledge domain.

9. Specific examples of concepts can be attached to the concept labels (e.g., golden retriever is a specific example of a dog breed).

10. Concept maps could be made in many different forms for the same set of concepts. There is no one way to draw a concept map. As your understanding of relationships between concepts changes, so will your maps.

Appendix II:
Procedures for Teaching
VEE Diagramming

1. Select a laboratory or field event (or object) that is relatively simple to observe and for which one or more focus questions can be readily identified. Alternatively, a research paper with similar features can be used after all students (and the teacher) have read it carefully.
2. Begin with a discussion of the event or objects being observed. Be sure that what is identified is the event(s) for which records are made. Surprisingly, this is sometimes difficult.
3. Identify and write out the best statement of the focus question(s). Again, be sure that the focus question(s) relate to the events or objects studied and the records to be made.
4. Discuss how the questions serve to focus our attention on the specific features of the events or objects and *require* that certain kinds of records be obtained if the questions are to be answered. Illustrate how a different question about the same events or objects would require different records to be made (or a different degree of precision).
5. Discuss the source of our questions, or our choice of objects or events to be observed. Help students to see that, in general, our relevant concepts, principles, or theories guide us in choosing what to observe and what questions to ask.
6. Discuss the validity and reliability of the records. Are they facts (i.e., valid, reliable records)? Are there concepts, principles, and theories that relate to our record-making devices that assure their validity and reliability? Are there better ways to gather more valid records?
7. Discuss how we can transform our records to answer our questions. Are certain graphs, tables, or statistics useful transformations?
8. Discuss the construction of knowledge claims. Help students to see that different questions could lead to gathering different records and performing different record transformations. The result may be a whole new set of knowledge claims about the source events or objects.
9. Discuss value claims. These are value statements such as X is better than Y, or X is good, or we should seek to achieve X. Note that value claims should

derive from our knowledge claims, but they are not the same as knowledge claims.

10. Show how concepts, principles, and theories are used to shape our knowledge claims and may influence our value claims.

11. Explore ways to improve a given inquiry by examining which element in the Vee seems to be the weakest link in our chain of reasoning, that is, in the construction of our knowledge and value claims.

12. Help students see that we operate with a constructivist epistemology to construct claims about how we see the world working, and not an empiricist or positivist epistemology that proves some truth about how the world works.

13. Help students see that a world view is what motivates or guides the investigator in what he or she chooses to try to understand, and controls the energy with which he or she pursues the inquiry. Scientists care about value and pursue better ways to explain rationally how the world works. Astrologers, mystics, creationists, and others do not engage in the same constructivist enterprise.

14. Compare, contrast, and discuss Vee diagrams made by different students for the same events or objects. Discuss how the variety helps to illustrate the constructed nature of knowledge.

References

Achterberg, C. L. (1986). *The meaning of food and nutrition in families with young children: A study of social cognition.* Unpublished doctoral thesis, Cornell University, Ithaca, NY.

Achterberg, C. L., Novak, J. D., & Gillespie, A. H. (1985). Theory-driven research as a means to improve nutrition education. *Journal of Nutrition Education, 17*(5), 179–184.

Alaiyemola, F. F., Jegede, O. J., & Okebukola, P. A. O. (1990). The effect of a metacognitive strategy of instruction on the anxiety level of students in science classes. *International Journal of Science Education, 12*(1), 95–99.

American Association of University Women. (1995). *Growing smart: What's working for girls in schools.* Washington, DC: AAUW.

American Psychological Association. (1995). Learner centered psychological principles: Guidelines for the teaching of educational psychology in teacher education programs. *Newsletter for Educational Psychologists, 19*(1): 4–5; 8.

Anderson, J. R. (1990). *The adaptive character of thought.* Hillsdale, NJ: Lawrence Erlbaum Associates.

Anderson, J. R. (1983). *The architecture of cognition.* Cambridge, MA: Harvard University Press.

Argyris, C., & Schon, D. A. (1978). *Theory in practice: Increasing professional effectiveness.* San Francisco: Jossey-Bass.

Arzi, H. (in press). More than walls, benches and widgets: Enhancing science education through laboratory environments. In Fraser, B. J., & Tobin, K. G. (Eds.), *The International Handbook of Science Education.* Dordrecht, Netherlands: Kluwer.

Ausubel, D. P. (1962). A subsumption theory of meaningful verbal learning and retention. *Journal of General Psychology, 66,* 213–224.

Ausubel, D. P. (1963). *The psychology of meaningful verbal learning.* New York: Grune & Stratton.

Ausubel, D. P. (1968). *Educational psychology: A cognitive view.* New York: Holt, Rinehart & Winston.

Ausubel, D. P., Novak, J. D., & Hanesian, H. (1978). *Educational psychology: A cognitive view* (2nd Ed.). New York: Holt, Rinehart, & Winston.

Baranga, C. B. A. (1990). *Meaningful learning of creative writing in fourth grade with a word processing program integrated in the whole language curriculum.* Unpublished masters thesis. Cornell University, Ithaca, NY.

Bauer, L., & K. Borman. (1988). *A review of educational foundations courses offered in U.S. colleges and universities.* Unpublished manuscript, University of Cincinnati.

Belenky, M. F., Clinchy, B., Goldberger, N. R., & Tarule, J. M. (1986). *Woman's ways of knowing: The development of self, voice, and mind.* New York: Basic Books.

Benbow, C. P., & Stanley, J. C. (1982). Consequences in high school and college of sex differences in mathematical reasoning ability: A longitudinal perspective. *American Educational Research Journal, 14,* 15–71.

Berne, E. (1964). *Games people play.* New York: Grove Press.

Best, R. (1983). *We've all got scars: What boys and girls learn in elementary school.* Bloomington: Indiana University Press.

Bierlein, L. A., & Mulholland, L. A. (1994). The promise of charter schools. *Educational Leadership, 52,* 34–35, 37–40.

Bloom, B. S. (1956). *Taxonomy of educational objectives—The classification of educational goals, Handbook I: Cognitive domain.* New York: David McKay.

Bloom, B. S. (1968). Learning for mastery. *UCLA Evaluation Comment, 1*(2), 1.

Bloom, B. S. (1976). *Human characteristics and school learning.* New York: McGraw-Hill.

Bloom, B. S. (1981). *All our children learning: A primer for parents, teachers, and other educators.* New York: McGraw-Hill.

Bonner, J. T. (1962). *The ideas of biology.* New York: Harper.

Brandt, R. (1993). Overview: A consistent system. *Educational Leadership, 51*(1), 7.

Bretz, S. (1994). *Learning strategies and their influence upon students' conceptions of science literacy and meaningful learning: The case of a college chemistry course for non-science majors.* Unpublished doctoral thesis. Cornell University, Ithaca, NY.

Bridges, E. M. (1986). *The incompetent teacher: The challenge and the response.* Philadelphia, PA: Falmer Press.

Bridges, E. M. (1992). *The incompetent teacher: Managerial responses.* Philadelphia, PA: Falmer Press.

Bronfenbrenner, U., & Ceci, S. J. (1994). Nature–nurture reconceptualized in developmental perspective: A bioecological model. *Psychological Review, 101*(4), 568–586.

Brown, A. L. (1994). The advancement of learning. *Educational Researcher, 23*(8), 4–12.

Brown, J. S., Collins, A., & Duguid, P. (1989). Situated cognition and the culture of learning. *Educational Researcher, 18*(1), 32–42.

Bush, V. (1945). *Science: The endless frontier.* Washington, DC: U.S. Government Printing Office.

Cañas, A. J., & Ford, K. (1992). An environment for collaborative knowledge building. Paper presented at the Workshop on the Technology and Pedagogy for Collaborative Problem Solving as a Context for Learning, Toronto, June.

Cañas, A. J., Ford, K. M., & DeBessonet, C. (1993, April). Intelligent support for collaborative modeling. Proceedings of the Sixth Florida Artificial Intelligence Research Symposium, FLAIRS '93. Fort Lauderdale, FL.

Cannon, W. B. (1932). *The wisdom of the body.* New York: Norton.

Carey, S. (1985). *Conceptual change in childhood.* Cambridge, MA: MIT Press.

Chi, M. T. H. (1983). Network representation of a child's dinosaur knowledge. *Developmental Psychology, 19*(1), 29–39.

Clery, D. (1994). Element 110 is created, but who spotted it first? *Science, 266,* 1479.

Commoner, B. (1971). *The closing circle: Nature, man, and technology.* New York: Knopf.

Crosby, P. B. (1992). *The eternally successful organization.* New York: Mentor Books.

Cullen, J. F., Jr. (1983). *Concept learning and problem solving: The use of the entropy concept in college teaching.* Unpublished doctoral thesis. Cornell University, Ithaca, NY.

Dethier, V. G. (1962). *To know a fly.* San Francisco: Holden-Day.

Donaldson, M. C. (1978). *Children's minds.* New York: Norton.

Drucker, P. F. (1993). *Post-capitalist society.* New York: Harper.

Dunn, B. R., Novak, J. D., Hill, R., MacQueen, K., & Wagner, L. (1989). The measurement of knowledge integration using EEG frequency analysis. Paper presented at the 1989 annual meetings of the American Educational Research Association, San Francisco, March.

Dunn, J. (1987). Understanding feelings: The early stages. In J. Bruner & H. Haste (Eds.), *Making Sense* (pp. 26–40). New York: Methuen.

Edmondson, K. M., & Novak, J. D. (1993). The interplay of scientific epistemological views, learning strategies, and attitudes of college students. *Journal of Research in Science Teaching, 32*(6), 547–559.

Educational Policies Commission. (1961). *The central purpose of American education.* Washington, DC: National Education Association.

Edwards, J., & Fraser, K. (1983). Concept maps as reflectors of conceptual understanding. *Research in Science Education, 13,* 19–26.

Farrell, W. C., Johnson, J. H., Jones, C. K., & Sapp, M. (1994). Will privatizing schools really help inner-city students of color? *Educational Leadership, 52*(1), 72–75.

Fedock, P. M., Zambo, R., & Cobern, W. W. (1996). The professional development of college science professors as science teachers. *Science Education, 80*(1), 5–19.

Feldsine, J. E., Jr. (1987). Distinguishing student's misconceptions from alternative conceptual frameworks through construction of concept maps. In J. D. Novak (Ed.), *Proceedings of the second International Seminar on Misconceptions and Educational Strategies in Science and Mathematics.* Ithaca, NY: Cornell University.

Feynman, R. P. (1985). *"Surely you must be kidding, Mr. Feynman": Adventures of a curious character.* New York: Norton.

Flavell, J. H. (1985). *Cognitive Development* (2nd ed.). Englewood Cliffs, NJ: Prentice-Hall.

Ford, K. M., Cañas, A., Jones, J., Stahl, H., Novak, J. D., & Adams-Weber, J. (1991). ICONKAT: An integrated constructivist knowledge acquisition tool. *Knowledge Acquisition, 3,* 215–236.

Fraser, K. (1993). Theory based use of concept mapping in organizational development: Creating shared understanding as a basis for the cooperative design of work changes and changes in working relationships. Unpublished doctoral dissertation, Cornell University, Ithaca, NY.

Freire, P. (1970). *Pedagogy of the oppressed.* New York: Searbury Press.

Freire, P. (1985). *The politics of education: Culture, power and liberation.* South Hadley, MA: Bergin and Garvey.

Fromm, E. (1955). *The Sun society.* New York: Rhinehart & Company.

Fromm, E. (1973). *The art of loving.* New York: Avon Books. (Original work published in 1956)

Fuata'i, K. (1985). *The use of Vee maps and concept maps in the learning of form five mathematics in Samoa College, Western Samoa.* Unpublished masters thesis, Cornell University, Ithaca, NY.

Gabel, D. (1994). Learning: Alternative conceptions. In D. L. Gabel (Ed.), *Handbook on research in science teaching* (pp. 177–210). New York: Macmillan.

Gage, N. L. (1963). *Handbook of research on teaching: A project of the American Educational Research Association.* Chicago: Rand McNally.

Gamoran, A., Nystrand, M., Berends, M., & LePore, P. C. (1995). An organizational analysis of the effects of ability grouping. *American Educational Research Journal, 32*(4), 687–715.

Gardner, H. (1983). *Frames of mind: The theory of multiple intelligences.* New York: Basic Books.

Gardner, H. (1993). *Creating minds.* New York: Basic Books.

Gates, B. (1996). *The road ahead.* New York: Penguin.

Gazzaniga, M. (1989). *Mind matters: How mind and brain interact to create our conscious lives.* Boston: Houghton Mifflin.

Gazzaniga, M. (Ed.). (1995). *The cognitive neurosciences.* Cambridge, MA: MIT Press.

Georgi, H. (1996). Cited in Glantz, J. (1996). How not to pick a physicist? *Science, 274,* 710–712.

Geraci, B. (1995). Local decision making: A report from the trenches. *Educational Leadership, 35*(4), 50–52.

Gerber, J. A. (1992). *Promoting excellence in elementary school teaching: Theory driven practitioners.* Unpublished doctoral dissertation, Cornell University, Ithaca, NY.

Getzelsz, J. W., & Jackson, P. W. (1962). *Creativity and intelligence: Explorations with gifted students.* New York: Wiley.

Gilligan, C. (1982). *In a different voice: Psychological theory and women's development.* Cambridge, MA: Harvard University Press.

Glanz, J. (1996). How not to pick a physicist? *Science, 274,* 710–712.

Glasser, W. (1994). *The control theory manager.* New York: HarperCollins.

Goleman, D. (1995). *Emotional intelligence: Why it can matter more than I.Q.* New York: Bantam.

Gonzales, F. M., & Novak, J. D. (1996). *Aprendizaje significativo: Tecnicas y aplicaciones.* Madrid: Ediciones Pedagogicas.

Goodlad, J. I. (1984). *A place called school: Prospects for the future.* New York: McGraw-Hill.

Gould, S. J. (1981). *The mismeasure of man.* New York: Norton.

Gowin, D. B. (1970). The structure of knowledge. *Educational Theory, 20*(4), 319–328.

Gubrud, A. R., & Novak, J. D. (1973). Learning achievement and the efficiency of learning the concept of vector addition at three different grade levels. *Science Education, 57*(2), 179–191.

Guilford, J. P. (1959). Three faces of intellect. *American Psychologist, 14,* 469–479.

Guilford, J. P., & Christensen, P. R. (1973). The one-way relationship between creative potential and IQ. *Journal of Creative Behavior, 7*(4), 247–252.

Gurley-Dilger, L. I. (1982). *Use of Gowin's Vee and concept mapping strategies to teach responsibility for learning in high school biological sciences.* Unpublished doctoral thesis, Cornell University, Ithaca, NY.

Hagerman, H. (1966). *An analysis of learning and retention in college students and the common goldfish (Carassius auratus, Lin).* Unpublished doctoral thesis, Purdue University, Lafayette, IN.

Halpern, D. E. (1989). *Thought and knowledge: An introduction to critical thinking* (2nd ed.). Hillsdale, NJ: Lawrence Erlbaum Associates.

Hamel, G., & Prahalad, C. K. (1994). *Competing for the future.* Boston: Harvard Business School Press.

Hamilton, W., Sir. (1853). *Discussions on philosophy* (2nd ed.). London: Longman, Brown, Green.

Hammer, M., & Champy, J. (1993). *Reengineering the corporation: A manifesto for business revolution.* New York: HarperCollins.

Hangen, J. (1989). *Educational experience as a factor in bulimia and anorexia.* Unpublished masters thesis, Cornell University, Ithaca, NY.

Hanushek, E. A. (1981). Throwing money at schools. *Journal of Policy Analysis and Management, 1,* 19–41.

Hanushek, E. A. (1989). The impact of differential expenditures on school performance. *Educational Researcher, 18*(4), 45–65.

Harris, T. A. (1969). *I'm OK, you're OK: A practical guide to transactional analysis.* New York: Harper & Row.

Hedges, L. V., Laine, R. D., & Greenwald, R. (1994). Does money matter? A meta-analysis of studies of the effects of differential school inputs on student outcomes. *Educational Researcher, 23*(3), 5–14.

Hegarty, S. (1996, November 21). Science, math study renews call for reform. *St. Petersburg Times,* p 1A, 10A.

Helms, H., & Novak, J. D. (1983). Overview of the international seminar on misconceptions in science and mathematics. In H. Helm & J. D. Novak (Eds.), *Proceedings of the International Seminar on Misconceptions in Science and Mathematics* (pp. 1–4). Ithaca, NY: Cornell University.

Herman, J. L., Aschbacher, P. R., & Winters, L. (1992). *A practical guide to alternative assessment.* Alexandria, VA: Association for Supervision and Curriculum Development.

Herrnstein, R. J., & Murray, C. (1994). *The bell curve.* New York: Free Press.

Herrigel, E. (1973). *Zen in the art of archery* (R. F. C. Hull, trans.). New York: Vintage Books.

Hibbard, K. M., & Novak, J. D. (1975). Audio-tutorial elementary school science instruction as a method for studying of children's concept learning: Particulate nature of matter. *Science Education, 59*(4), 559–570.

Higgins, J. M. (1993). *Innovate or evaporate.* Winter Park, FL: The New Management Publishing Co.

Hoffman, B. (1962). *The tyranny of testing.* New York: Crowell.

Holden, C. (1992). Study flunks science and math tests. *Science, 258,* 541.

Houston, W. R. (Ed.). (1990). *Handbook of research on teacher education.* New York: Macmillan.

Howe, K. R. (1995). Wrong problem, wrong solution. *Educational Leadership, 56*(6), 22–23.

Hughes, B. F. (1986). *Knowledge, beliefs and actions of Elmira Water customers related to groundwater, contamination of groundwater.* Unpublished master's Thesis, Cornell University, Ithaca, NY.

Hyde, J. S. (1991). How large are cognitive gender differences? *American Psychologist, 36*(8), 892–901.

Jensen, A. R. (1969). How much can we boost IQ and scholastic achievement? *Harvard Educational Review, 39,* 1–123.

Johnson, D. W., Johnson, R. T., & Holubec, E. J. (1988). *Cooperation in the classroom* (Rev. ed.). Edina, MN: Interaction.

Jonassen, D. H., Beissner, K., & Yacci, M. (1993). *Structural knowledge: Techniques for representing, conveying, and acquiring structural knowledge.* Hillsdale, NJ: Lawrence Erlbaum Associates.

Kaestle, C. F. (1993). The awful reputation of education research. *Educational Researcher, 22*(1), 21–31.

Kahle, J. B. (Ed.). (1985). *Women in science: A report from the field.* Philadelphia: Falmer Press.

Kahle, J. B., Douglas, C. B., & Nordland, F. H. (1976). An analysis of learner efficiency when individualized and group instructional formats are utilized with disadvantaged students. *Science Education, 60*(2), 245–250.

Kahn, K. M. (1994). *Concept mapping as a strategy for teaching and developing the Caribbean Examinations Council (CXC) mathematics curriculum in a secondary school.* Unpublished doctoral dissertation, The University of the West Indies, Barbados, West Indies.

Kamin, L. (1974). *The science and politics of IQ.* Hillsdale, NJ: Lawrence Erlbaum Associates.

Katzenbach, J. R. (1995). *Real change leaders.* New York: Times Books.

Keating, D. P. (1984). The emperor's new clothes: The "new look" in intelligence research. In R. J. Shavelson (Ed.), *Advances in the psychology of human intelligence* (Vol. 2, pp. 1–45). Hillsdale, NJ: Lawrence Erlbaum Associates.

Keddie, N. (Ed). (1973). *The myth of cultural deprivation.* Baltimore, MD: Penguin.

Keller, E. F. (1983). *A feeling for the organism: The life and work of Barbara McClintock.* New York: Freeman.

Keller, E. F. (1985). *Reflections on gender and science.* New Haven, CT: Yale University Press.

Kerr, P. (1988). *A conceptualization of learning, teaching and research experiences of women scientists and its implications for science education.* Unpublished doctoral dissertation, Cornell University, Ithaca, NY.

Kitchener, R. F. (1986). *Piaget's theory of knowledge: Genetic epistemology & scientific reason.* New Haven, CT: Yale University Press.

Klausmeier, H. J., & Harris, C. W. (1966). *Analysis of concept learning.* New York: Academic Press.

Kozulin, A. (1990). *Vygotsky's psychology: A biography of ideas.* New York: Harvester Wheatsheaf.

Krajcik, J., Spitulnik, M. W., & Zembal, C. (in press). Using hypermedia to represent student understanding: Science learners and preservice teachers. In J. Mintzes, J. Wandersee, & J. D. Novak (Eds.), *Teaching science for understanding.* San Diego: Academic Press.

Kuhn, T. S. (1962). *The structure of scientific revolutions.* Chicago: University of Chicago Press.

Lakoff, G., & Johnson, M. (1980). *Metaphors we live by.* Chicago: University of Chicago Press.

Lawler, A. (1994). NSF takes leap into school reform. *Science, 266,* 1936–1938.

Lewis, M. (1995). Self conscious emotions. *American Scientist, 83,* 68–78.

Likert, R. (1932). A technique for measurement of attitudes. *Archives of Psychology, 40* (whole issue).

Macnamara, J. T. (1982). *Names for things: A study of human learning.* Cambridge, MA: MIT Press.

Mandler, G. (1967). Verbal learning: Introduction. In *New directions in psychology III,* by G. Mandler, P. Mussen, K. Kogan, & M. A. Wallach (pp. 3–50). New York: Holt, Rhinehart, & Winston.

Marshall, H., & McCombs, B. L. (1995). Learner-centered psychological principles: Guidelines for the teaching of educational psychology in teacher education programs. *Newsletter for Educational Psychologists, 19*(1), 4–8.

Marshall, R., & Tucker, M. (1992). *Thinking for a living: Education and the wealth of nations.* New York: Basic Books.

Martin, D. (1993). *Team think: Using the sports connection to develop, motivate and manage a winning business team.* New York: Penguin.

Martin, M., Miller, G., & Delago, J. (1995). Portfolio performance: Research results from California's Golden State Examinations science portfolio project. *The Science Teacher, 62*(1), 50–54.

Maslow, A. H. (1984). *Motivation and personality.* New York: Harper & Row.

Matthews, G. B. (1980). *Philosophy and the young child.* Cambridge, MA: Harvard University Press.

Matthews, G. B. (1984). *Dialogues with children.* Cambridge, MA: Harvard University Press.

Matthews, L. (1995). *Gravitropic responses of five Maize Zea Mays.* Unpublished doctoral dissertation, Cornell University, Ithaca, NY.

Mayeroff, M. (1972). *On caring.* New York: Harper & Row Perennial Library.

Mazur, J. M. (1989). *Using concept maps in therapy with substance abusers in the context of Gowin's theory of education.* Unpublished masters thesis, Cornell University, Ithaca, NY.

Miller, G. A. (1956). The magical number seven, plus or minus two: Some limits on our capacity for processing information. *Psychological Review, 63,* 81–97.

Ministry of Education and Science. (1989). *Li͏bio Blanco la Reforma del Sistema Educativo* (White Book for the Reform of the Educational System). Madrid, Spain: Ministry of Education and Science.

Minkin, B. H. (1995). *Future in sight.* New York: Macmillian.

Mintzes, J. J., Wandersee, J. H., & Novak, J. D. (in press). *Teaching science for understanding.* San Diego: Academic Press.

Moll, L. C. (Ed.). (1990). *Vygotsky and education: Instructional implications and applications of sociohistorical psychology.* New York: Cambridge University Press.

Molnar, A. (1994). Education for profit: A yellow brick road to nowhere. *Educational Leadership, 52*(1), 66–71.

Molnar, A. (1995). The bell curve: For whom it tolls. *Education Leadership, 52*(7), 69–70.

Moloney, W. J. (1996, December 11). Reading at the 8th-grade level in college. *St. Petersburg Times,* p. 18A.

Moore, J. F. (1996). *The death of competition.* New York: HarperCollins.

Moore, R. (1996). Teachers unions. *The American Biology Teacher, 58*(5), 260–262.

Moreira, M. M. (1977). *The use of concept maps and the five questions in a Brazilian foreign language classroom: Effects on communication.* Unpublished doctoral dissertation, Cornell University, Ithaca, NY.

Muller, H. J. (1958). *The loom of history.* New York: Harper.

National Commission on Excellence in Education. (1983). *A nation at risk: The imperative for educational reform.* Washington, DC: U.S. Government Printing Office.

Nicolini, D., & Meznar, M. B. (1995). The social construction of organizational learning: Conceptual and practical issues in the field. *Human Relations, 48*(7), 727–746.

Nonaka, I., & Takeuchi, H. (1995). *The knowledge-creating company.* Oxford, England: Oxford University Press.

Nordland, F. H., Lawson, A. E., & Kahle, J. B. (1974). A study of levels of concrete and formal reasoning ability in disadvantaged junior and senior high school science students. *Science Education, 58*(4), 569–575.

Novak, J. D. (1958). An experimental comparison of a conventional and a project centered method of teaching a college general botany course. *Journal of Experimental Education, 26,* 217–230.

Novak, J. D. (1963). What should we teach in biology? *NABT News and Views, 7*(2), 1. Reprinted in *Journal of Research in Science Teaching, 1*(3), 241–243.

Novak, J. D. (1964). Importance of conceptual schemes for science teaching. *The Science Teacher, 31*(6), 10.

Novak, J. D. (1969). A case study of curriculum change—Science since PSSC. *School Science and Mathematics, 69,* 374–384.

Novak, J. D. (1972). Facilities for secondary school science teaching. *The Science Teacher, 39*(3), 2–13.

Novak, J. D. (1977a). *A theory of education.* Ithaca, NY: Cornell University Press.

Novak, J. D. (1977b). An alternative to Piagetian psychology for science and mathematics education. *Science Education, 61*(4), 453–477.

Novak, J. D. (1979). Applying psychology and philosophy to the improvement of laboratory teaching. *The American Biology Teacher, 41*(8), 466–474.

Novak, J. D. (1980). Learning theory applied to the biology classroom. *The American Biology Teacher, 42*(5), 280–285.

Novak, J. D. (1987, June). *Proceedings of the Second International Seminar on Misconceptions and Educational Strategies in Science and Mathematics.* Ithaca, NY: Cornell University.

Novak, J. D. (1988). The role of process and content in science teacher education. In P. F. Brandwein & H. Passow (Eds.), *Gifted young in science—Potential through performance* (pp. 307–319). Washington, DC: National Science Teachers Association.

Novak, J. D. (1990). Concept maps and Vee diagrams: Two metacognitive tools for science and mathematics education. *Instructional Science, 19,* 29–52.

Novak, J. D. (1991). Clarify with concept maps. *The Science Teacher, 58*(7), 45–49.

Novak, J. D. (1993). Human constructivism: A unification of psychological and epistemological phenomena in meaning making. *International Journal of Personal Construct Psychology, 6,* 167–193.

Novak, J. D. (1994). A view on the current status of Ausubel's Assimilation theory of learning, or "La teoria dell'appendimento per assimilation di D. P. Ausubel. Le proopsettive attuali." *CADMO* (Giornal Italiano di Pedagogoa sperimentale, Didattica Doc imologia, Tecnologia dell'Instrusione) 2(4), 7–23. Also in Novak, J. D. (Ed.), *Proceeding of the Third International Seminar on Misconceptions and educational Strategies in Science and Mathematics (August 1–4, 1993).* Published electronically.

Novak, J. D., & Abrams, R. (Eds.). (1993, August). *Proceedings of the Third International Seminar on Misconceptions and Educational Strategies in Science and Mathematics.* Ithaca, NY.

Novak, J. D., & Gowin, D. B. (1984). *Learning how to learn.* New York: Cambridge University Press.

Novak, J. D., Gowin, D. B., & Johansen, G. T. (1983). The use of concept mapping and knowledge Vee mapping with junior high school science students. *Science Education, 67*(5), 625–645.

Novak, J. D., & Iuli, R. I. (1995). Meaningful Learning as the foundation for constructivist epistemology. *Proceedings of the Third International History, Philosophy and Science Teaching Conference* (Vol. 2). Minneapolis: University of Minnesota.

Novak, J. D., & Musonda, D. (1991). A twelve-year longitudinal study of science concept learning. *American Educational Research Journal, 28*(1), 117–153.

Novak, J. D., & Wandersee, J. H. (Eds.). (1990). Special issue on concept mapping. *Journal of Research in Science Teaching, 28*(1), New York: Wiley.

Nussbaum, J., & Novak, J. D. (1976). An assessment of children's concepts of earth utilizing structured interviews. *Science Education, 60*(4), 535–550.

O'Neil, J. (1995a). On lasting school reform: A conversation with Ted Sizer. *Educational Leadership, 52*(5), 4–9.

O'Neil, J. (1995b). On schools as learning organizations: A conversation with Peter Senge. *Educational Leadership, 52*(7), 20–23.

Papalia, D. E. (1972). The status of several conservation abilities across the life span. *Human Development, 15,* 229–243.

Penfield, W. (1952). Memory mechanisms. *A.M.A. Archives of Neurology and Psychiatry, 67,* 178–198.

Perkins, D. N. (1992). *Smart schools: Better thinking and learning for every child.* New York: The Free Press.

Peters, T. J. (1992). *Liberation management.* New York: Knopf.

Peters, T. J. (1994). *The Thomas Peters seminar: Crazy times call for crazy organizations.* New York: Vintage Books.

Piaget, J. (1926). *The language and thought of the child.* New York: Harcourt Brace.

Piaget, J. (1972). *Psychology and epistemology* (A. Rosin, trans.). New York: The Viking Press.

Piaget, J. (1976). The child and reality: Problems in genetic psychology. New York: Penguin.

Pines, A. L., Novak, J. D., Posner, G. J., & VanKirk, J. (1978). *The clinical interview: A method for evaluating cognitive structure* (Research Report #6). Ithaca, NY: Cornell University.

Polyani, M. (1966). *The tacit dimension.* New York: Doubleday.

Postlethwait, S. N., Novak, J. D., & Murray, H. T., Jr. (1969). *The audio-tutorial approach to learning through independent study and integrated experiences* (2nd ed.). Minneapolis, MN: Burgess.

Postlethwait, S. N., Novak, J. D., & Murray, H. T., Jr. (1972). *The audio-tutorial approach to learning through independent study and integrated experiences* (3rd ed.). Minneapolis, MN: Burgess.

Prestowitz, C. V., Jr. (1988). *Trading places.* New York: Basic Books.

Puckett, M. B., & Black, J. K. (1994). *Authentic assessment of the young child: Celebrating development and learning.* New York: Macmillan.

Qin, Z., Johnson, D. W., & Johnson, R. T. (1995). Cooperative versus competitive efforts and problem solving. *Review of Educational Research, 65*(2), 129–143.

Resnick, L., & Nolan, K. (1995). Where in the world are world-class standards. *Educational Leadership, 52*(6), 6–10.

Ridley, D. R., & Novak, J. D. (1983). Sex-related differences in high school science and mathematics Enrollments: Do they give males a critical headstart toward science- and math-related careers? *The Alberta Journal of Educational Research, 29*(4), 308–318.

Ripple, R. E., & Rockcastle, V. N. (Eds.). (1964). *Piaget rediscovered*. Ithaca, NY: Cornell University.

Robertson, M. T. (1984). *Use of videotape-stimulated recall interviews to study the thoughts and feelings of students in an introductory biology laboratory course*. Unpublished masters thesis, Cornell University, Ithaca, NY.

Rossiter, M. W. (1982). *Women scientists in America: Struggles and strategies to 1940*. Baltimore: John Hopkins University Press.

Rowan, B. (1994). Comparing teachers' work with work in other occupations: Notes on the professional status of teaching. *Educational Researcher, 23*(6), 4–21.

Rowe, M. B. (1974). Wait-time and rewards as instructional variables: Their influence on Learning, Logic and Fate Control. I. Wait-time. *Journal of Research in Science Teaching, 11*(2), 81–94.

Ruiz-Primo, M. A., & Shavelson, R. J. (1996). Problems and issues in the use of concept maps in science assessment. *Journal of Research in Science Teaching, 33*, 569–6.

Ryle, G. (1949). *Collected papers, Vol. II. Critical essays*. London: Hutchinson.

Sadler, P. (1995). Astronomy's conceptual hierarchy. In J. Percy (Ed.), *Astronomy education: Current developments, future coordination* (pp. 46–60). San Francisco: Astronomical Society of the Pacific.

Sarason, S. B. (1993). *The predictable failure of educational reform*. San Francisco, CA: Jossey-Bass.

Schneps, M. (1989). *Private universe project*. Cambridge, MA: Smithsonian Center for Astrophysics.

Schön, D. A. (1987). *Educating the reflective practitioner*. San Francisco: Jossey-Bass.

Schwab, J. J. (1973). The practical 3: Translation into curriculum. *School Review, 81*(4), 501–522.

Sedlak, M. W., Wheeler, C. W., Pullin, D. C., & Cusick, P. A. (1986). *Selling students short*. New York: Teacher College Press.

Senge, P. M. (1990). *The fifth discipline: The art and practice of the learning organization*. New York: Doubleday.

Shayer, M., & Adey, P. (1981). *Towards a science of science teaching: Curriculum development and curriculum demand*. London: Heinemann.

Shedd, J. B., & Bacharach, S. B. (1991). Tangled higherarchies: Teachers as professionals and the management of schools. San Francisco: Jossey-Bass.

Shuell, T. J. (1993). Toward an integrated theory of teaching and learning. *Educational Psychologist, 28*(4), 291–311.

Shulman, L. S., & Keislar, E. R. (Eds.). (1966). *Learning by Discovery*. Chicago: Rand McNally.

Simon, H. A. (1974). How big is a chunk? *Science, 183*(8), 482–488.

Skinner, B. F. (1938). *The behavior of organisms: An experimental analysis*. New York: Appleton-Century-Crofts.

Skinner, B. F. (1987). What ever happened to psychology as the science of behavior? *American Psychologist, 42*(8), 780–786.

Slavin, R. E. (1982). *Cooperative learning: Student teams*. Washington, DC: NEA Professional Library.

Smith, B. E. (1992). Linking theory and practice in teaching basic nursing skills. *Journal of Nursing Education, 31*(1), 16–23.

Songer, N. B., & Linn, M. C. (1991). How do students' views of science influence knowledge integration? *Journal of Research in Science Teaching, 28*(9), 761–784.

Sonnert, G., & Holton, G. (1996). Career patterns of women and men in the sciences. *American Scientist, 84*, 63–71.

Stallings, J. A. (1995). Ensuring Teaching and Learning in the 21st Century. *Educational Researcher, 24*(6), 4–8.

Stecklow, S. (1994, December 28). Acclaimed reforms of U. S. education are popular but unproven. *The Wall Street Journal*, pp. A1, A4.

Sternberg, R. J. (1986). *The triarchic mind.* New York: Penguin.

Sternberg, R. J. (1988). *The nature of creativity.* New York: Cambridge University Press.

Sternberg, R. J. (1996a). *Successful intelligence.* New York: Simon & Schuster.

Sternberg, R. J. (1996b). Myths, countermyths, and truths about intelligence. *Educational Researcher, 25*(2), 11–16.

Suppes, P., & Ginsberg, R. (1963). A fundamental property of all-or-none models, binomial distribution of responses prior to conditioning, with application to concept formation in children. *Psychological Review, 70,* 139–161.

Swanson, D. B., Norman, G. R., & Linn, R. L. (1995). Performance-based assessment: Lessons from the health professions. *Educational Researcher, 24*(5), 5–11, 35.

Swiss, D. (1996). *Women breaking through.* Princeton, NJ: Petersons/Pacesetter Books.

Tannen, D. (1994). *Talking from 9 to 5: How women's and men's conversational styles affect who gets heard, who gets credit, and what gets done at work.* New York: Morrow.

Taylor, D. (1991). *Learning denied.* Portsmouth, NH: Heinemann.

Thorndike, E. L. (1922). The effect of changed data upon reasoning. *Journal of Experimental Psychology, 5,* 33–38.

Toffler, A. (1970). *Future shock.* New York: Bantam.

Toulmin, S. (1972). *Human understanding. Volume 1: The collective use and evolution of concepts.* Princeton, NJ: Princeton University Press.

Tronto, J. C. (1993). *Moral boundaries: A political argument for an ethic of care.* London: Routledge.

Tyler, R. W. (1977). Foreword. In J. D. Novak (Ed.), *A theory of education* (pp. 7–8). Ithaca, NY: Cornell University Press.

Vance, M., & Deacon, D. (1995). *Think out of the box.* Franklin Lakes, NJ: Career Press.

von Glasersfeld, E. (1984). An introduction to radical constructivism. In P. Watzlanick (Ed.), *The invented reality* (pp. 17–40). New York: Norton.

Vygotsky, L. S. (1962). *Thought and language* (E. Hanfmann & G. Vakar, Eds. & Trans.). Cambridge, MA: MIT Press.

Vygotsky, L. S. (1986). *Thought and language.* (A. Kozulin, Ed. & Trans.). Cambridge, MA: The MIT Press.

Wainer, H. (1993). Does spending money on education help? *Educational Researcher, 22*(9), 22–24.

Waitley, D. (1995). *Empires of the mind: Lessons to lead and succeed in a knowledge-based world.* New York: Morrow.

Wallace, J. G. (1976). The course of cognitive growth. In U. P. Varma & P. Williams (Eds.), *Piaget, Psychology, and Education* (pp. 15–30). London: Hodder & Stoughton.

Wandersee, J. H. (1990). Concept mapping and the cartography of cognition. *Journal of Research in Science Teaching, 27*(10), 923–936.

Wandersee, J. H., Mintzes, J. J., Novak, J. D. (1994). Learning: Alternative conceptions. In D. L. Gabel (Ed.), *Handbook on research in science teaching* (pp. 177–210). New York: Macmillan.

Waterman, R. H. (1995). *What America does right.* New York: Penguin.

White, J. B., & Suris, O. (1993, September 21). New pony: How "skunk works" kept mustang alive—On a tight budget. *Wall Street Journal,* pp. A1, A12.

Whorf, B. L. (1956). *Language, thought and reality. Selected writings of Benjamin Lee Whorf.* Cambridge, MA: MIT Press.

Wiggins, G. (1989). Teaching to the authentic test. *Educational Leadership, 49*(7), 45.

Wilshire, B. (1990). *The moral collapse of the university: Professionalism, purity, and alienation.* Albany: State University of New York Press.

Wilson, K. G., & Davis, B. (1994). *Redesigning education.* New York: Holt.

Wittrock, M. C. (1974). Learning as a generative process. *Educational Psychologist, 11,* 87–95.

Woodruff, R. B., & Gardial, S. F. (1996). *Know your customer: New approaches to understanding customer value and satisfaction.* Cambridge, MA: Blackwell.

Zaltman, G., & Higie, R. A. (1993). *Seeing the voice of the customer: The Zaltman metaphor elicitation technique.* Cambridge, MA: Marketing Science Institute, Report No. 93–114.

Author Index

Subject Index

for research productivity, 97, 99*f*
teaching diagramming of, 229–230
for team learning, 149–153

L

Language acquisition, 44
Language labels, 35–37
   in concept learning, 40–42
Leadership
   management *versus,* 214–215
   for reform, 208–209, 211–212
Learners
   age impact, 68
   as Child, 155
   choice for meaningful learning, 9, 19, 51, 53*f*,
      113, 224
   in constructivist education of teachers, 126*t*
   customers as, 221–226
   as education element, 10–11*f*
   empowerment of, 9, 14*f*–15*f*, 27, 113, 212
   interaction with the teacher, 13–14*f*
   perspective of, 13–16, 14*f*
   in traditional education of teachers, 125*t*
Learning
   affective, *see* Affective learning
   in businesses, *see* Corporations; Organiza-
      tional learning
   characteristics of, 20*f*
   cognitive, *see* Cognitive learning
   of concepts, *see* Concept learning
   cooperative, 147–148
   by discovery, 56–59, 163
   evaluation of, *see* Evaluations
   knowledge creation and, 92–96, 157–159,
      213, 221–226
   meaningful, *see* Meaningful learning
   nature of, 3–4*f*
   organizational, *see* Organizational learning
   as a process, 209
   propositional, *see* Propositional learning
   psychomotor, *see* Psychomotor learning
   rate of, 62*f*
   representational, *see* Representational learn-
      ing
   rewards for, *see* Rewards
   rote, *see* Rote learning
   superordinate, *see* Superordinate learning
Learning disability
   case study of, 135–142
   concept map of, 138*f*
   of corporations, 177–178, 212
Learning theories, *see specific theory*
Likert Scales, 188–190
Literacy
   empowerment from, 31–32
   universal, 2
Long-term memory (LTM), 22–23

Loving
   the art of, 156–159
   in capitalistic society, 156–157
LTM (long-term memory), 22–23

M

Managers and management
   as autocratic, 177
   as effective, 112–152
      necessary conditions for, 114*f*–116*f*
   limited conceptual understanding in, 119–123
   problems of education by, 12
   site-based, 176–177
   as teaching, 5, 17
   total quality, *see* Total Quality Management
   trust and honesty of, 143–147
Materials
   conceptual opaqueness of, 162–164
   role in meaningful learning, 19, 53*f*, 162–164
Meaning
   construction of new, 35–48, 36*f*
   meaning of, 35–36
   negotiation of, 13–14*f*, 38, 113, 118
   principal units of, 40
Meaningful learning
   advantages of, 61
   creativity from, 20*f*, 73*f*–75
   defined, 13–15*f*
   disadvantage of, 61
   elements of, 36*f*–48
   empowerment through, 31
   evaluation of, *see* Evaluations
   introduction to, 3–8
   as knowledge creation, 92–96
   learners role in, 9, 13–16, 19, 113
   per assimilation theory, 51–56, 69
   prior knowledge needed for, *see* Prior knowl-
      edge
   recall in, 61–62, *see also* Tests
      failure to, 60*f*
   requirements for, 19, 53*f*
   rote learning in contrast to, 19–20*f*, 58*f*, 61
   teachers role in, 13–16, 113
Measurement
   of cognitive learning, 181–183
   key concepts and relationships in, 189*f*
   reliability of, 184, 192, 194, 198
   validity of, 184–185, 192, 197–199
Memory
   long-term, 22–23
   nature of, 4
   neural cells role in, 51–53*f*
   perceptual, 22
   short-term, 22–23
   systems of, 4, 22–24, 23*f*
Metaphors, as communication tools, 164
Money, as factor in education, 11–12